GIVE ME TOMORROW

A young girl's ordeals
during the WWII
Russian invasion of
eastern Germany

To Hans,

in heimatlicher Verbundenheit!

Ingrid Stabins

a memoir

Ingrid Stabins

GIVE ME TOMORROW
A young girl's ordeals during the WWII Russian invasion of eastern Germany
A memoir by Ingrid Stabins

Copyright © 2012 Ingrid Stabins

ISBN: 978-1-484028-48-3

Designed by Maine Authors Publishing, Rockland, Maine

www.maineauthorspublishing.com

First U.S. Edition: August 2012

Printed in the United States of America

I dedicate this book to my kind and gentle father
who never knew he lost his homeland
and my loving mother
who endured life with a broken heart.

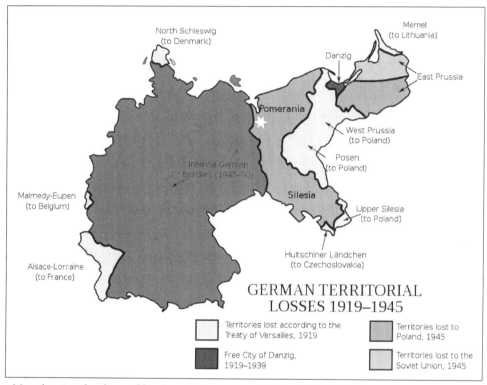

GERMAN TERRITORIAL
LOSSES 1919–1945

North Schleswig
(to Denmark)

Memel
(to Lithuania)

Danzig

East Prussia

Pomerania

West Prussia
(to Poland)

Posen
(to Poland)

Internal German
borders (1945-90)

Malmedy-Eupen
(to Belgium)

Silesia

Upper Silesia
(to Poland)

Alsace-Lorraine
(to France)

Hultschiner Ländchen
(to Czechoslovakia)

Territories lost according to the
Treaty of Versailles, 1919

Territories lost to
Poland, 1945

Free City of Danzig,
1919–1939

Territories lost to the
Soviet Union, 1945

Map showing the changed borders of Germany and Poland, 1919-1945.
Star indicates the location of Köselitz.

ACKNOWLEDGEMENTS

This book is the fruition of more than ten years of writing. My heartfelt thanks go to my children Martina and Henning for their unwavering encouragement and support and belief in my abilities and the outcome. A warm thank-you to the many friends who prodded me along, answered questions, and provided supportive input along the way. My grateful thanks also extend to June Calender who offered her time to read and edit my story, to Carol Bright who wanted to know more about my experiences, and to Stephanie De-Ferie who was there when I needed to talk about publishing. A warm thank-you also goes to my sister Christa in Germany, who I could always call on for dates and names. Pam Hunt deserves a special remembrance, as she was a dear friend who stood by me right from the beginning.

"They can take everything from us,

but they can't take our land."
—Paul Buchholz, Ingrid's father

"But they did."
—Ingrid Stabins

CONTENTS

PROLOGUE 3

FOREWORD 5

chapter one | KÖSELITZ 7

chapter two | AS YOUNGSTERS ON OUR FARM 29

chapter three | SCHOOL YEARS 59

chapter four | THE BEGINNING OF WORLD WAR II
IN 1939 67

chapter five | THE SHIFT OF THE WAR 75

chapter six | 1944: THE WAR COMES HOME 81

chapter seven | LEAVING KÖSELITZ IN 1945 93

chapter eight | MY ORDEAL 119

chapter nine | SEARCH FOR MY FAMILY 157

chapter ten | THE FAMILY'S RESETTLEMENT
IN TANGERHÜTTE 185

chapter eleven | OUR FAMILY REUNITED 195

chapter twelve | THE MOVE TO WEST GERMANY 203

chapter thirteen | BAMBERG YEARS 209

chapter fourteen | MAKING PLANS FOR AMERICA 245

chapter fifteen | VOYAGE 253

chapter sixteen | AMERICA 261

Epilogue | 1996: KÖSELITZ REVISITED 279

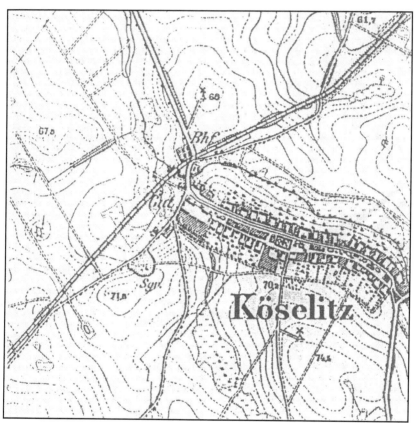

Map from the National German Archive depicting the village of Köselitz.

PROLOGUE

"He who has a why to live can bear almost any how."
—Friedrich Nietzsche

My children urged me to put down the legacy of my experiences for them and the generations to come. At this stage in my life, I can look back on all of it. To tell my story, I have selected important events and highlighted episodes my family knew very little about. I describe growing up in a rural area of Germany, our heritage and traditions, the way we lived, and the closeness of the extended families in the rural setting.

My sister, Christa, recorded dates and times, which helped me tell my story as it gradually evolved. She stayed in touch with many hometown friends and established a record of all the families and names of Köselitz, our hometown.

In the summer of 1945 after the end of World War II, my family became part of the largest expulsion of a people from their homeland in recent history. These were Germans from their homeland in the provinces of Pomerania and Silesia, the land east of the Oder River. Millions of people were uprooted from land that generations before them had called home. We, who lived in Pomerania, lost our homeland where generations of our family had farmed. Losing one's homeland can be one of the biggest tragedies in a person's life.

In early February of 1945, the invading Russian forces detained all the men and young boys who were still at home and transported them to Russia. My father was one of them, and like most of them, he never came back. In the first weeks of March 1945 under the Russian occupation, I was separated from my mother and siblings. I was sixteen years old and suddenly on my own; I grew up instantly. I spent many months in a Russian camp, where they intended to transport us to Russia to work.

My story will describe the brutal acts of cruelty women suffered at the hands of the Russian Army. It shows how inhuman that war was as the Russians fought their way through Eastern Germany on the way to Berlin.

These writings are echoes of the past. Parts of my life story are like footprints on the beach. Tides have swelled and receded and washed away much sadness. During those years, significant events occurred at crucial times in my young life, and the memories have stayed with me. The events transpired during my formative years, and completely changed my life forever.

Over fifty years ago, I put my roots down in America. I have spent most of my life here on lovely Cape Cod. I still consider Pomerania my homeland, even after all these years and events. I have vivid images of the beautiful land, rich in Prussian tradition, of the golden wheat fields, rural landscapes, and the wandering dunes along the Baltic Sea.

FOREWORD

During my childhood, I learned about my German heritage through my mother's stories of her family, my experiences, and the trips we made to visit relatives. The stories evoked great interest, but the significance of them was sometimes lost on my young age. Even though my last childhood trip to Germany was at the age of ten, these family visits had a great impact on my future life outlook. This was enhanced by my mother's stories, and led to an interest in her experiences and a desire to know more. Later, as a young adult, I thought back on my visits, especially to East Germany, and the differences between those experiences and my German family's lifestyles, freedoms, and opportunities.

After my mother's first trip back to her homeland in 1996, it became a dream to visit her hometown with her. I wanted to see with my own eyes the scenes she had painted in her stories—the village setting, the fields her family farmed—and to have her relay more details as we would walk together down the same village streets she did as a child. This dream became possible in the spring of 2009, when we traveled to Germany for a family reunion and her cousin Arno offered to take us to Pommern. My anticipation was great.

When we approached my mother's homeland, my mental vision didn't disappoint me. The flat and gently rolling rural landscape was comprised of green farmland in full spring growth and rape fields blooming a sea of vibrant golden yellow. Köselitz was nestled among the fields, visible as an island of house and barn roofs scattered among the village's trees. I had seen photos of Köselitz, but now I could savor every sight with my own eyes. My mother made sure to remind me how different things were back in the pre-war times. Though fifty years of communist Polish rule had not been kind to the infrastructure of the town, one could see and imagine how the place would have appeared at one time with up-kept homes, tidy streets and courtyards, and well-tended gardens and fields.

Henning and Ingrid Stabins, Köselitz, 2009.

As we stood in front of my mother's house and viewed the large brick barns surrounding the inner courtyard, the stories of her experiences became much more real. A complex mix of feelings overwhelmed me as I tried to connect the many stories in my mind. Now I could better imagine both the fun moments she described as a youngster on her farm, caring for baby goats, playing ball, and winter sleigh rides, and the horrors of the Russian invasion and her ordeal that started in this very spot. Though we only had a short hour or two to spend there, we had many special moments: seeing the front yard elm tree she played in still alive after all these years, seeing a stork nest on the building that used to house the horses, and visiting the train station that she used when traveling to her Pyritz school.

These memoirs are a true treasure for our family. They will help all the grandchildren and future generations know and understand what led to the values and life outlook that have been instilled in them. My children have now begun to hear the stories from Oma. I so look forward to visiting Köselitz again with my children someday, so they too can see for themselves an important part of the family's history.

—Henning Stabins

chapter one

KÖSELITZ

Maikäfer fliege.
dein Vater ist im Kriege,
deine Mutter ist im Pommernland,
Pommernland ist abgebrannt,
Maikäfer fliege.

Fly little Maybug, fly.
Your father is at war,
Your mother is in Pommernland,
Pommernland has burnt,
Fly little Maybug, fly.

It was about eight o'clock one evening in the spring of 1963 on Cape Cod when the telephone rang and a voice called out, "Ingrid? This is Hannelore Bliese." For a moment I was speechless.

All I could ask was, "Hannelore, where are you?"

"I am in Connecticut." I was astounded. This was incredible; tears rolled down my cheeks and I could hardly speak. I had grown up with Hannelore Bliese in Germany. We had started first grade together; her father was a teacher in my hometown. We often played together. They lived just across the street from us in the school building. When we were in second grade, they moved away because her father had accepted a teaching position in another town. At that time we were too young to keep in touch, but a few years later when we were about twelve years old we had a wonderful surprise when we met again. We both started boarding school in Pyritz, our county seat, and were classmates until the war was practically on our doorstep.

It was just before Christmas in 1944 when we parted for Christmas school vacation. Until this phone call, that was the last time we had heard from each other.

I thought our paths would never cross again. Almost twenty years had passed; the Russian invasion had shattered everyone's dreams and scattered people all over the country and world. Of all the classmates, she was the one I would have least expected to leave Germany and come to America, but here she was. Our teary voices soon changed to excitement. Connecticut wasn't that far from Massachusetts, and we promised to visit very soon.

As fate would have it, Hannelore became one of my dearest friends in America. During our school years in Pyritz, we were not very close. She had friends in the dormitory and it seemed I bonded with friends who came from other towns and were commuting with me on the train.

She and her husband Bill Bitz had settled in Connecticut in 1961 where he was offered a job. Hannelore's mother came to visit from Germany and on her return home, she found my American address in the school newsletter. She contacted Hannelore and told her the news. While sightseeing in Massachusetts and surrounding areas, Hannelore noted that Cape Cod wasn't far from Connecticut. And so started this wonderful friendship later in our lives.

Reconnecting with Hannelore brought back my happy school memories, and I thought of the time when Hannelore and I parted. We were sixteen years old and getting ready for Christmas vacation, and didn't know whether we would come back to school. The Russian front was not far away anymore. Several girls came from quite a distance away and definitely wouldn't leave home since they lived in the eastern part of Pomerania. I was a commuting student taking the train from Köselitz every day, and had more flexibility.

What popped into my mind were the sandwiches we swapped on our breaks. Because I came from the farm, I had delicious sandwiches with homemade ham and salami. Most of the girls had to contend with the meager sandwiches the dorm provided. Many times I took an extra sandwich for a special friend. I tried to recall the nicknames Hannelore and I had for our teachers. Looking back now, fifty years have gone by, but the memories came rushing back.

I remember the cold winters with lots of snow, and the wonderful carefree summers with the long days when the evening seemed to last forever. We girls often skipped down shortcuts on narrow dirt roads, and walked beside fields of golden wheat gently swaying in the summer breeze as we picked bouquets of cornflowers and poppies. Nature had endowed them with such striking colors; how could we not be tempted to pick them? I remember the many times I rode on the bicycle paths that ran along the sandy dirt roads. They were so narrow I could not take my eyes off the path. We picked chamomile blossoms growing along the paths and dried them for tea.

This was Köselitz, the small village where I was born. It was a farming village in the middle of the county of Pyritz, or "Pyritzer Weizacker" (Pyritzer Wheat Fields), away from any major road and in tranquil harmony with nature, until a terrible war changed it all.

Köselitz belonged to the county of Pyritz, an agricultural area located in the heart of the Province of Pomerania (Pommern). The large Oder River split the province in half into Vorpommern and Hinterpommern. Our county was about fifty kilometers east of the Oder River in Hinterpommern. Pyritz was known for its fertile land. Indeed, it had rich soil, and the farmers did very well. I heard my father once say that the rye stood six feet tall. The grain ears were larger, and therefore led to more harvestable grain. The straw was important, too; it provided feed for the livestock. How proud the farmers were at the end of the seasons when all their hard efforts paid off.

History and Traditions

Archeological finds proved that primitive farming in this area was already going on over a thousand years ago. With the gradual development of improved farming tools, early tribes began to settle in the area. A class structure developed with landowners and serfs. Farmers were serfs, and were obliged to deliver a percentage of their harvest to the landowners. Eventually nobility became established, including knights and counts. As time went on, the landowners looked for more prosperity or better land, and moved on. They gathered their serfs, moved east, and settled in new, sparsely populated areas.

Old records have shown that in 1229, a form of the name Köselitz had already appeared. In 1628, the name, the way it was spelled when I lived there, was already established. It seemed that Köselitz was an old settlement, and had maintained its village status despite wars and plagues throughout the centuries. About a thousand inhabitants lived and worked in our little village, a mix of farmers and the families who worked for the farmers. These worker families were given free housing by the farmers. In the old days, the women wove their linen and the farmers grew their tobacco. Life was simple. When I was small, we still had some primitive implements for preparing flax fibers for spinning. Flax hadn't been grown since grandmother's early days, and we still had a large loom in the attic, along with several trunks holding homespun linens.

It was common in those days for people to wear fancy costumes on special occasions, and probably going to church too. The costume in our area was called the "Weizacker Tracht," the Wheat Field costume. The women's was a red pleated skirt and several layers of underskirts, a white blouse covered by a handsome vest, and a fringed scarf with large flowers draped around the shoulders. A delicately embroi-

Example of Weizacker Tracht.

dered white apron covered the front. The headdress was a little black or blue cap with ribbons. Red hand-knitted stockings with embroidery down the front and black shoes finished the outfit.

The men looked very handsome and elegant in their long, blue coats with red silky-looking lapels and tight-fitting pants, often in light colors, tucked into black boots. Their wide-brimmed hats had little ribbons reaching down in the back. Interestingly, all the larger villages had their own unique version of this costume.

Another custom in those days were journeymen. Journeymen are an age-old tradition which began in the fifteenth century. They were traveling tradesmen who had finished their apprenticeships, and were now moving around to perfect their knowledge and skills. They were not allowed to have any possessions except what they carried in a bundle on a long stick over their shoulders.

Their costumes had evolved over the centuries, and they were easily recognized. They wore wide-legged pants, looking more like sailor's pants, and a top hat. The eight shiny buttons on the vest represented the hours of the working day, while the six buttons on the jacket were for the six days of the work week. The three buttons on the sleeves were for the three years of their travel. The professions were mainly woodworking, masonry, and smithing, especially in the earlier centuries. This tradition was forbidden a few times in history, but it never died out.

This is an old folk song from Pommern.

Das Pommernlied
Wenn in stiller Stunde Träume mich umweh'n
bringen frohe Kunde Geister ungeseh'n
reden von dem Lande meiner heimat mir
heller Meeresstrande düstern Waldrevier.

Weisse Segel wiegen auf der blauen See
weisse Möven fliegen in der blauen Höh,
blaue Wälder krönen weissen Dünensand,
Pommernland, mein Sehnen ist Dir zugewandt.

Aus der Ferne wendet sich zu dir mein Sinn,
aus der Ferne sendet trauter Gruss er hin.
Traget laue Winde meinen Gruss und Sang,
wehet leis und linde treuer Liebesklang.

Bist ja doch das eine auf der ganzen Welt
bist ja mein, ich Deine treu dir zugestellt,
kannst ja doch von allen, die ich noch geseh'n
mir allein gefallen, Pommernland so schön.

Jetzt bin ich im Wandern, bin bald hier bald dort
doch aus allen andern treibt mich's immer fort,
Bis in dir ich wieder finde meine Ruh'
Send ich meine Lieder dir o' Heimat zu.

Adolf Pompe – 19. März 1852

Pommernlied

This song is about the dreams of a journeyman.
Many decades ago, journeymen of many trades
wandered from place to place to see the land
and perfect their skills.

They lived a carefree life, walked most of the time
and were often far away from home.
Their special black outfits and hats
made them always recognizable.

The song is about a young man far away from home,
dreaming and visualizing his home, the blue sea
with gulls flying above the dunes edged with trees.
He is longing for his Pommernland.

His thoughts are traveling from distant shores and he

begs the wind to carry his greetings and gentle love song.

He is yearning, "you are mine and I am yours, my wonderful Pommernland."
Wandering here and there, but his thoughts drive him on,
singing his love song until he finds his rest at home again.

Pommern was part of Prussia, and the Prussian traditions had been handed down from generation to generation. The Prussians were a proud people. Their German dialect "Plattdeutsch" was always maintained in the northern areas.

A song in "Plattdeutsch" about the Baltic Sea.

Wo die Ostseewellen trecken an den Strand,
Wo de gale Ginster beugt im Dünensand,
Wo de Möven schriegen gell in Stormgebrus.
Dor is mine Heimat,
Dor bin ick tau hus.

Where the waves are trekking to the shore,
Where the yellow broom is bending to the dunes,
Where the gulls are shrieking in the roaring storm.
That is my homeland,
There is my home.

Pyritz

The history books tell us that Pyritz and the surrounding area were settled by the Wends, or Sorbians as they are also called, who came from the East and honored heathen gods. They gradually melded with the tribes who were there at the time. Later, German settlers came from the west; they established and laid out villages and divided the land amongst the people who wanted to farm.

Bishop Otto from Bamberg in Bavaria came in 1124 to Christianize the population. It is said that he stayed for twenty days. He christened the people at a natural spring in what was then already a settlement in Pyritz. In later years, the natural spring was named after him, the Ottobrunnen, meaning the Otto well. Centuries later, it was made into an open-air shrine with a plaque telling what took place there. Big old trees near the well offered welcome shade on a hot day, and stone benches along a low wall invited the stroller to relax and listen to the soft babble of the spring. It became a landmark that everyone knew.

By approximately 1270, the rulers of the land had endured many small wars and raids from neighboring provinces. In order to protect their homes, they built a thick, high wall around the core of the settlement with a moat and embankment. To the north and south were huge towers with smaller ones in between. Pyritz was almost like a large fortress. The gates at the towers would be closed in times of danger. The gates also served as checkpoints to control who was coming and going.

These fortifications served the little town of Pyritz well through the Middle Ages. The town was a wonderful and charming place.

Pyritz wall and tower, 2009.

Many of the side streets were still paved with cobblestones and had narrow sidewalks when I grew up there. Some of the street names were most likely taken from the trades that once existed there, for example "Alte Weberstrasse," Old Weaver Street, comes to my mind. The smaller, in-between towers all had names. I often passed through the "Eulenturm," Owl Tower, which opened into the inner town, when going to school.

When I was young, the wall and towers were still standing for the most part, but had been repaired here and there. The moat was turned into gardens, and the embankment was a promenade with large old trees lining the sides. Going on a stroll here was delightful any time of the year. With a little imagination, one could picture what it would have looked like seven hundred years ago. I walked part of it on my way to school every day. A few times in art class, we went out there to draw a tower or a particular section of the wall which was dotted with embrasures that were wonderful nesting places for birds.

Pyritz was the center of education. In those days, it was the only place for higher education in the area. There were separate elementary schools for boys and girls. Villages with fewer students did not have schools, so the children had to walk to the next larger village. In that time, typical elementary education continued up to eight years; after that one looked for a job or learned a trade. Higher education beyond eight years of elementary schooling was available to those who wanted to pursue a degree. I transferred after fifth grade to the all-girls school in Pyritz, a special school to prepare one for higher education. Although it was a boarding school, I lived so close I commuted by train every day.

The gymnasium, the boy's school for higher education, was a well-established institution; its history reached back over a century. The impressive building had columns in front and a Latin inscription on the façade. Bright boys entered this school after four years of elementary school, then spent eight more years in the gymnasium. The girls' school I attended also lasted eight years. Students who wanted to go on to a university had to have this education. The boys had to take Latin and Greek along with English and French. After graduating from this school, they were able to go right to their chosen studies at a university. Boys wore caps in different colors to identify the grades they were in, and of course the caps gave them a distinction and status. Wearing caps was banned when the Socialist Party took over; it was considered discrimination, and this didn't fit into their philosophy.

The Lyceum was the upper class girls' school for well-to-do families. The Lyceum wasn't a very large school; it was organized like the gymnasium. My mother and her two sisters attended this school. It still existed when I started, but it didn't have the upper grades. A new school was built on the outskirts of town in a lovely park and contained dormitories to house the out-of-town students. That was a big improvement. They gave the school a fancy name, "Oberchule für Mädchen in Aufbauform." This was the school I attended.

In the forties, the structure of education changed; for example, only one foreign language was required. No one wanted to take French, so the whole class opted to take English. Instead of a third language, classes in art history were added. In 1944, cooking classes and gardening were also added. These classes were not to interfere with the academic classes. All these new subjects were mandatory, so they were added in the afternoon. For the gardening class, we dug up a corner in the park; most of the time was spent digging and raking. There was not much incentive to start growing things, since too little time was available. We mostly just went through the motions, and the teachers had more than they could handle. Their interest was academic teaching, and now some of them had to do both. The cooking class was a dilemma too. What could we cook, and where could we do it? A hot plate was set up, and all I can remember was a cabbage soup we cooked. Cabbage was abundant, and about the only thing the teachers could purchase without ration coupons. There just weren't ration cards for cooking classes. We all hated this.

A part of the socialist philosophy was that the women should be more domestic and not take jobs away from men. We clearly understood the intentions and the direction that education for women was headed.

Our Village

The village was a "Langdorf" or long village because it was long and narrow. It stretched about one kilometer, and had two parallel streets. The houses were nestled close together along the sides of the streets, with the farm buildings and farmyards behind them. The fields were spread around the village. Nobody had all their land in a single place. Some fields were quite far away. Horse-drawn buggies or wagons were the primary transportation. Of course, for visits to neighboring towns or for going to Pyritz, a carriage would be used; these had comfortable seats and looked nice. For special outings, we had a very fancy carriage called a landauer. Not every farmer had one, but ours had been passed down through the family, and we all loved it. Our landauer was navy blue with blue upholstery and leather lap covers, and a movable top with beautiful brass lanterns on either side. It took two horses to pull.

Almost every farmer employed one or two families to work for them in the fields. These families lived in separate houses that the farmers provided for free. The families also received produce, milk, and grain as payment for their work. Many of the families kept a goat or two and sometimes a pig, which they butchered as needed. An unspoken division existed between the farmers and the workers. In retrospect, nobody thought anything of it; this was the way it had always been. The itinerant families moved around; they would quit one farmer and move to another. The farmer could dismiss his workers if there were disagreements, but it seemed they never left the village. The young woman from one of our families worked for us first as a maid, then later, after she got married, both she and her husband continued to work for our family, and moved into one of the apartments.

Young farmer boys and girls often married someone in the village or someone from a neighboring village. Very few people moved far away. Quite a number of farmers had the same last name, and most of them were related. This often caused confusion, so sometimes, for clarity, a nickname was added related to where they lived or their profession.

Like all the other villages around, ours had its own post office.

I am not sure if the mail came by train or if there was already a mail truck in the area, but mail was delivered to the house every day. For a while, the post office was across the street from us as part of a home, apparently part of the family's living room. In a little hallway was the public phone. At that time, hardly anyone had a private telephone. One had to go to the post office to make a call. There was no privacy; the post lady operating the switchboard always listened in and was of course well-informed. We didn't have a phone, so we were forced sometimes to use the public phone. Mother hated it, and often asked me do the telephoning.

Everything in the village was close by, although from a child's perspective it seemed always too far. We children were often sent to run errands or take messages to friends or businesses. Without a phone, this was the quickest way. Many times, my sister and I argued about who should go or whose turn it was. However, for a visit to Knaack's market, the village store, we were both eager to go. We were quite young, maybe six and seven, when mother would give us a list of items which we handed to the storekeeper. They were items like sugar and salt that a household ran out of regularly and that we could carry in our basket—which we both held on to. We loved it when we had to wait for the storekeeper to fill the list. It gave us time to walk around and look at toys, pretty dolls in fancy boxes, glass bowls, or gifts for grownups. I begged father once for money so I could buy mother a vase for Mother's Day. I had seen this pretty blue vase and had fallen in love with it; to me it was the nicest I had ever seen. I must have been eight or nine years old, and the thought of giving her this on Mother's Day was so exciting. With all my anticipation and joy, I could hardly wait for the day. On our way to the store, my sister and I hoped the purchase was big enough to warrant a free little bag of hard candies. Sometimes Mr. Knaack would hand us these with a big smile as a surprise, and we would hurry home and divide the candy faithfully between the three of us.

Another shop we enjoyed was the butcher. I will never forget the wonderful aroma in the store. We seldom went to the butcher because father butchered our own animals at home. But sometimes mother thought we should have a change from our homemade sausages. Wie- ners and the butcher's own cold cuts were always a special treat; he had quite a variety. If Christa and I went along with mother, we had a hard time picking out the cold cuts; we each had our favorites. One favorite was always Jagdtwurst. At butchering time, liverwurst, blood- wurst, and salami were the sausages mother always made—the tradi- tional sausages on the farms. Of course, we always had the wonderful smoked ham. But the butcher's sausages were special because they weren't the kind we had at home.

The most important trades in the village were those pertaining to farming equipment. The village had at least two cartwrights, wheel- wrights, and blacksmiths. It was awesome to watch the blacksmith swinging a big hammer, pounding a piece of red-hot iron with the sparks flying about. His big doors were always open, and one couldn't help looking in when going by.

The railroad station was at one end of the village. Several trains came every day from both directions. The train was our connection

One of the two main streets in Köselitz, 1980s.

with the larger outside world. If we took the train to Pyritz, we could then travel in several directions. We could hear the noisy puffing steam engine from quite a distance, and many times I ran alongside, shouting, "Wait for me!" I went to school on the train, and if I missed the train, I missed school. The engineer often had to wait a moment for a straggler to hop on. In the evening came "Molly," a one-car diesel train. It was always fun riding Molly because it seemed so quiet and so much faster. It had just one big car where everyone rode together.

Sunday was the day of rest. Going to church was always a solemn and dignified time. Everyone belonged to the Lutheran faith, and went to church every Sunday morning. Men and women sat separately; children sat in the balcony, where the schoolteacher played the organ. This big old stone church was always very cold in the winter, even though the janitor fired up a large iron stove early in the morning.

After we were confirmed at the age of fourteen, we could sit with our parents. Our family always sat in the same pew. On special occasions, father would dress up with a top hat; he looked so formal. A plaque on the organ commemorated the donor, a Werner related to our family, who was the uncle of my grandfather and who gave my grandfather the family farm. This uncle loved children, but didn't have any and for many years he arranged a "Children's Fest" in the summer, paying for everything.

Our church seemed as old as the village. The building stood in the middle of the village, and was part fieldstone and part wood. The wooden steeple held two bells, and had turned black with age. A thick fieldstone wall around it also attested to its age. Between the church and wall was a long-forgotten graveyard; the gravestones had disappeared long ago. Tall trees offered shade. At each end of the graveyard was a big iron gate which was never locked. We often used pathways through the churchyard as a shortcut.

Life in the village seemed very well arranged. At each end of the main street was a pub. Meetings were held in the pubs, and once in a while in the winter, father went there to play billiards. Both places had ballrooms with a stage. Before Christmas, the teachers and school children usually staged a play, entertaining the whole town. In first grade, I had to recite a poem about St. Nikolaus in the play; what jitters I had! Parents admired the talents of their offspring, and the farmers relaxed and took time out for socializing.

The holiday season was also the time to visit with friends and relatives. Mother's sister Adelheid lived in Naulin, and we visited often, especially during the slow time of the year. Naulin was only four kilometers from Köselitz. Many times these visits were unannounced, and what a calamity it was when there was nothing baked in the kitchen! Father and Uncle Hans would sit and smoke a cigar. Mother and Aunt Adelheid would dash into the kitchen and quickly bake waffles; something that was quick to make. There had to be something to go along with the tea or coffee.

Even the smallest villages had a "Buergermeister" (mayor). Usually a farmer held the position. Most of his duties concerned farming. Our village also had a town crier—named Polzin—whose duty was to make village announcements. Polzin rode his bicycle to several designated stops. He had a list and a big brass bell; he shouted out what he wanted everyone to hear. Of course, everyone who heard the bell rushed to the front door and listened. There must have been town meetings, but I don't remember that.

Polzin was also the village's night watchman, and performed this duty on his bicycle, too. I remember my father asking him once to check on a pregnant mare in the stable at night. Polzin eventually knocked on my parent's bedroom window and reported that all went well; the little newborn foal was waiting by the stable door. It gave my father an awful scare; the foal had staggered around in the dark and could have been accidentally hurt by the other horses.

How the scary moments stay with us! One I clearly remember was when I was about twelve years old. I came home on the midnight train from my big summer vacation. I was the only one getting off the train. My fear of dogs running loose in the street was my biggest worry, because most of them would bite. Many farmers had the dogs for herding, or as watchdogs, and they were kept outdoors at all times. After being tied up all day, the dogs were very excited when they were let loose at night. I had good reason to be scared.

This was a wonderful moonlit night, and I gingerly tip-toed down the middle of the cobblestone street in my white dress, with my suitcase in hand. Suddenly, in the distance I saw a man on a bicycle coming towards me. At first it frightened me, but I soon figured it could only be Polzin, the night watchman. He, on the other hand, had no idea who or what was coming towards him. He dismounted his bicycle and walked very slowly towards me. I couldn't wait to meet up with him, and wondered why he was so slow. He told me later he was actually a little frightened because he thought he was seeing a ghost. I will never forget the words he called out as he came closer: "Wem is denn dat?" (in Plattdeutsch, *who is that?*). We were both relieved when we met. He offered to walk me home, and I gladly accepted. His helpfulness and kindness reached far beyond his position. He did all kinds of favors for people, and tried to look out for everyone. If he saw a bicycle left outside at night, he took it into the courtyard, or he closed someone's front door if it was open.

Winter was the time of rest, when people pursued their own interests. Women knitted and mended clothes, catching up with things that had been put aside during the busy season. Men came together for a card game or met in the pub for a round of billiards and beer. The farmers' daughters took advantage of their leisure time, and signed up with seamstresses in Pyritz for sewing lessons. This was not dressmaking; they learned how to make practical everyday garments such as underwear, shirts for men, and nightwear. White cotton or even homespun linens were used. Many sewed for their hope chests. Girls had fun meeting up with the boys who were going to Pyritz for agricultural classes. The young people all enjoyed the train rides to the city; for a day here and there, boys and girls had a good time away from their farm life.

Very little crime occurred in those days, so not every village had a policeman. The Köselitz policeman lived in Beyersdorf, about ten kilometers away. He was in charge of three or four villages; we didn't have a police or fire station. I am not sure whether there was a police station in Beyersdorf, or if he worked out of his home. His transportation was also a bicycle. His rotund body swayed on the bicycle as he rode along the sidewalk. He never looked like he was in a hurry, and always wore his uniform with shiny buttons and a fancy helmet with a chamois tuft on top.

One incident, though, put our little village on the front page all over the country. Our village was quite fortunate to have a lumberyard, the only one around. Mr. Papenfuss had a thriving lumber business. He also had the biggest construction business in the area. Besides lumber, he also had carpentry shops where doors and windows were made, as well as all the other items for home and barn construction. His house was beautiful; the loveliest in the village. I use to go by there every day on my way to the railroad station, and always wished I could live in a house like that. It had a front yard with beautiful flowers and white picket fences. The house was painted white; so different from most of the other red brick houses. I often wished I could have a peek inside.

Once a year in the fall, the "Farmer's Ball" was held in one of the pubs' large ballrooms. The ballroom was decorated with plants; tables and chairs were set up around the sides. A live brass band played. Everyone looked forward to this festive occasion. Those who didn't participate came to watch. The ladies dressed in their best gowns. It was probably for many the once-a-year dance party. Children with beaming faces took the first dance steps with their fathers. For the young single adults, it was a chance to mingle with the eligibles. Mother's older sister met her husband at such a dance. He came from a neighboring village to join in the fun. This was often the case, where young people explored the "neighborhood" to find a suitable partner.

One memorable year, I was old enough to remember the ball. It was in the evening and already dark. The dance came to an abrupt halt when a man came running in shouting "FIRE!" People ran outside to see where the fire was burning. An orange glow illuminated a dark smoke cloud. Whose house or barn could that be? There was great confusion. Several men were shouting orders and urging others to hurry. Of course, everyone was on foot. Some ran to the fire and others ran home to gather firefighting items. Horses had to be harnessed to pull the water wagon. Others ran to the shed where the water wagon and the pump were stored. The shed was the only enclosed facility, placed near a small water hole. Young men rolled up their sleeves and pumped, two or three on each side pulling the big handle up and down. The wooden ladders were stored in a lean-to against the church wall.

Schulze's barn down the street was burning. It was full of straw and grain from the recent harvest, and it quickly burned almost to the ground. As if that wasn't enough, in the next couple months, several other barns burned down too, always the old dilapidated ones. Some still had thatched roofs. Mr. Papenfuss, the lumberyard owner, was seen everywhere; lots of business was coming his way. The farmers who had lost their "old" barns were in high spirits. They had insured all their buildings and farm equipment. Some had even put all the farming equipment in the barns to make sure it would be lost, too. Many rumors started to go around. It didn't take long for the law to get to the root of it. Mr. Papenfuss wanted more business; he had persuaded these farmers to go along with his idea to burn down the barns and collect the insurance money. He would then build them new and better barns. It must have sounded very convincing to the farmers he had picked out to go along with this proposition. A farmhand was bribed to start the fires. The arson became the biggest scandal our sleepy little village ever had. It was written up in many newspapers all over Germany. The embarrassment for the families was indescribable. Otherwise well respected families were branded with this terrible crime. The farmers had to go to jail, and Mr. Papenfuss went to the penitentiary where he stayed until his death.

Our Farm

Our farm was considered medium-sized for that era; we had about one hundred sixty acres. The land was fragmented into several different parcels, all having their own names so that someone could be sent to a certain field by just its name. These names were probably handed down from the previous generations. My mother inherited the farm because there was no male heir, and my father married into it. My grandfather had inherited the farm from the childless uncle.

Usually a son would be chosen to be the heir, to hold up the tradition and the name, but my grandparents had three daughters. In this case, my mother, the middle daughter, was chosen to inherit the farm. New laws had been made so that farms couldn't be sold but only passed on within the family. Farms couldn't be divided either—if there were more than one boy in the family, one son, usually the eldest, was chosen to be heir. The others, if they wanted to stick to farming, had to try to marry into a farm. There was always the chance to go to school and further your education or become an apprentice and learn a trade. Children from the working class families sometimes preferred this trade option. There were plenty of opportunities even in these small villages.

My mother was probably chosen to inherit the farm because

Buchholz home (left) and farm help home (right), 2004.

her older sister, Adelheid, fell in love with a young farmer in the next village. Adelheid married very young, when she was only nineteen. This young man, Uncle Hans, had been working in a business in the city because his older brother was the heir to their farm. But the older brother died in World War I, and Uncle Hans had returned home to become a farmer. Uncle Hans would have preferred the city job; he never became a good farmer.

Grandmother had sent her three daughters to the Lyceum in Pyritz for higher education. She was determined to have her daughters well-educated, even though they didn't plan to attend the university. They boarded in Pyritz with a widowed lady, Mrs. Christian, who took in students and also taught them the finer things in life. Mother learned French and English, and especially loved French, using it many times instead of German words. Mother talked often about these school years and how she enjoyed being with Mrs. Christian and living in Pyritz. Besides school, the girls had piano lessons. Mother was quite accomplished. Their boarding school routine included being picked up in Pyritz by grandfather on Saturdays and returned on Sunday afternoon. Mother always talked fondly about these years going to school in Pyritz.

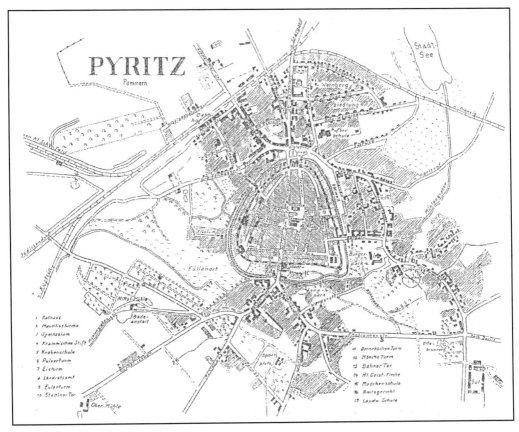

The ancient wall surrounding the center of the town.

Chapter Two

AS YOUNGSTERS ON OUR FARM

M y first memory from childhood is the birth of my brother Werner. He was born on June 13, 1932. Mother had spent three weeks in a Women's Clinic in Stettin, our provincial capital, and returned home with the baby. I wasn't quite four years old, but I remember this special occasion very well.

Grandmother prepared us for mother's homecoming with a new baby. It was one of those delightful sunny spring days. Christa and I were dressed in our Sunday dresses and white pinafores, and were each given a little flower bouquet to greet mother. Waiting for her arrival was a test of patience. Grandmother wanted us to be ready, but no one knew exactly when she would arrive. Father had hired a limousine to pick her up. Stettin was very far away for us little children; we couldn't go there with horse and buggy. We sat on the front steps where the old elm trees offered welcome shade. Time went by very slowly. Grandmother made up little stories, especially about the storks who brought babies and were nesting on the many barns. She kept encouraging us when our patience ran out; she didn't want us to get our dresses dirty, so we had to sit and wait. The flowers in our little bouquets, held so tightly in our hands, began dropping their heads. Finally, the car drove up. It was always a big excitement to see a car in our little village, since no one at that time had a car. Then mother stepped out with a bundle in her arms. She called out to us to come closer; she had a present. I should have been jumping for joy seeing mother again, but instead I became very shy and hid behind grandmother. It felt strange to see mother after she had been away for three weeks. She coaxed us to come closer and, of course, when she mentioned that she had a present, we quickly changed our minds. We wanted to see the present. Then she held out our little baby brother. Of course, we believed storks brought babies, and since we had many storks around, this had fastened our belief. It took us a little while to understand that this little baby was now part of our family. This was such a special event at my young age that it stayed with me all my life.

The baby was named Werner, which is mother's maiden name. Since there were no male heirs in her family, they wanted to hold on to the name. Lukas, my grandson, the son of my son, now carries the name as his middle name. Perhaps the name will continue to thread through future generations.

Buchholz family, Martha and Paul, Ingrid, Werner, and Christa, 1930s.

Grandmother

Traditionally, grandparents stayed with the child who inherited the farm or homestead. Our house was older and not very large, but grandmother had her own room and a small ante-room where she could retreat whenever she wanted. There were no nursing homes around, especially not in the country. Before Aunt Lydia, mother's younger sister, was married, she lived in the house, too.

Grandmother was always dressed in dark clothes; her long black skirts reached almost down to her ankles, and deep side pockets held her keys and handkerchief. I can still picture her with her sleeves rolled up, working in the kitchen with her hair tightly pulled back in a bun. On special occasions, she dressed up in a black velvet dress and wore a small velvet ribbon tightly around her neck, sometimes with a pretty broach.

Oftentimes this traditional arrangement didn't work out well, and caused much unhappiness. Such was the case with mother's older

Wilhelmine Reckner Werner, 1934.

sister, Adelheid, who lived in the next town of Naulin. There was no other place for her parents-in-law to go to; she had married the only son. They all had to live under the same roof, and this required tolerance on both sides.

Grandmother, or "Oma" as we called her, was still active and helped with the everyday chores in the household and garden, which was a great help for mother. If she wanted to travel to town alone or have her peace of mind, Oma was there to take care of us, the best possible babysitter.

We grew all our vegetables, so planting the garden in the spring and early summer was a huge task that grandmother assisted with. Oma expertly laid out the beds for the planting. She loved gardening, and gardened for a good part of her life. We children bent down right next to her as she taught us which were the new seedlings and which were weeds. Right then and there she planted the seed in me that grew into my love of gardening.

Lettuce and radishes were seeded quite early, but the different cabbage plants were bought from a garden business, which sold them by the piece. The gardener had an array of flats with seedlings. He pulled out as many as we asked for, always added two or three plants for good measure, and then wrapped the bare roots in newspaper. We had to be prepared to get these tender little plants into the ground right away, or they would quickly wilt. Watering was the biggest chore, because water had to be carried in buckets and watering cans from the pump in the farmyard to the garden. Carrying the water to the garden was a cumbersome task. Christa and I had our little buckets and helped. Oma taught us how to water each plant carefully, just a little bit, and not to spill the water.

Christa and I often spent time with Oma, because running a farm household kept mother very busy. Mother would just say, "Go see Oma," and off we trotted down the hallway. Oma was always happy to see us. Occasionally she would say, "Let me see what I can find in my secret drawer." Then she asked us, "Can you possibly eat a cookie?" I still remember her favorite cookie: an almond macaroon. Whenever mother went to town, she would buy a big bag of them for Oma.

The long dark winter afternoons were often spent in Oma's cozy room. On one wall was a red plush sofa with pillows she had embroidered, and over the sofa hung a large picture depicting a tranquil landscape. By the window was a table and chairs with a hand-crocheted tablecloth. In the summer, she always had a vase with flowers from our garden on the table. An imposing white tile stove, almost reaching to the ceiling, took up a corner of the room. These tile stoves were built by special stove fitters; the tiles were ceramic and beautifully glazed, and came in various shapes and colors. Often, the last row around the top was ornate. The stoves had to be connected to chimneys. If all the rooms required heat, the house would have several chimneys.

Halfway up the middle on the stove was an opening that was also tiled on the inside. This "warming oven" was a very practical way to keep food warm in the winter. We often roasted apples in this opening, wafting a wonderful aroma through the room which reminded us to check if they were ready. Apples were from our own trees and stored in the attic. They were laid out as a single layer on a sheet so that part of the attic smelled sweet and fruity. Even after the apples were gone, the fragrance lingered.

If we came in with cold hands, we darted right to the stove and warmed our hands; each room in the house had a stove. Sometimes the tiles were so hot that we couldn't directly lay our hands on them, so we stood on our tiptoes and searched higher up for a cooler spot. The warmth also dried our mittens after coming in from playing in the snow. In the evening, little sacks filled with grain were warmed in this opening, and placed in our beds to warm our sheets so we could snuggle our feet against them.

In front of the stove was a bench where Christa and I often sat in the evenings or on a cold and rainy day. Oma usually read to us as we sat there. I don't remember many children's books, but we at least had *Grimm's Fairytale* book. Oma would also read booklets of Greek myths which had been saved from mother's childhood. How we loved those stories of the vicious dragons! Zeus and Hercules became very real to us. Oma often didn't finish a story so that we were anxious to come back the next day.

When I was in first grade, I recall quite well how she oversaw my homework and practiced reading with me. I used to quickly memorize the lines, and when my finger didn't follow fast enough, a gentle tap on my head would result; she didn't have much patience with poor behavior. Learning was very important to her; she had sent her three daughters to boarding school for higher education, which was unusual for farm girls in the early 1900s.

Once in a while, Grandmother spent a few weeks with her youngest daughter, Lydia, and her family who lived in Seefeld, about 50 kilometers away. It was always exciting for us children to visit Seefeld because we had to travel there by train, changing trains in Pyritz and also Stargard, the next larger train station. She died in Seefeld at her daughter Lydia's home in the summer of 1936; she was sixty-eight years old and the only grandparent I ever knew.

Mother had a loving relationship with her mother, and she wore only black mourning clothes for a time. It was the custom in those days that one would mourn in black clothes for about a year and then gradually change. No one would have dared to do otherwise. Decades later, the daughter of the minister who married Aunt Lydia and Uncle Ewald in 1932 sent me their wedding picture. Apparently, the minister in those days was often a friend of the family and was given a wedding picture. I was thrilled because Oma is in the picture. It is the only picture I have of her.

Spring

Springtime was especially wonderful. We couldn't wait to trade our heavy stockings for socks and shed our hand-knitted sweaters. Snowdrop flowers that braved the snow and cold delighted us as the first sign that spring was on the way. Crocuses and narcissus were waiting for the sun to warm the earth. Soon came the time when the chickens, ducks, and geese hatched. Little cozy baskets were set up in a warm place in the house. Hatching all the broods always took quite a while, sometimes weeks, since the eggs didn't hatch all at once. The tiny creatures had to be kept warm before they were returned to their mothers. Sometimes we taught them to eat, and we had to be very gentle picking them up. Holding them to my face was delightful; they were so soft and warm.

Mother knew from experience to look for hens in the farmyard who made a clucking sound, an indication that they were ready to

Christa and Ingrid, 1930s.

sit on eggs. In the carriage house was a special section enclosed with a lattice wall. This was the breeding room for the hens. Several long wooden cages with lids were set up along the walls to keep the hens in place. The insides were divided into five or six small individual sections, just big enough for each hen. In each section a soft nest was prepared with straw and hay, and here the hen was placed on about a dozen eggs. The hens plucked some of their own soft feathers and made the nests even softer. More hens were added as mother searched them out. Dates were recorded, and a daily routine was started. This was mother's job, and she went twice a day to check them. The lids were opened, and the hens waited patiently as she grabbed them one by one to lift them out so they could eat and drink. These hens were in their own world as they clucked constantly to familiarize their brood with their sound. After a while, mother went back to put them onto their nests again.

One year we were given two little baby goats. We fed them milk from a bottle, and were delighted when they followed us around. We even persuaded Father to let us sleep with them in the stable for a night where we made little beds with hay and blankets.

Christa is only a year younger than I; we practically grew up as twins during our pre-school years. But that doesn't mean we were always the best of friends. We had our share of fights, like many young siblings. At times, mother couldn't figure out who was at fault and punished us both, sometimes with spankings. I can still hear her preaching, "Always tell the truth even if it means there will be punishment." That was often tough to stick to. She laid the groundwork for shaping our lives and guiding us to be responsible for our actions.

Farming people depended much on the weather, and Easter was usually the start of the busy season. Church also played a big role in this holiday. We all belonged to the Lutheran Reformed Church. After Easter, confirmations took place. We all looked forward to this celebration. We especially looked forward to the end of Bible school; two years of classes were held once a week in the afternoon by the local minister. These classes helped us prepare for confirmation between the ages of 12 and 14.

In 1941, when I started going to Bible school, we were already at war and our young minister was drafted. The established routines had to change. The older ministers from the surrounding towns shared the preaching in parishes where the younger ministers were in the military service. A minister from Pyritz had taken on our church. He came on Wednesdays, the Bible school day. He rode the same train I took home from school. The class was held in the village school. It was always a mad rush. I ran most of the way to the school, and in my mind I went over what I had just read during the fifteen-minute train ride. We were always given homework, such as memorizing hymns and Bible passages. I was hoping that I could quickly check again what I needed to know before the minister stepped into the classroom.

For the eighth graders, confirmation signaled both the end of Bible school and the religious celebration of being received in the church. Everyone had parties. For most youngsters, this meant entering the adult world. Some started working on farms, and others learned a trade—usually something related to farming like smithery, carpentry, or wheelwrighting. In my day, not a single boy went on to higher education.

Easter was a big two-day holiday. Several days before, we decorated our Easter baskets with colorful little ribbons and had them ready for the big event. Mother traveled to Pyritz, and shopped for wonderful decorated Easter eggs and filled chocolate eggs and chocolate bunnies in all sizes. We could hardly wait to have these delectable treasures in our baskets.

To go "stüppen" was an old custom in our region. One needed budding spring green twigs to tie together into a switch. If we couldn't find any with budding leaves, some days before we would place some twigs in water to force the first little green leaves out. With the switch, the children would go to neighbors' or friends' houses and recite the little rhyme: "*Stüpp stüpp Osterein, gibst du mir kein Osterei, stüpp ich dir den Rock entzwei.*" They gently tapped or pretended to hit the neighbor or friend with the switch until they were given sweets or real eggs. We all hoped for a sunny warm day so we could wear our new Easter dresses. The little girls wore big bows in their hair. Part of the fun was to wait for other children to come to our house and then *stüppt* each other. Our eggs were hidden by mother in the garden behind trees and in the low boxwood hedges surrounding the flower garden. Sometimes when the hedges were trimmed later in the year, here and there a missed Easter egg was found.

The two-day Pentecost holiday came next. Ascension Day was a few weeks later, in late May or early June. These were Protestant holidays that everyone celebrated; we had no Catholics in our village. We all went to church on Sunday morning, especially on Pentecost Sunday. A two-day holiday was wonderful. People dressed nicely and enjoyed the second day by visiting or just resting. We were ready to say good-bye to the nasty cold spring weather and wear summer dresses. Many front doors were decorated with birch branches—a custom in the area. It made the village look very green and festive. We strolled up and down the street in our Sunday dresses to see who had the most attractive door decorations.

Ascension Day, an old custom, was the day of our big annual village picnic. What a worry we had about the weather! We needed a warm and sunny day because it was an outing into the nearby forest where we would meet with family and friends, including our cousins from Naulin and mother's sister Adelheid. Mother was in charge of the picnic, and father got our best carriage out. He dusted it off and polished the brass lanterns. We didn't really need the lanterns, but they made the landauer look so much more elegant. The harnesses were rubbed with oil and all the brass polished until it gleamed.

As soon as we arrived at the forest, we ran around to locate Aunt Adelheid and Uncle Hans and the cousins so that we could picnic next to them. They had about the same distance from Naulin to the forest as we had from Köselitz. Blankets were spread under shady trees, and a wonderful picnic was laid out, with ham and liverwurst sandwiches, stuffed eggs, and lots of cake. Soon we children ran off to look for our friends. The game warden's hunting lodge was always one of the first places to visit, to see if new trophy antlers and stuffed animals had been added to the wall displays. We bought ginger ale and ice cream at the nearby old-fashioned restaurant—another place we explored. All this was part of our annual excursion, but the excitement was always new again. This was also the time to pick the wildflower woodruff. It was just about to bloom, making it the right time for picking. It had always been part of the outing. The plant had a lovely fragrance and also a special taste; we used it for tea or just a cold drink. We also dried it and made little bundles to put into drawers and closets so the fragrance would keep moths away.

As all good times must come to an end, so did our picnic afternoon. We had feasted and played enough but one more fun time was still to come: decorating the carriage for our ride home. It was just about the time when the beech trees sprouted their first leaves. These small, shiny leaves felt like silk, a little fuzz still covering the underside, and when the leaves moved in the breeze, a silvery gleam waved through the air. We picked the prettiest and silkiest branches and dec-

Stork nest on the Köselitz church, restored after the war, 2009.

orated the carriage and the horses. We stuck little branches into all the spaces we could find on the carriage, such as behind the lanterns and especially on the back and sides. Even the horses' harnesses were not spared. As we waved "Good-bye" to our cousins and friends, everyone was happy that this day had turned out so splendidly.

A wonderful sign of spring was the return of the storks. Some farmers still had thatched barn roofs, which were the stork's preferred nesting sites. Some even had a nest at each end of a barn. We loved to watch the storks repairing their nests and later hatching the young. In later years environmental scientists would come and band the young before they were ready to leave the nest. Seeing the young storks practice flying was fun to watch. Often the nest seemed too small for all the activity. We believed for the longest time that storks brought the babies to our village, and we had a little song that we would sing while watching the storks. *"Klapperstorch du Guter, bring mir ein kleinen Bruder, Klapperstorch du Bester, bring mir eine kleine Schwester."*

In back of our gardens was a little creek called the Bruchgraben, with a wetland on either side which was the perfect feeding ground for the storks. We had an adventure one day catching a stork in the tall wetland reeds. It hopped, but didn't seem to be able to fly. It was hard for us to walk in the mushy reeds, too, but we were determined to get to the stork. As we approached, we realized it had a broken wing. Now we had a goal: to save the stork. My sister ran up to the house to fetch our little wagon, then, with the friend who was with us, we chased the stork until we grabbed him. He was much bigger on the ground than he looked on the roof. We also discovered when he bit my hand that he was a fierce fighter. But we managed to set him into our little wagon, and two of us held him down. Our parents were not very happy; they didn't allow us to keep the stork. Mother explained that the wing wouldn't heal by itself and that he could never fly again. It had never entered our minds that this wonderful stork, our trophy, could die. We decided to find someone who could take care of him, because we didn't want him to die. Father suggested the shepherd in the town. We took the stork there, and the shepherd promised to catch frogs and mice to feed him. It had never occurred to us that taking care of a stork was such a big task and that a broken wing would not heal by itself.

A few years later on a sunny fall day I had an unexpected encounter. I was riding my bicycle through the fields when I heard the loud, familiar sound of clapping storks. As I drew closer, I realized this must be the day the storks were gathering to leave on their long journey to the Nile Delta in Egypt. The bare, flat field in front of me was their gathering place. I immediately knew this was very special, and quickly lay down my bike to sit and watch; I knew I might never witness this again. There must have been fifty or more storks jumping up and down. Their long, red legs seemed like rubber bands, their heads were thrown back, and their long beaks clapped incessantly. Perhaps they were electing a leader to guide them safely across the Mediterranean Sea. Finally, they flapped their wings and became airbound. Waves of air swooshed over me as they ascended into the sky. My eyes followed this black and white cloud, still unorganized and very noisy, until they were just little dots on the horizon.

In May came the invasion of the "Maikaefers," large bugs similar to June bugs found in America. They seemed to come from nowhere, and appeared all in one day. It was a plague the adults dreaded. They ravaged trees and hedges with their big appetites for tender new leaves. For us youngsters, this was a time for fun and pranks. Normally the bugs were mostly brown, but we looked for the ones who had more white on the wings and called them "millers." We stored them in matchboxes or cigar boxes, and actually played with them. Boys sneaked up on us girls and stuffed a handful into the back of our shirts; a not-so-pleasant experience which resulted in laughing and screaming. All this happened in the evenings when the bugs came out; they slept during the day under the leaves.

The maple tree in front of our house was one of their favorite trees. The bugs were safe at night, but in the morning father would shake the bugs from the branches. They were quickly swept into a large bucket and fed to the chickens or pigs.

Summer

Summer was embraced with open arms. Six weeks of school vacation was a marvelous gift of free time. The big garden with its many berry bushes and fruit trees was a haven where we could always find a juicy strawberry or raspberry; whatever was in season. Climbing the cherry tree and eating to our hearts' content was part of summer. We met with the neighborhood children and played ball and jump rope in the street. One ball game comes to my mind that was a simple game of agility. One would use different parts of the body to hit a ball on a flat wall, starting with one hand, then both hands, and then a knee, and so forth. If one dropped the ball before one did it ten times in a row, the partner had her turn. We played this game endlessly.

In the evening when more children were around, we formed teams and played "drive ball." The aim was to throw a ball as far as we could to the opposite team, who tried to drive it back. A good ball-thrower was important, and a good catcher, too. We didn't have organized sport teams in school. Sometimes the boys here and there formed teams and played soccer.

Bicycles were our best friends, but all of them were old enough to be retired to the junkyard. We had no other transportation, so we had to take care of them the best we could. It seemed that something always needed to be fixed. The bicycles had to last, since there was no way to buy a new one, so we oiled and cleaned them carefully. We became good at putting the chains back on. We learned quickly never to leave without the bicycle pump.

Adele, a friend in the neighborhood, and I were born on the same day. We had another thing in common: we liked to sew for our little dolls. We must have been seven or eight years old. She lived next to a dressmaker, and always had lots of scrap material. Our dolls were about five or six inches tall. We sewed tiny clothes for them, and were delighted with our creations. Many times we sewed while sitting on the ground by her house or on the doorstep. Perhaps this laid the groundwork for my interest in sewing in later years.

Days were long in the summer, and breakfast was early. Around ten o'clock we had a midmorning break. Everyone, including the farm hands, would eat a sandwich and have a cool drink. It was like a second breakfast. A similar break also happened in the afternoon. The day's biggest meal was served at noon. Mother didn't like it if we ate at a friend's or neighbor's house. If we were hungry, we were supposed to come home. But who wanted to go home when you were having fun with your friends and you were offered a snack at their house? We were really tested. We were to say, "No thank you, we are not hungry." Who believed that? It didn't always work; food tasted so much better at someone else's house.

Aunt Lydia's Wedding

Wedding bells were ringing for Aunt Lydia. The festivities took place in our home in 1934 on a wonderful sunny day in June. These farm weddings were usually celebrated in the homes. Aunt Lydia had lived with us at times; this was her home, too. Since grandmother lived with us, it was only natural the wedding would be at our house. Aunt Lydia was marrying Ewald Spieckermann from Seefeld, a small town a little farther away. He had a small farm and a position in the town government.

Preparations for the wedding started weeks in advance. This was the third wedding grandmother had to arrange and carry out, but of course this time she had the help of my mother. A cook was hired to help plan the meals; cakes and tortes were selected and ordered from the local baker, who didn't just bake bread, but was also a talented pastry baker. Fresh fish came from a distant relative who had fishing rights on a lake. One or two fish courses were always offered at festivities like weddings. A large basket of live eels was delivered and left in the farmyard. The eels wiggled out of the basket, to the delight and excitement of us children, and were soon all covered with sand stuck to their skin. They had no resemblance to eels anymore. A quick retrieval was forthcoming.

Eel was prepared in aspic for a special touch to the evening meal. Mother kept praying for good weather. Even though the festivities were inside, much was also going on outside. A rainy day would be terrible. Our house wasn't very large, so furniture had to be removed from the rooms to make space for tables and chairs.

The celebration began on the eve of the wedding. It was the "Polterabend," an old custom where broken crockery, glass, and dishes were further smashed at the front door of our house for good luck for the bride and groom. The custom also called for the bride and groom to clean up the smashed pieces. Of course, it was the farm hands early the next morning who were busy with shovels and rakes to take the mess to the town dump. For the townspeople, the Polterabend was a fun occasion and not missed by many. Everyone who wanted to and could participated; they lingered outside until platters of cake were passed around. Large sheet cakes had been baked especially for this occasion. Many guests had arrived to join this evening of fun and merriment that included reading funny poems and telling silly stories. People even dressed up for skits. The party lasted into the wee hours of the morning.

Early the next morning, the farmyard was swept and tidied up. The farm hands ran around to check and see if anything had been overlooked. The stable doors were closed, and space was made for the guests who arrived with horse and buggy. For the out-of-town guests, overnight stays had been arranged in friend's houses. Many townspeople were also invited, including neighbors and distant relatives who lived in the village.

By midmorning, the guests started to gather outside the house,

Lydia and Ewald wedding processional, 1934.

waiting to form the procession to the church for the ceremony. Neighbors introduced themselves to the out-of-town guests. Relatives who hadn't seen each other for awhile stood around in small groups chatting and passing on family news. The ladies wore long gowns, and the men, not to be out-done by the ladies, wore tuxedos and top hats. The four of us—the two cousins and my sister and I who were part of the procession—couldn't wait for the start.

Finally, the bride and groom stepped out of the front door and slowly made their way to the street to start the procession. The church was very close by, and we all walked. My sister Christa and Cousin Sigismund, the flower children, strew flower petals on the cobbled street. Cousin Hans Dietrich and I, just a year older, walked behind the bride and groom holding up the veil and train of the bride's dress. Grandmother and Ewald's mother and father were the first ones to walk behind us and the bride and groom. Grandmother kept an eye on us to stay in step with the bride and groom and make sure we weren't letting the train sweep down on the street. All the other guests walked in pairs behind them. Christa and I had white organdy

Lydia and Ewald Spieckermann wedding photo in front of the Buchholz barn, 1934. Ingrid is the third child from the left on the blanket.

dresses on, and were told over and over again not to get dirty before the picture-taking, which was on the return from the church. I don't remember the ceremony except that we couldn't wait for it to be over.

Setting up the group photo took a long time. It was arranged in front of one of the large barn doors; benches were placed for the group in the back. We youngsters sat on blankets in front of the first row, the little ones on one side and the bigger boys on the other. It really tested our patience to sit still for what seemed like an eternity.

The feasting took all afternoon, starting with a big dinner at noontime. I don't know how many courses were served, but they included soups, beef, pork, chicken, and fish. Then, in the afternoon, came the coffee with fancy cakes and tortes. In between meals, the guests went for walks and visited with each other. Like most weddings, there was music and dancing. A brass band had played in the afternoon sitting outside by the door, and then at night, the real fun began. The guests strolled to the pub which had been reserved for dancing in the evening. Aunt Lydia's wedding made an indelible impression; never again have I been to such a generous and lavish wedding.

Aunt Lydia left with her husband and made her home in Seefeld. To visit her, we had to take the train, so we didn't get to see them very often. We missed Aunt Lydia; she had been a big part of our young lives. After a while, they bought a car and Aunt Lydia learned to drive. She came to visit more often after that. Uncle Ewald was an early member of the National Socialist Party. Sometimes he wore his uniform and looked very important to me. He had a picture of Adolf Hitler hanging right over the old-fashioned desk in his office.

Many horse and buggy rides were made to Naulin where mother's older sister, Adelheid, lived. They also had a farm. She was married to Hans Schmerse. Since it was only four kilometers away, we often walked there, spent a few hours, and returned home. Later, when we had bicycles, we children biked. When visiting as a family, we would always go by horse and buggy. Of course, these visits were reciprocal, and often unannounced. Our cousins Brigitta and Elisabeth were eight and nine years older than we were, and often had other plans, but we would always have fun with the boys Hans Dietrich and Sigismund who were our age.

No one had much time during the summer to visit due to the farm work, but birthdays were always celebrated. Mother's birthday was at the busiest time, in early August, right in the middle of the harvest. Her birthday celebration often would be on the following Sunday. Big announcements were not made and invitations were not sent out either. Then it would be guesswork who might come. These surprise visits were not always welcomed, but that was the way it was done. The thought behind the surprise visits was to keep the hostess from going through a lot of meal planning and extra work. There was always plenty of food on hand, but the cake for the afternoon coffee was sometimes a problem. I can still see my mother quickly mixing up a batch of dough and deep-frying something like doughnuts. We called it "Schuerzkuchen." The soft dough was rolled out and cut into oblong pieces, and then one end was twisted through a slit in the middle. I often helped with this, and couldn't wait to eat the first one; they were especially delicious when still warm and sprinkled with confectioner's sugar.

Our trips did not extend very far. Visiting was always a happy time, no matter how close by. Most of our trips were with horses and buggy. Father's sister Minna lived in Bahn. Bahn was about 20 kilometers away, and we didn't go there often. I remember the last visit in the middle of winter. Father loved to go there in the winter since it was a time when everyone rested and had plenty of time. The horses were frisky, and needed a good run. They had cabin fever just like people when there was no outlet for stress and exercise.

It was a long ride to Bahn. Since the days this time of year were short, we left very early in the morning and came home late at night. The three of us children were bundled up in wool blankets and fur foot warmers, little sacks where we put both feet in. Warm scarves and hats covered the rest of us. Our parents had fur-lined coats.

The air was cold and crisp. We pulled our scarves over our mouths and noses. It hurt to breathe in the icy air. A layer of frozen snow covered the road. We listened to the crunchy sound of the horses' hooves on the road. Now and then, they would have to snort in the cold air. Despite the cold weather, it was a marvelous night coming back. Father always tried to pick a day when he knew there would be enough moonlight for the late ride home. The black sky was studded with sparkling stars. The longer I looked, the more stars seemed to appear; I felt closer to the stars than ever before. We counted shooting stars and made secret wishes. This was in 1943. Who would have thought that it was the last time we saw our relatives?

Fall

Fall was just as busy a season as the summer. Apples, pears, and plums ripened. Mother kept us helping with the picking. Much of the fruit was preserved and canned for the winter. It seemed she had just finished slaving over making jams and jellies from the currants when more chores waited for her.

The harvest of potatoes and beets had to be brought in. This was hard work because the potatoes were picked by hand after being plowed out. Three weeks of school vacation was timed around this work. Older children helped during this time, because hired help in the last two war years was especially scarce. Christa and I had to help, too. It was dirty work; we dreaded to climb on the wagon in the morning, wearing several layers of clothes, old shoes, and pants. Many times, it was still foggy and damp, and it was always cold. Old gloves were saved for this, and came in very handy. When the potatoes were plowed up, earth still clung to them as if the potatoes did not want to let go of what had nurtured them all summer. Sometimes the men would set fire to a pile of dry potato stalks and we would roast potatoes. I really disliked being out in the field at this time of year. Christa, a year younger than I, was taller and stronger. We worked together as a team. Father gave us one row at a time. Together we picked up the potatoes from the plowed row and placed them in a big basket. In order to dump the potatoes into a sack, we both had to hold on to the full basket, which was large and bulky. Then one of the men would tie them up, and load the sacks onto a wagon. Some were taken home for storage, but most were sold. By the end of the day, the tired driver was bent over on the hard wooden seat of his wagon. The horses hung their heads, and with a monotonous clop-clop, pulled home the last wagon of the day. One sensed that they were tired, too.

Other tasks we helped out with included herding the cows. It was not an easy task to walk them to the grazing fields. We were just fourteen and fifteen years old. Usually, father hired a young man for this, but in 1943 and 1944, all the young men were in the service. Christa and I had to help out where needed. I sometimes chose to herd the cows. I packed my little knapsack with a sandwich and a drink along with my book or some handiwork, but most of the time I read. I would be out with the cows all day, reading. Our wonderful dog, Strolch, who was trained to herd, was a dear companion, and always ready to chase a cow that had strayed into the neighbor's field back to the herd. In our area, the division between properties was just a narrow strip of grass and weeds, and if there was something more tasty on the neighbor's field than what was on ours, the cows quickly headed that way. Everyone knew their field's borders.

Mother, and for that matter I, too, worried about the trains. Even though I drove the herd on dirt roads through fields, I had to cross the railroad tracks sometimes twice before I came to the designated grazing field. There were no guardrails or warning signals at the railroad crossings. Many times mother said, "Wait ten more minutes so you don't have to worry about the train." It didn't always work out, because many times freight trains came in between the regular trains. If this happened and I saw the train coming, there was no other way but to chase the herd with shouting and waving arms across the tracks; stopping the cows in their walk was impossible.

On one of my herding days, a cow wandered off on the railroad tracks, which had steep banks on either side. She rambled along on the track. I just couldn't get by her to make her turn around. Then I heard the train in the distance. The more I tried to get by her, the faster she walked. The train engineer had seen this dilemma and had to stop the train. A disgruntled look let me know he wasn't very happy. Finally, I got in front of the cow and made her turn around.

What a relief it always was to finally arrive at the field for the day. Father would sometimes stop by to see if all was well. One time, I let the cows graze in a clover field because they love clover. Father had warned me not to let them graze too long, since it causes gas, and can kill a cow. Later, I noticed a cow struggling to stay on her feet. I was very scared, and dashed off to find father. The cow was dragged home on a platform with a runner which was made for this purpose. Father knew what to do to relieve the gas, and the cow recovered after a while.

Every farmer had his own pastures, but not everyone herded the animals. Quite often, we would meet up with someone else's herd. Since milking time was usually around five o'clock in the afternoon, we often met other herds at the small pond in the middle of the village as they too headed back to the milking.

Actually, it was more a watering hole than a pond. Here, nothing could stop the cows. After not having anything to drink all day, they dashed for the water, and the different herds became all mixed up. I could never tell one cow from another, but when they had enough water, they would regroup and trot back on the cobblestone street, each herd finding its way home. It was just amazing. They proceeded to the cow stable, where they found exactly their own station to be chained and milked. They were used to this routine, and would hold their heads still while the chain was placed around their necks.

In 1944, Werner turned twelve years old in June. Father thought he was old enough to take on a man's job. It was time for the grain harvest to be brought in. This was a year of testing everyone's ability. There was very little farm help, and enormous pressure from the government to produce as much as possible.

The weather always played a great role. Sudden thunderstorms and hail could flatten the field and ruin the grain. The grain, still on the straw, had to be dry since it had to be stored in the barn for threshing in the winter months. Wet straw would mold in a very short time. For bringing in the grain, the wagons were modified to "ladder wagons" with sides that spread out to hold more straw.

Werner would sit on top of a loaded wagon, guiding it home from the field. Sometimes the load was packed so high that it swayed back and forth on the uneven cobblestone road. One hardly saw him in the midst of all the straw which was piled so that he could only look straight ahead. Mother was worried, and feared for his safety. She waited by the door when she thought it was time for him to come. These big loads sometimes tipped over; horses could get skittish when something startled them. Werner was very proud to do a man's job.

Winter

Winter came early in these northern regions. Many times it started to snow in late November. We always looked forward to a white Christmas with plenty of snow. During the weeks before the holidays, the household churned to prepare for the winter months. The Pfefferkuchen dough for Christmas had to be prepared. A large amount of dough was made and preserved in a big brown crock pot for whenever cake was needed; it lasted for weeks if kept in a cool place. The dough was made with honey, which colored it an amber color, and provided a distinct fragrance and flavor. The mixture of spices, which included cinnamon, nutmeg, and cardamom, were sold in little packs at the market. Mother just cut off a chunk of dough, rolled it out, and baked it on a large cookie sheet. Sometimes she sprinkled on almonds or other nuts that she happened to have on hand. A variation of the dough with more butter and sugar and honey was also made for cookies, and then we children could let our artistic ideas flow. We didn't want to just cut out stars and hearts; we formed shapes of little people and animals, using raisins for buttons and eyes. Each of us had her own assortment, and we made sure that after baking they were ours. This was the once-a-year treat at Christmastime.

Early winter was the best season for the important task of butchering, since it was cold and we had no refrigerators. The meat was preserved in different fashions. Father did the butchering. The pig, for its unceremonious death, was chosen quite early, and fattened up. Its belly almost hung to the ground.

A few days before the planned date, father gathered all the large knives, and took them into his workshop to sharpen them. Usually one of us had to go out with him to turn the old-fashioned grinding wheel. But a hand-sharpening stone was always on hand in the kitchen. The knives needed to be sharpened more than once, since a lot of cutting happened during the holidays.

Everyone dreaded the dicing of onions, and there were plenty of them. No one ever volunteered, so mother always ended up doing it herself. It was an endless crying session. One time I came home on the day before the butchering and saw mother and Christa wearing old eyeglasses while peeling a large bowl of onions. I burst out laughing. They didn't think it was funny; their wet cheeks were glistening and their eyes were red. They both had a large handkerchief next to them. They invited me to help them and join in the crying and sniffling.

On the day of the butchering, the household awoke into full swing very early in the morning. Father was the first one up. The butchered pig had been hung outside on a ladder to cool. He brought in the pieces of meat on a wooden tray that had been saved for this task. The tray had been used many times, perhaps even when mother was a little girl.

Now mother and her helpers went to work. Everything was done by hand. The meat grinder (now probably a museum piece) needed a strong arm. Nothing was electrified. That's when father came in handy. The women worked fast, with sweaty brows and red faces. The kitchen was like a steambath. The window panes were fogged up due to the cold air outside, and little rivulets of water ran down onto the window sill.

Nothing was wasted. Large pots of meat were boiling on the stove to make sausages. All the fatty parts were boiled into lard, which was spiced with thyme and onions. Lard and butter were the only fats we used for cooking.

All kinds of jars and herbs and spices had been checked and lined up days before. Their fragrances mixed with the smell of boiled meats. The mixtures for the liverwurst and bloodwurst were important. Lots of wursts were made. Mother had to use her talent to mix the flavors just right. "Maybe a little more thyme and salt and pepper," she would say out loud. She took pride in her skill; she wanted everyone to compliment her on her delicious sausages.

Some of the mixtures went into sausages, and some were preserved in jars. Fancy sausages were fried brown and crispy, and also preserved in jars for future meals. We all liked the homemade salami, which required a mixture of meats; extra beef was bought for this.

Mother's job was to taste all the mixtures. Every family had their own recipes, and often they were handed down from mother to daughter. Hams and bacon sides had to be brined before they were ready for smoking. A great many sausages were also smoked to preserve them, especially the salamis. The smoke chamber was in the attic.

Certain good friends looked forward to sampling the fresh sausages and special meats, so baskets with several different kinds of food were put together as gifts. For a few days, every doorknob in the house felt greasy and sticky. I really didn't like to be around at this time.

This was also the time the geese and ducks were butchered; mainly geese, since we didn't have many ducks, and the ducks were often saved for Sunday dinners. One or two geese were saved for Christmas, because Christmas dinner always included the traditional roasted goose stuffed with apples.

Killing the geese was a task for the women. They had no qualms about killing the geese; I still don't know how they did it. They wouldn't let us watch them. Oftentimes, the neighbors helped each other, especially when it came to plucking the feathers. That was such a monotonous job. Plucking had to be done immediately while the geese were still warm; otherwise, the feathers left awful quills in the skin which were almost impossible to remove.

With scarves tied tightly around their hair, the women set out to the washhouse. Here, it didn't matter; the feathers could dance all over everything. The last bits of down were singed off over a kerosene flame. The feathers were stuffed into pillowcases or big bags, and saved for the long winter evenings when friends and neighbors were invited to the "Federreissen" party, which was an old custom. During the plucking, the feathers and down were mixed just the way they came off the goose. Down was highly valued, and it took a while to save up enough for a wonderfully soft quilt.

Mother had saved up feathers for a few years, then surprised us with her plan to have a Federreissen party which was also a social get-together with friends and neighbors. This was exciting for us children, since we had never participated in one. Mother promised us that we were old enough to stay up. There wasn't much going on in the winter, and anything that brought a little diversity was very welcomed.

Everyone helped prepare for the event. The upholstered furniture had to be removed from the room, since down would stick on them. Think of "light as a feather." Just exhaling deeply made the down fly all over. A long table was set up in the middle of the room, with the mix of down and feathers piled on it. The ladies sat around separating the feathers from the down, putting each into the appropriate container; usually a pillowcase. The larger feathers were stripped from the quill and put in a separate container for use in bedding and pillows.

For the ladies, the fun began with getting their mother's or grandmother's neatly stored-away dresses out. Nothing would stick to these shiny silk dresses. The hair had to be covered, too, which resulted in another fashion statement. Little silk hats or scarves had been saved for these occasions. This was not a boring work party; it was a hilarious story-telling time. It was the best entertainment. Christa and I were old enough to stay up and join the ladies.

We laughed with hands held in front of our mouths and tears running down our cheeks. The younger women talked about funny encounters with the opposite sex, telling stories one didn't think possible in our little village. I still remember some of them. Afterwards, the table was cleared—but the evening wasn't over. Refreshment time came next. A favorite was a freshly baked "Berliner," a jelly-filled doughnut. In the old days, sometimes young men joined the event near the end of the night for dancing.

Even though the winter days were short and it was very cold, farm work always had to be done. Threshing the grain began as early as possible after the last harvest. What a dusty and noisy job that was! One winter when everything was done, father set to work to build a wagon. We were all so proud of his accomplishment; he also built a two-piece working sled. I think it was his own design. It was used to bring logs for heating from the woods. A sled lent itself much better to this type of transportation than a wagon. We had snow all winter; it started in early December, and sometimes even in November.

Mounds of snow on the sides of the road remained there all winter. The snow plowing was done with horses; the farmers had to take turns. But despite the plowing, the road was never clean of snow.

Sleighs could be used almost all winter. Horses were shoed with special cleats to keep them from sliding or falling. It was always exciting when father announced on a nice day that we were going to take out the sleigh and visit our relatives in Naulin. For our own family's pleasure, we used our little sleigh, which looked just like the ones on Christmas cards; like a relic of the past. It was quite small, with straw mats around the inside. This little sleigh was usually used for visiting, but once in a while father traveled to Pyritz with it. He had a certain place where he left the sleigh or the buggy in the town. This place had a livery stable for the horses. It reminds me of an old-fashioned way station. It also had a pub— a welcome sight in the winter. A hot toddy was much appreciated on a cold day after sitting on the open sleigh or buggy. Father then went on foot about his business in town.

After being used to hearing the clop, clop of the buggy horses on the cobblestones, the sleigh was almost noiseless. Could it be that's why there are sleigh bells? We never left without the bells. They were polished until they gleamed in the sun. If I close my eyes, I can still hear the jingle. It was the only real sound on the snow-covered road.

Sleigh rides, sledding, and skating were our main winter activities. When we were younger, we built igloos and snow forts in the mounds of snow on the side of the road, and poured buckets of water over them so they would ice up and become quite sturdy.

The bigger boys plugged up the culverts of the "Bruchgraben" creek that ran around the village. It was muddy, not good for swimming. We were always warned not get too close or venture to cross the creek on the skinny board the neighbor had put across. The land on either side was swampy and wet. Bright yellow buttercups with shiny green leaves covered the wetland in the spring, and tall, lush grass and cattails took over in the summer. But in the cold winter season, it was flooded, and became a wonderful skating surface. All we had to do was walk a few hundred yards behind our gardens and we were there. Our parents never had to worry that we might fall through the ice. Since it was shallow, the worst that could happen was wet feet. Though we were always reminded not to skate on the creek itself, we did not want to take a chance of falling in due to the muddy and dark water below. The creek was always a mystery to us. We often stood on the edge and fantasized what creatures might live in it. We saw frogs in the summer, but what else was living on the bottom in all that muck? The thought of falling in and getting stuck was terrifying.

We didn't have fancy skates. We used mother's and Aunt Lydia's; she had left them with us when she moved away. These skates were adjustable, so they fit on our smaller boots. We had a skate key which we carried on a string around our neck. The skates were a big bother because we had to screw them on; it seemed we were always adjusting them, and they were always coming off. They ruined our boots, causing deep groves in the heels; sometimes the whole heel came off. Despite it all, we learned how to skate. When we were smaller, mother came with us and we all shared the skates.

While sledding with our friends one winter afternoon, someone had the idea to see if we could secretly arrange a sleigh ride after dinner. One of our friends had relatives in Heinrichshorst, a little village about four kilometers away. When everyone was settled in the house, my sister and I very quietly pushed our sleigh out into the street. Then, with the help of friends we pushed it down the road to someone else's house, where a boy already waited for us with a pair of horses. The horses were eager for a good run, and in no time at all we were ready to go. We left so fast that the last person barely managed to jump on. It was a crisp clear night with a big moon above. The black sky looked so vast and the stars so close one wanted to reach up and touch them. We counted "Sternschnuppen," the shooting stars, and made wishes. The trees sparkled as if "Frau Holle," our snow fairy, had just sugarcoated them for us. The snow crunched and glistened like a carpet of diamonds. It felt like we were gliding into a white fairyland. We must have all been moonstruck. I think I remember it so clearly because it was a perfect night.

Of course, we arrived there unexpected and without an adult, and on top of it, in the evening. We were glad they didn't ask too many questions; we didn't want them to know that our parents had no knowledge of our excursion and whereabouts.

"Come and sit down and warm your hands and feet," the aunt offered. She came back with warm milk while we warmed our hands on the big tile stove. The boys soon became restless; they worried about the horses standing outside in the cold. They urged us to get going again, and with that excuse, we thanked the relatives and scrambled back into the sleigh, huddling close together to keep warm. Soon we started discussing what to say when we arrived home. We had been gone far too long to keep our adventure a secret. So when we came home, cold and with red faces, we told our parents where we had been. They were astounded, and of course had been wondering where we were, since it was getting late. Had we asked for permission, they most likely would have let us do it, but it would not have been so exciting. The secrecy of it made us all feel like "buddies-in-arms."

My last sleigh ride was a few years later, right after New Year's in 1945, when father took me to school after Christmas break. All the school buildings were crowded with refugees. We had no classrooms, and started to meet in the schoolyard once a week to hand in our homework and receive our new assignments. We gathered around the teachers in the freezing cold with our papers in hand. This once-a-

Köselitz postcard from the 1930s.

week meeting had already started before Christmas vacation. The few teachers who remained in town tried to keep some education going. The students from farther away never came back after the holidays. Only the students who lived in Pyritz and the commuters from nearby villages showed up. The dedication of the teachers was incredible. No one was in charge anymore to stop these pointless meetings. The front was perhaps fifty to eighty kilometers away, and we still had homework and were concerned about returning it to the teachers. I thought, if I can get there I should go; what excuse did I have? All the boys from the Gymnasium, sixteen and older, had been drafted. Every effort was made to uphold the routines. Was it denying the seriousness of the situation or did the teachers see it as their duty to hold out to the last minute?

chapter three

SCHOOL YEARS

It was wonderful for us to have the school so near our home. Located just across the street and through a little alley, we were there in two or three minutes. How we loved that on rainy or snowy days. Many times, I dashed across and met the teacher just as he was entering the classroom. He shook his finger, and said, "I saw you galloping over here, young lady!"

The eight-year school system was strictly enforced. Dropping out was not allowed, even though some of the eighth-graders already worked on the farms during the busy time when school was still in session.

Schoolhouse in Köselitz, 1930s.

Most village schools had two classrooms. Four grades were taught in each at the same time. Two teachers shared the education. The teachers were very organized. While they taught one grade, the students in the other grades had reading or writing assignments. The students in the different grades were able to finish their assignments, and then participate with the next grade, especially if the teacher was working with the next higher grade.

The sturdy wooden desks had the benches attached. On top was a little well for pencils and pens, and at the right side, a little hole for the ink well. The old stubborn ink stains on the desks could tell interesting stories. Perhaps a little boy or girl ink-stained an assignment near its completion, causing a flow of tears. Here and there, an initial was carved in; that was, of course, against the rules. It could have been done by someone a generation before us. These desks were very old. I sometimes wondered if mother, as a little girl, had sat here, too, since she had attended this school as well.

After using slate and chalk, and then pencil, we learned to write with pen and ink. Perfecting this took much practice. Our hands and clothes attested to our trials and errors. We had ink stains all over, and the ink-soaked blotting paper made even more stains. Oftentimes, just as I was almost finished with the schoolwork, an inkblot spoiled it all, bringing frustration and tears. We had boxes for our pens, and a little one for the nibs, which came in different sizes. The nibs seemed to wear out very fast, and we were forever running to the grocery store for new ones. We had to buy all our school supplies since nothing was furnished by the school.

The classrooms were very ordinary. They contained just the necessary furniture: a desk and chair for the teacher and the benches for students. A large brown tile stove stood like a sentry against the wall. In the winter months the custodian, a man of all trades, came in during the morning sessions and fed the fire with coal from a big bucket. It was his job to keep the classrooms warm, clean, and tidy. Both teachers lived in the school building, which stood in the middle of town, giving the teachers a good handle on what was going on.

We all feared the teacher of the upper-grade classes. He did not have much patience; especially with the boys. He allowed no excuses for not having homework finished. Surprisingly, this middle-aged man, with his round belly, could quickly leap on top of the desk, grab a boy by his shirt, hold him between his knees, and spank him so furiously that sometimes his bamboo switch flew through the classroom. He was a WWI veteran, and had a crippled hand. In anticipation of the flying switch, we quickly held our hands over our heads to avoid being hit. In those days, the parents were mostly on the side of teachers concerning discipline in school.

Werner, my brother, received a spanking in school one day. I always thought of him as my little brother who could not do any wrong. What could he have done to deserve this? The spanking made me very angry, and I marched right to the schoolhouse to find out. Mother pretended to ignore it, but I wanted to know. I can't remember exactly what it was, but I never forgot how surprised the teacher was when I showed up.

Confirmation

Graduating from school was not really celebrated. It was the church confirmation which was the big celebration. Most youngsters were happy to leave school behind them. We lived in an all-Protestant area. For us, confirmations were always the big celebration, occurring soon after the Easter holidays. My confirmation was in 1943, and plans had to be made in advance due to the wartime rationing. Food for the party was not a big problem for us since we had the farm, but clothing and shoes were almost impossible to buy. The country was in the fourth year of war. The stores were pitifully empty. If we were lucky and had connections, we perhaps could get material for a dress; even then we had to barter for it. Tradition was that we wore a black dress to church and another dress for the afternoon party. Mother decided to have my black dress made from one of my grandmother's dresses stored away in the attic.

For the second dress, I had new blue material. Mother let me decide how I wanted my dresses. I wanted to have smocking on the front of my blue dress. Off I went to the seamstress. This had to be done quite early, since we only had two seamstresses in town, and confirmation was their busiest time. It seemed they made every girl's dresses. These seamstresses were marvelous—artists in their own right. The woman I went to didn't mind having to take grandmother's dress apart. She took my measurements, wrote them down, and that was it. She did not use patterns or pictures. Weeks later, after a few fittings, I had just the dresses I wanted.

Finally the confirmation Sunday arrived. With butterflies in our stomachs, we sat in front of the altar for the examination. The boys had fresh haircuts, and suits that barely fit or were a little too big. Girls with their new black dresses had their long hair pulled back, and some wore a black bow. What a somber group we were. I studied the minister's face: will he ask me something I might not remember? In a classroom, I wouldn't have been so nervous, but here in church, in front of my parents and the congregation, I would be very embarrassed if I didn't know the answer. All this was very important for a fourteen-year-old. My heart took a leap when I heard my question. I remembered the answer—what a relief! —then I relaxed. The sermon that followed told the confirmands about our future as good Christians. Finally, the ceremony ended, and congratulations were offered. Everyone smiled. Most youngsters were glad the end of school was near. We received our first communion, and with that we became members of the church. We could now sit with our mothers and fathers. We no longer sat in the loft where one of the teachers played the organ, and where the older boys took turns working the bellows.

We made our way home slowly. The out-of-town guests had already arrived, and soon the party began. Preparations for dinner had been started several days before; mother worked very hard to prepare delightful meals. Several courses were offered, such as roast beef and pork roast; one course was always fish. Dinner lasted a long time. I was the celebrity, and received many toasts; I had my first glass of wine. Relatives visited with each other after the meal and took walks down the street. Several of them lived far enough away that they didn't often see each other. I had invited my best friends, and the cousins from nearby were all present. The whole town celebrated. We took a stroll around the neighborhood, where we showed off our new dresses to our friends. Later in the afternoon, the tables were readied for coffee and cakes. It seemed there was no end to the eating. Much later in the evening, a meal with cold cuts and salads was served. The party continued until late into the night. Finally, the next day I had time to admire the gifts I had received.

My school day began very early. There was only one train, around seven in the morning, which I took every day, and I even had school on Saturdays. Köselitz was the last stop on the line to Pyritz. The train ride was only twenty or twenty-five minutes. With my eyes strained to the windows as the train rolled in, I tried to catch a glimpse of a friend's face so I could have someone to sit with. Many students came from towns down the line. I much regretted that my ride was so short. Many friendships were formed over the years. Eva Borchardt, who lived in Gross Moellen, the previous train stop to Köselitz, became my best friend. Because of the regional nature of the school, friendships crossed town lines.

Leaving for school was especially hard during the cold months of winter. One winter during the war, the clocks weren't turned back in the fall. It was pitch dark in the morning walking to the train station; the streetlights were turned off due to the war blackout. I carried a lantern which I left at the train station and picked up on my way home. Mother made a heavy wool scarf for me, which I wrapped around my head and face. I trudged to the station faithfully every morning with my heavy school bag. We had to bring most of our books to and from home to complete homework.

Then came that fateful day when military people investigated the possibility of transforming the school into a military hospital. Since I arrived at school early due to the train schedule, I happened to be in my classroom when this occurred. Military officers were walking through the classrooms with the school director, and I overheard what their intentions were. I was shocked to hear what was going to happen to our wonderful school building, and wondered where we would go.

Soon this change was announced, and our quiet island under

the oak trees away from the war and the bustle of everyday life was dealt a big blow. Every student's and teacher's life changed drastically, especially the boarding students. It was a nightmare for the director and teachers. We became a school without classrooms. The boarding students had to be placed in private homes, which added a wrinkle to monitoring the welfare and safety of these students. Life in the dormitory was orderly, with meals on time and curfews. The teachers, who had also been dormitory mothers, now roamed the streets to make sure that their flocks did not go astray.

However, this was fun and games for some. By this time, most of the girls were fifteen and sixteen years old, and there were many handsome boys in the Gymnasium. After school meetings became a hide-and-seek game with lots of whispering in class. No more signing out and telling the dorm mothers where they were headed. I once overheard a teacher asking a student to bring a slip from her parents giving her permission to interact with boys.

Pyritz was just a small town, but it was really a school town with many opportunities. Now other schools had to relinquish some classrooms for us. During the breaks, we had to hurry from one school building to another, often just for one subject, which was especially

Pyritz postcard from the 1930s.

hard in the winter. We also had classes in the boys' Gymnasium where all the labs were located. One of the problems at the Gymnasium was keeping the girls and boys separate on breaks in the schoolyard. Girls were on one side and boys on the other; even when going back to the classrooms, we couldn't walk together. I had cousins in the Gymnasium, and if my mother wanted me to relay a message, I had to ask for permission from the teacher to talk to them.

The Youth Movement started after Adolf Hitler came to power. It was supposed to be voluntary, but soon pressure was put on parents to sign their children up. The boys had their own organization, and the girls had the "Jungmaedchen" —JM for short. It didn't seem like a big political organization, especially not in our little town. I must have signed up in 1939 when the war started. Most of our summer meetings were spent outdoors on the sports field, often in competitions with other groups who would come from neighboring villages. We were proud of our nice facility; a small building had been erected for us near the sports field. One year we staged an evening with funny skits and invited our parents. Our repertoire was quite limited, but the parents were a wonderful audience. I made dance skirts out of crepe paper and hats to match.

As the war went on, our emphasis changed to lending a helping hand in a small way. One of the things we were asked to do was to collect medicinal plants. This was a good opportunity to take another look at the weeds around us and learn that many were considered healing plants. We dried and stuffed them into bags that were later picked up. For us youngsters, life had changed to a more serious tone. Everywhere we looked, we were reminded of the sacrifices our soldiers made. Many families in the village had already lost a family member in the war.

Our JM group also made toys for small children. Some of us had fretsaws, and cut out little animals and then painted them; these were given to little children at Christmas. Toys were not part of the war effort and not available in stores. We also made little packages, mainly of food, for the soldiers. I don't think the packages actually reached the soldiers. The packages were required to be so small, it didn't seem worth the effort. We didn't even have proper paper to wrap them. I had a soldier pen pal for a while who had the same last name as I did; we tried to find out if we were related.

Surprisingly, despite the food shortages, summer camps were offered. The government and the youth movement tried hard to keep the young people healthy. I had a chance to go to a camp which was located on a lake. I had a wonderful time there. We went swimming every day. Köselitz didn't have a lake for swimming nearby, so this opportunity was a real treat. I tried my best to learn how to swim, but the time was too short. Pyritz had a swimming pool but we hardly ever went because it was a little too far to go there and swim and come home. During the week and on Saturday, we were busy with school. That left only Sundays, which was when we caught up with friends, rested, had fun, and enjoyed our families. Of course, the chores on the farm had to be done whether it was Sunday or not; the livestock had to be taken care of and mother had to do the cooking. But we always put our Sunday clothes on and often went to church. The Sunday dinner usually was quite special. We helped to set the table with nice china, and mother always used her favorite crystal sugar and cream set. In the fall, roasted duck was often served.

Mid-afternoon was tea or coffee time. Mother usually baked a sheet cake for the weekend, since there were many mouths to feed. But often she made something special for us for Sunday afternoon. In the summer, it would be a torte with fruit from the garden. If we were around the house or farmyard, we were expected to join the family at tea time. For father, this was a relaxing time with the family, especially in the wintertime.

chapter four

THE BEGINNING OF
WORLD WAR II IN 1939

It was early in 1938 when father's decision to build a new house for the farm help gradually took roots. The old house must have been over a hundred years old. I remember the inside of the kitchen was very small and the chimney was next to the stove. It looked so dark and spooky in the kitchen. Mother told us that the people smoked their bacon in the chimney.

The construction started with taking down the old house. It was sheer muscle power that completed the demolition. The new two-family house was to be all brick. Gradually the walls went up, and when the rafters were in place, a sign of a certain stage of accomplishment, the carpenters nailed a large wooden crown with colorful ribbons on the highest spot. This was the "Richtfest"—the topping-out ceremony—a day to celebrate with special food and beer. By the end of the year the house was finished. Father was happy that all had gone well. The deadlines had been met, and the two families, who had patiently waited over a year, could now move in.

But not all was well in the world. Dark clouds hung over the horizon; a lot of talk and whispering was going around about war. We read and heard about atrocities in Poland. What was happening? Hadn't we lived peacefully as neighbors all these years? These stories became very important and worrisome to our family—especially to father. He was born in former West Prussia, a German Province, which Germany had lost to Poland after the First World War in 1918. He came from a family of twelve children, six boys and six girls, and several of his sisters still lived there. One sister had inherited the homestead, another had a grocery store, and two married into businesses. No one at that time wanted to abandon the properties. They stayed in Poland rather than move into Germany. The young men in the family were asked by Poland's government to swear allegiance to their new country. To avoid that decision, all six boys left Poland and moved to the motherland. Father was the youngest; he had already served four years in the German military before World War I, and then saw active combat in Russia during that war. When he moved to Germany, he joined an older brother who was already established in Pyritz.

Now his biggest concern was for his siblings and their families who had stayed in Poland. Reports of atrocities continued. The bubble burst in the middle of the summer. Many young men received draft orders; names spread quickly through the village. We wondered, will these men have to go to war? Everyone asked questions, and many tears were shed. Again and again people asked why this sudden shift was occurring.

It had not been that long since the First World War; no one wanted to believe another war was already looming. Our province, Pomerania, shared a border with Poland; should we have to worry? Mounting propaganda discussed incidences of clashes between Poles and Germans. We children were too young to worry. Mother was glad my brother was still a little boy, and that father had passed the draft age; he had just celebrated his fiftieth birthday.

It was September 1st when the propaganda minister announced the start of war. We were grateful that no one in our immediate family had been called up; all my cousins were too young. Listening to the news now became very important. Of course, our soldiers' successes were cheered and celebrated. The war with Poland was over in an unbelievable eighteen days. Men came home victorious.

Father, plagued by the uncertainty of the fate of his family, anxiously awaited news from them. Finally, communication was established, but the news was sad; his brother-in-law, his sister Ida's husband, had been killed by the Poles. The rest of his relatives were unharmed. His homeland had once again returned to Germany, and he wanted to see it for himself.

A trip was planned as soon as it was allowed, and my sister and

I were to accompany him. We were excited; we had never taken a day-long train trip like this would be. We would meet some of our relatives for the first time, including cousins who were much older than we were. The visit was planned for late fall. How we looked forward to it! Preparations included a shopping trip to Pyritz, where mother bought new coats and dresses for us. She let us help pick out what we liked. This was the first time she thought we were old enough to have that responsibility. This added a new aspect to the shopping trip and we had much fun looking at so many coats and dresses. Of course, it took a little persuasion to have us agree on the same identical outfits; mother insisted on that. Finally, after all the waiting and counting the days, the moment came to board the train. Christa and I always tried to find a window seat; we never tired of looking out the window. The countryside was much like our own. It was late fall, and the fields were bare. We passed through many small towns which didn't have train stops. The distances between towns never seemed very far. Mother had packed plenty of sandwiches. For long trips like this, we brought our own food, unless we had a longer delay at one of the larger stations that had a restaurant. We kept munching on our sandwiches.

Our destination was Hohenkirchen, where three of my father's sisters lived. I was surprised, since it wasn't a town like ours. All I knew were villages in our area which resembled our town. Here in Hohenkirchen, the houses were not neatly in a row like in Köselitz; the farmers had their buildings where their land was.

It was wonderful to see my father so happy with his family; soon we were taken with horse and buggy from one relative to another. There were lots of new faces for us children: cousins, aunts, uncles, and even second cousins. Father had quite a time explaining it all to us. We stayed with Aunt Emma Henning, father's sister, who had inherited the homestead which was father's birthplace. Pauline, an older sister, had married a miller who owned a windmill that sat on a little hill close to their house. We went there by horse and buggy, too. Their household was bustling when we arrived. They were making sauerkraut, which was new to me. I had never heard of anyone making their own sauerkraut. It was not part of our store of winter staples, though mother would buy it a few times in the winter, and always served it the same way, with mashed potatoes, mashed yellow peas, and homemade sausage.

The size of father's family was astounding. Sister Ida had the grocery store in Hohenkirchen. Her husband was the one who was killed just before the war broke out with Poland. On one of our visits with her, she said to me, "How about visiting me when you get a little older during school vacation"? This was an invitation I didn't forget.

Summer Vacation in Hohenkirchen

Aunt Ida's invitation to visit during my summer vacation had really taken hold of me. In 1941, about two years later, I was twelve years old. I began earnestly to ponder this invitation, but first I needed to convince mother and father that I was old enough to travel there by myself. Mother didn't want to hear anything about it. She had a dozen excuses: it was too far, I was too young, and with the military people traveling, eastbound trains would be overcrowded. Father began to weaken. He must have had a lot of faith in me. Finally, after much begging and many promises, mother gave in. I was so proud, and felt very grown up. Father had sent all the necessary traveling information to his sister, and they were ready to meet me at the destination. I had packed my suitcase weeks before, and was never more excited in my life than at this time. My train schedule was stored in a safe place, and I had looked at the map many times and memorized the stops and changes. When the day came, I was ready. The trains were crowded; mother was right. I had quite a time getting on at stations where I had to change trains. Soldiers on their way to the Russian front had first priority. All went well, though, and after almost a daylong trip I arrived safely in Hohenkirchen. I stayed with Aunt Ida. She didn't have children of her own, and really spoiled me. I loved to help her in the grocery store. Times weren't any different there than in Köselitz; everyone had ration cards. In the evening, we sat down and sorted all the coupons so she could apply them for her next deliveries. The plan was to stay for just two weeks, but I stayed through my whole summer vacation. Mother sent a telegram to come home for cousin

Brigitta's wedding, but not even that could persuade me to leave. I had a wonderful time.

The Henning family also lived in Hohenkirchen. Paul Henning had married father's sister Emma, who had died in 1939 from tuberculosis. She was the one who inherited the farm homestead, and had left behind a son, Paul Jr., who was a year or so younger than me.

I bicycled back and forth between the relatives. Paul Jr. raised angora rabbits. I fell in love with these soft little creatures. They were gray, and their fluffy, silky fur made them look larger than they really were. Some rabbits had escaped their pens, and roamed around in the nearby yard, but no matter how hard we tried to catch them, we couldn't outrun a rabbit. No wonder they wouldn't let us catch them; they preferred the open space to their small cages.

I knew my brother, Werner, would have lots of fun with these rabbits. Stroking them made me think of how wonderful a sweater would feel made out of angora yarn. This idea started to grow in my mind. I imagined myself knitting an angora sweater. I knew taking one with me was impossible, but perhaps I could send one. At that age, I believed anything was possible if I put my mind to it. Didn't I convince mother and father that I was old enough to travel here by myself?

When I told Paul Jr. about my plan, he thought it was a great idea. He certainly could spare one rabbit. We immediately began to search for a wooden box. There was no stopping us. I peddled to the train station to find out if it was possible to ship a live rabbit. "Sure," the station master said with a big grin. "Just make sure you have a sturdy box, and don't forget to include some food," as if we didn't know that. Now we went full steam ahead. It took us a little while to find the right design but in the end we made a box with a little door. The whole thing was rather small, but then we only wanted to ship one rabbit. Now came the moment to pick one. I chose the woolliest one. We stuffed the box with plenty of clover and carrots, and off we went to the train station. Paul Jr. had a sturdy bicycle that he used to take to school. We tied the box on his bicycle rack. Communication with home was only by mail, so I had written my family that I was sending them a rabbit by rail delivery. I only hoped that we did everything right and it would get there alive. Our big plan worked, and the rabbit arrived just fine. I wished I could have been there to see my brother's surprised face.

The Henning family employed an English prisoner of war on the farm. I finally became brave enough to say one evening as he left for his camp, "Sleep good." I wanted to practice my English. He turned around and said, "It is sleep *well*." I was so embarrassed. Needless to say, I never made that mistake again.

Rationing

Peace didn't last very long. The shock of war with Russia caught us all by surprise, since Germany and Russia had signed a non-aggression pact. Father was troubled to see the Germans taking on the Russians again. He had fought four years in Russia in the First World War, and knew about fighting in the harsh winter climate. He feared the worst.

Ration cards for food and certain other goods were part of the war effort. But in the country, we had plenty to eat, and lived mostly as before. The daily news was upbeat, with lots of propaganda. Our soldiers were victorious on the front that moved deeper and deeper into Russia. Italy and Japan became Germany's allies. France and England then declared war on Germany. German troops overran Holland and Belgium, and conquered France in a short time. This war became larger and scarier. The draft age was extended; every man up to his late forties was either drafted into the service or worked in the war factories. Farmers had to hire foreign workers; most were young Poles or Ukrainians, who were forced to work in Germany. At one time, we had French prisoners of war working for us during the harvest. The ballroom of one of the village pubs was converted into their quarters. Mother tested her school French on them to see what she remembered. The government ordered segregation between different nationalities during meals. The German laborer who took care of the horses was not supposed to eat with the rest of the help. The Polish and Ukrainian maids and men could eat at the same table, but a class distinction was made. The French prisoners of war were only allowed to eat with the Germans. It was a real challenge for mother to accommodate everyone. Although my parents deeply resented the government holding the hatchet over our heads, they were afraid to go against the rules.

Rationing became strictly enforced as the war progressed, and included not only food, but also clothing and shoes. It reached the point where bribing someone in the store was necessary and became commonplace. We were much better off than many others because we lived on the farm. We could bribe shopkeepers with ham or bacon, or even a chicken. People in the cities had a hard time. Our attic held several huge trunks from grandmother's time, full of assorted clothing and linens. These proved very helpful as time went on. The maids, who also were foreign help, had very few possessions, and mother had to find clothing for them. Experience from the past war and the subsequent inflation had been a good teacher; nothing was wasted.

During my grandmother's days, flax was grown and woven into linen. We had a large loom in the attic, and rolls of homespun linen. At one time my sister and I had, for lack of other fabric, little suits made from this linen.

The German armies were deep in Russia; the winters were grueling, and unbelievable sacrifices were demanded of the soldiers. The government started collecting winter clothing for them. Women knitted socks, mittens, and scarves. It became apparent that the economy was stressed to its breaking point. The country had to be self-supporting, and there were too many people to feed.

Farmers were forced to sell almost everything they grew. Inspectors calculated how much the households could keep for themselves, and snooped around unannounced, counting the livestock. They figured out how many eggs per chicken on average we had to deliver. It would have been nice if the chickens had cooperated, but some old hens laid only a few eggs a year. The quotas were always too high. Many times, when the word came around that the inspectors were in town again, mother would catch a few chickens, stuff them into a sack, and hide them in the attic. We would all hold our breath, hoping they wouldn't make a noise, or that the inspectors, who could go wherever they wanted, would not decide to check the attic.

We were only permitted to keep a small amount of milk in the house. In order to prevent farmers from churning butter, some parts of the centrifuge and the butter machine had to be delivered to a collection place. Even so, the inspectors still came around to check pantries. Our parents lived in fear that the help would report them to the authorities for breaking the rules. Everybody broke rules; the resourcefulness of people proved unlimited. Mother found a way to make butter by skimming the cream of the little milk she could keep, aging it, and then rolling it in a large bottle on her lap until it turned into butter. It was a slow, monotonous task. She even found a way to color the homemade butter so it looked more like it was store-bought. One time she fell asleep and dropped the bottle; what a mess, but worse, what a waste.

It was a blessing that father could butcher. Meat was also very strictly rationed, and only a certain weight was permitted depending on the size of the household. There was never enough from one slaughter to the next. My father provided the wrong animal count when the controllers came around to count the livestock, because it meant a calf or sheep was hidden somewhere so it would not be missing at the next count. All the preparation had to be done secretly. Then, when the day came, excuses were found to get all the help out of the house and property. The doors were locked, and we children became lookouts. We were scared; we knew if anyone discovered this and reported us, father would go to jail. We were always afraid that the help, all foreigners, might know what was going on and denounce us. One never knew who had a grudge; the workers were all forced to leave their homeland and work in Germany. They were certainly not happy with their circumstances.

One time, father loaded a big pig on the wagon and drove to his brother's place, a more secluded farm just outside of Pyritz. They butchered the pig there. It was terrible for mother, who was alone in performing the task of quickly using and preserving the meat. There was no way she could accomplish this in one day, and therefore much was hidden. But mother always managed.

chapter five

THE SHIFT OF THE WAR

The German Army had penetrated deep into Russia; they had reached the outskirts of Moscow and St. Petersburg. Huge desperate battles were fought during the long, bitter cold winters. Gradually, this terrible war climaxed at Stalingrad in late 1942. The German army was defeated. They had been encircled so that neither provisions nor weapons could reach them. It was a heroic fight on both sides. Hundreds of thousands of men died in these battles. The German army started to retreat. It was a bitter pill to swallow for the German military and for the people who had already sacrificed so much.

This was the turning point of the war. The German army was exhausted. For us young people, life went on. The war fronts were still far away. The propaganda machine lured us to believe that the Russians would be pushed back and the victory would eventually be ours. They pointed out that we would never let the Russians step on German soil. Radio and newspapers were our only source of information.

Our lives hadn't changed much; we all went to school every day, though perhaps we all were a little more sober. My sister Christa's confirmation was in the spring of 1944. Normally, this would have been a joyous and happy celebration; mine had been just a year before, and we had celebrated with relatives and friends and plenty of good food. Mother went again to Pyritz, and bribed a storeowner with a package of ham and bacon to buy material for a confirmation dress. Christa was sad; her party was small and family and friends weren't able to buy gifts. But we were still better off than many people. The cities had serious food shortages despite the ration coupons. Often, people stood in line for many hours for food that wasn't there, and endured the air raids almost every day.

There was another plight farmers were confronted with once a year. Military men came around, and every farmer had to bring his horses to a designated place for mustering. The fittest horses were taken, and this brought more hardship for the farmers. Even if you had a tractor, the horses were important, since there was no gasoline. Some farmers resorted to working with oxen. Father also decided to buy a pair of oxen. The idea was very experimental. Gradually, the men who worked with the oxen adjusted to a slower pace, since the oxen plotted along at their own speed. My father was glad this new venture was a success.

Many families in the villages had already lost more than one family member. Our lives became more and more subdued. We went to school every day, and tried to have as much fun as we could. Sometimes I went to the café after school with my commuting school friends. We brought bread coupons with us so we could buy a piece of cake; nothing fancy, just plain sheet cake. Mother baked a much better cake. It was more like a little diversion to brighten the ordinary day, from drudging to school and getting home with loads of home-work. We drank a cup of coffee which was "Ersatz," a kind of roasted grain even children could drink.

Many of us had soldier pen pals; efforts were always made to keep up the soldiers' morale. I should have been going to school danc-es, but all that was curtailed. Movies were generally only for those eighteen and older. Köselitz was so small it never had a movie theater; we hadn't grown up with it and didn't miss it. But one time I met my cousin Elisabeth in Pyritz. I skipped my regular train going home and met her so I could go to the movies with her. She was old enough, but I was not, so we waited until it was dark inside, and then we qui-etly entered. I was very nervous, thinking that any minute someone would come and order me out. Authorities claimed that if youngsters under eighteen watched love stories, it would lead to immoral behav-ior. Films were limited to nature films for us youngsters. According to the government, the morals of the German youth had to be kept untarnished and clean.

Following the course of the war, the names of the embattled Russian cities soon became familiar to us again, but this time it was on the slowly retreating path of our troops. The thought that we could lose the war surfaced more often, especially when we gradually realized that the propaganda could not be trusted. We were always grateful our lives were kept as normal as possible, that we didn't have to worry about air raids, and had enough to eat. Father planted more than ever, and the harvests were good. Of course, he had to sell almost all the crops; we were only allowed to keep the small amount prescribed by the government. By now we had learned to be resourceful and thrifty, and to do without the things that were no longer available. Clothing and shoes were the worst shortage. The taste of oranges and bananas was long forgotten. We used to buy oranges and bananas from the man who picked up the eggs every week, but they were among the first items to disappear. However, we had fruits from our garden, and didn't even think of oranges and bananas anymore. Mother could no longer buy real coffee.

The front crept closer, and the death tolls kept mounting. Younger and younger men were drafted; they were really boys. In the Gymnasium, the sixteen-year-olds were drafted to replace soldiers who operated aircraft searchlights. Young women were also drafted for the same task. My cousin, Hans Dietrich from Naulin, was only sixteen, just a year older than I, when he was called up. Not long before that, we had bicycled through the fields to visit each other. As the oldest son, he was to inherit the farm, and was already a much-needed helper for his father. He loved horses, and had great plans for the future.

After the United States entered the war, air raids on the cities increased. The big cities were bombed relentlessly. Schools were evacuated to small country towns. Homeless mothers with children had to be placed with families in the country after their houses and apartments were bombed. We hosted a mother with two little boys in our house for a while. There was no war industry in our immediate area, so it became a preferred part of the country to temporarily relocate people. Not far from Stettin was Penemuende, a city shrouded in secrecy. It turned out that the V II missiles were launched from there to England. It was Germany's secret weapon developed near the end of the war and was the forerunner of the modern missile.

For the last year and a half, Stettin, our provincial capital, became a bombing target. It had plenty of industry and an important shipyard open to the Baltic Sea. We regularly saw and heard the planes flying over. The droning noise, like no other sound, is still in my ears. Seeing the planes, and knowing that in a few minutes the bombs would fall, was always a scary moment for us children, but we realized we were far enough away and safe. As it turned out, we weren't as safe as we thought.

On a clear summer day, we had a little air-raid test. We were in the garden, and watched the enemy planes flying overhead. They were tiny specks in the sky. Suddenly, a plane began tumbling down from the formation above. It looked like it was falling out of the sky, and started shooting. Between Köselitz and Pyritz was a little airfield. It had only a few buildings and a few small planes; none were warplanes. Boys in the Youth Movement had glider training there, and used these planes to pull up the gliders. The planes must have been spotted as the enemy flew over. We were terrified as we watched this. Empty shells were flying all around us. It happened so fast; we stood there as if we were planted in the ground. We didn't think of running for protection. It was over in a few minutes.

What was so amazing was that even being over a hundred miles away at night, we could see from our backyard the glowing red-and-orange sky. A faint distant rumble of the explosions carried all the way to us. It was painful to watch, and very frightening. When it was all over, we quietly went back into the house. That event brought the horror of the air war much closer, but still we had not experienced it directly, and I could not picture myself in this fiery and deadly situation.

In the fall of 1943, Uncle Hans from Naulin went to a spa to treat his asthma, and Aunt Adelheid went to visit and pick him up. The two boys, Hans Dietrich and Sigismund, were in charge of the farm. Cousin Elisabeth came home from school in Heidelberg to take care of the household. This was a great opportunity for me to see her again. I arranged that, instead of taking the train home after school, I would take the train to Naulin to visit with them, stay overnight, and go from there to school the next day. We were looking forward to an evening without parents. After dinner, we sat around the warm stove while Elisabeth talked about the beautiful city of Heidelberg where she studied. I dreamed of perhaps going there, too. After much talking, Sigismund and I quickly finished our homework, since we had to wake early the next morning to take the train to school.

I had just gone to bed when I heard the humming drone of a plane. The noise was irregular, and I guessed there was something wrong with the plane. As I listened, it became louder and louder. I sensed that something was going to happen any second; it seemed right on top of us. I held my breath, and then came a tremendous bang. The glass in the window shattered, and there was fire outside. The plane had crashed right in the middle of the cobblestone street in front of the large building housing their farm animals. A few feet more, and the plane would have fallen on the house. It was just as if lightning had struck, and above my bed there was a bullet hole in the wall. The exploding ammunition on the plane sent burning pieces of metal everywhere.

I jumped out of bed, and realized that there was no electricity; everything was dark. I groped in the hall for my coat; I didn't know which was mine, and just grabbed one. My cousins were yelling, "Get out of the house." Little metal pieces were burning all over the farmyard; it was an eerie sight. We were all in our nightgowns with coats thrown over them; we must have looked like ghosts in a midnight ritual. We ran to the sandbox (every family had one for exactly this reason), and threw handfuls of sand over these flames. The impact was enormous; the plane had dug a deep hole in the street, and was on fire. Pieces of metal had also pierced the roof of the house, and were burning in the attic. We didn't know where to run first. Smoke came out of the barn, and in no time at all the roof burst into flames. Dry hay stored in the attic of the barn had quickly ignited. People came to help, shouting, "Hurry get the animals out!" The horses and cows were just turned loose and chased down the street. It took a while to bring the water wagon around. Russian prisoners of war pumped the primitive equipment. There were no firemen, or one could say, everyone became a fireman. A big part of the barn and stable burned down. Needless to say, none of us could think of sleeping. When dawn broke, we set out to round up the horses and cows.

The plane was a German fighter plane that had been crippled in a fight over Berlin. The pilot tried to land on the little airfield near Pyritz/Köselitz, but he couldn't make it, and jumped before the crash to save himself. He came the following morning to investigate the damage. We were glad he survived, and he was glad that nobody was hurt in the crash.

I didn't go to school that morning, but took the train to Pyritz, and then I had to take another one to Köselitz in a roundabout way to go home by train. Some of my school chums were just getting off their trains. Of course, this was big news and everyone wanted to know what had happened. As I told them, we noticed a man standing very close by. All of a sudden it dawned on us that he could be a spy. Over the years we had become accustomed to warnings about spies, and his presence caught our attention. We stopped talking, and stared at him. He turned and left the building in a great hurry, with a bunch of eager girls behind him, trying to catch a spy. We never saw where he went. He had just disappeared into thin air.

chapter six

1944: THE WAR COMES HOME

Early in 1944, the eastern front came frighteningly closer. Uncertainty crept into everyone's mind. We didn't believe in winning the war anymore. Propaganda boasted about new weapons, but they were still on the drawing boards. Our parents must have spent many hours thinking and talking about the future. They listened at night to the BBC, which broadcasted news and events of the war in German. I can still hear the announcer starting off in English: "Germany calling, Germany calling." Our parents sent us children out of the room. They listened in secret because it was forbidden; nevertheless, almost everyone listened to the enemy broadcasts. Listening was a "public" secret that people didn't dare mention to each other. The German propaganda blasted away, telling us that the home front was strong and not to worry, and that the enemy would never set foot on German soil. The BBC contradicted these local broadcasts. We all wanted to believe the German broadcast very much, but the troops kept retreating, and many stories circulated about refugees becoming caught up in the conflicts.

By this time, the Russians already occupied the Baltic countries. The Baltic Germans who had lived there for centuries did not trust the Russians, and many fled to Germany. Some had had previous experiences of Russian occupation in past decades, when they had been sent to camps deep in Siberia. This time they were not taking any chances. Sadly, they had to leave everything behind. Germany was already crowded with displaced persons, including prisoners of war and refugees. The ones who had relatives in Germany were lucky to have a place to go, but many more had to be housed and fed. They were placed in empty garrisons, barracks, and storage warehouses;

many had to live a hand-to-mouth existence.

This situation added another strain to the German economy, since food and goods were already very scarce. Being asked to work in the war industry wasn't what they had expected either, and caused discontent amongst them. Huge camps with prisoners of war needed to be fed, too. Many prisoners were sent to the country to help on farms; however, many remained in camps. Much of the work almost everywhere was done by foreigners. Germans, who were not in the military, had to work in factories. Of course, Germans did not trust foreign workers in the war factories. We heard that they would sabotage whatever they could.

Food shortages were worst of all. Long lines formed in front of grocery stores. People waited often for hours, and even though everything was rationed, many things were not always available. Many city people traveled by trains to neighboring farming villages and bartered for food with items they could spare, like linens and fancy objects. I don't remember people coming to our village to barter; however, mother supported a cousin and her family in Pyritz. She also cared for the elderly lady with whom she and her sisters boarded during their school years, and whom she dearly loved. Mother sent me to her now and then with a package of food.

Towards the last year of the war, electricity was also rationed. I remembered I had to go to the dentist to have a cavity filled, and that afternoon the electricity was off. The dentist had to pedal an old-fashioned drill with his foot; perhaps for old times' sake, he had saved it in his attic.

The front was getting closer; we traced the movements of our troops on maps with little flags that we made. Our forces had retreated to Poland. For us children, this seemed still quite far away and didn't scare us, but father began to worry about his sisters, Ida and Anny, who had lived together since Ida's husband had died. Anny was single and had moved in with Ida. She had worked in Berlin, and was glad to get away from the horrible air raids. Anny was a slender, tall lady. I asked father once why she didn't get married, and, not wanting to make too much of it, he told me, "She couldn't find a husband as tall as she is." Most of father's siblings were all very tall.

We later found out that Paul Henning and his son Paul Jr. had died when the Russian troops moved through their village. Communication with them became slower and slower. We kept watching the news, and saw the front getting closer to their area, and wondered whether they stayed or left.

It was amazing that people were able to track down relatives and friends after the war. Mother found out that Ida had survived and had left Poland. Ida's sister Anny died on her struggle to escape the Russian front. Years later, on one of my visits to Germany from America, Mother and I had the opportunity to visit Ida. This was the time when East and West Germany were separate countries. Ida lived in East Germany, as did my mother. My heart ached to see her living under deplorable conditions in a single room. The situation in East Germany during the 1960s and 1970s was dire, and especially difficult for the elderly refugees.

Digging Trenches

In the middle of August of 1944, I received notice that I was drafted to dig trenches for our retreating soldiers. The government called it the Pommernwall (*Pomeranian Wall*). It was very different from the "Siegfried Line" at the border with France, which had taken years to build with bunkers and fortifications. This news really opened our eyes. The hope of winning the war had already faded, but now we understood the seriousness of the situation. I only knew trenches from pictures, which showed soldiers scurrying about, and wounded men finding shelter. Father was very upset. He examined the order and remarked, "Look at this, they don't even tell you where you will be going." I was fifteen years old. Mother begged me not to go. "Let's find an excuse." But what excuse could I have, as I was healthy, and that was all that counted? She was also worried that I would miss school. "How long will this digging take? It's only a few more weeks and school will start." She nervously tried to make her point. Despite all the propaganda, our parents were now deeply concerned. The unsure future weighed especially heavily on the farmers' shoulders. And now children were ordered to help in the war effort; it was a last desperate attempt.

I had to travel to an assembly point where I met a larger group of girls. A train took us to a little village near Schneidemuehl, which was on the border of Pomerania. We came from different towns and villages, and everyone was curious to see and hear what the trench-digging was all about. Of course, the youth movement had much to do with this undertaking. When we arrived in Alt Karbe, a little farming village, the leader announced enthusiastically, "This will be our home for now and our contribution for our brave soldiers. No sacrifice is too great." On and on she went. She noted that we would look back on this with great pride.

The large ballroom of the pub in this town was prepared for us by covering the floor with straw. We each picked a place to arrange our sleeping area and our belongings. It seemed like camping out; we all slept in rows. Of course, friends wanted to be together, and it took the rest of the day until everyone was settled. At this point, we hadn't looked at the whole picture. We were fired up and enthusiastic. All the up-beat talk about helping to protect our borders was still ringing in our ears. Soon, realization set in when we found out about our future spartan existence: no showers, no hot water, and the toilets were out-houses. This quickly put a damper on our enthusiasm.

After we became acquainted with our surroundings, we had our first drill. We received the work schedule, including the meal times, and were each issued a shovel or spade—the key item for this whole affair. Since it was August and very warm, we rose early to take advantage of the cool early-morning hours. Sunglasses and suntan lotion were no longer available; no luxuries of any kind could be had. The sun was beating down mercilessly on us; we were digging in plain open areas with no shade. It was hard physical work. None of us had ever done this, but we were too patriotic to complain, at least not very loudly. We soon had blisters on our hands, and our backs were sore. In fact, we ached all over, but we kept digging every day. One or two soldiers measured a length of ground for each of us, our assigned task for the day. The trench had to be two meters deep and one meter wide. The dirt was piled on the edges on top to give added height.

Boys were also drafted, but of course they were not near us. At one time, the line went through an old cemetery; it must have been very old because we didn't see any gravestones. After a few feet of digging, we discovered human bones. We were switched to another area, and the boys had to finish the cemetery trench.

To preserve my strength, I would lie down on a pile of sand during our breaks. I trained myself to fall asleep almost instantly. However, one day my face felt hot and strange; before I knew what was happening, it turned into big blisters. In a short time the blisters burst, and fluid ran down my face; I had a second-degree sunburn. What to do? It was very painful. I don't remember, but there must have been a nurse somewhere; my face was powdered and bandaged. It took a while to heal. I was lucky it healed without getting an infection. I resumed my shoveling as soon as I could. My face looked strange, with blotches of white skin surrounded by tan.

We all missed our mothers' home cooking. I often wrote home for someone to bring better food. Father took time off so he and Christa could come one Sunday; this was also our day of rest. Father was interested to see what was going on, and naturally was worried about my welfare, especially since I kept writing and asking for food. They brought a big food package. I enjoyed the homemade sausages and smoked ham. I was also delighted to see a big box of tomatoes. I sat on my straw bed and prepared the biggest tomato salad—my favorite salad. Tomatoes never tasted better! Christa gave me all the news about our friends, and I wished with all my heart I could go home with them.

I had also asked for a roll of string. String in these days was made of twisted paper, but the string my father brought was actually used for the harvester to bale straw. Someone had started to make macramé bags, and in no time at all, everyone who had connection to string was making bags. This was a fun diversion. We taught each other and made bags for everyone at home. We had plenty of free time, and I had a large roll of string to share.

Since we started work so early, we stopped at about two o'clock. Then we had our main meal, which we all looked forward to even though the food wasn't very good. We were hungry and ate heartily.

I began to wonder why they had so much meat; it seemed the same kind every day. Meat was a scarce food item, and it tasted different. Coming from a farm, I knew how beef and pork tasted. Being curious, I asked the cook, "How come we eat so much meat at every meal?" She was startled and said, "It's venison." I wondered who was out there shooting deer, but didn't give it more thought. Much later, I discovered it was horsemeat.

Every afternoon we had roll call and inspection. We called it the "Spatenappel." Our shovels and spades were our tools, and had to be in perfect condition. We polished them until they were shining.

Not only did we dig trenches for our German soldiers, we also dug tank traps, which were much wider and deeper, and were stabilized with wooden logs. The tank traps didn't make much sense to me as a youngster. I began to wonder if this huge endeavor would really keep the Russians from advancing into our homeland, and if our war-weary soldiers would find protection in these trenches if they should ever come this way.

The following is a poem written by Else Schlender from Kollin, one of the girls in the camp with me.

Here in the East far away
twelve pretty girls sitting under a Linden tree
dreaming about a happy future.

Early in the morning
by the first rays of sunrise.
We pick up our breakfast, shovels and spades,
in the hills of Alt Karbe we are digging the Pommernwall
to help our brave men
and to save their lives if we can.

At the hour of midday,
we eat our meal,
sitting in a frolicking round
where grass and moss abound.

When the whistle blows, it means back to work,
with blisters on hands and a back that hurts.

Hans, the good boy has told many jokes
and made fun of us.
Come evening we trudge back to our nest,
dreaming about our much missed featherbed.

This is the end of my little song,
with a little humor to go along,
thinking of the loved ones,
who are standing watch for us.

October was approaching. The air in the mornings was nippy, and we had to double-layer our clothes. The last thing we did was to prepare gun positions for the artillery. This involved making flat platform bases upon which to place the large artillery guns, which were then camouflaged with branches and little trees that were cut and delivered to our work areas.

Towards the end of this project, diphtheria broke out. We were immediately quarantined. This was something unexpected, since we were set to go home. Now it looked like we had to stay. Some girls already had sore throats and fevers. The project leader was frantically seeking medical help and urging everyone to gargle.

I already felt a little soreness in my throat, but I kept gargling with the mouthwash; it kept me from getting ill. After a few days, vaccine arrived, and we were all vaccinated. Although the trenching project wasn't finished and there were many more kilometers to dig, we were sent home after the quarantine period, near the end of October.

The Last Christmas in Köselitz

School had already started, and I was looking forward to my old routine. I wondered how much schoolwork I had to make up. The trains were still running, but everything else seemed to have changed. The boarding students returned only briefly after the fall vacation.

Some of the girls came from towns near what used to be the border to Poland. They were already much closer to the front.

Now parents felt it was important for children not to be too far away from home. Several teachers weren't there anymore. We had to rush more than before to the different schools for certain classes. The teachers also had to keep a close eye on their schedule, as they also had to run from school to school and were often late. The older male teachers had been drafted into the Volkssturm—the last sad attempt to have a few more men to fill the soldier gaps.

Miss Braun, an older retired teacher, came back to the Pyritz school due to the teacher shortages. She had taught my mother at the Lyceum several decades earlier. When I told my mother about our new teacher, mother looked at me in disbelief. She asked me to tell Miss Braun that I was the daughter of Martha Werner. Miss Braun had been one of her favorite teachers.

Around November, German refugees fleeing from their towns in the eastern parts of Germany ahead of the Russian front, appeared near our town. We had an early snowfall and the roads were poorly plowed, some not at all. Many of the roads were quite narrow. The weather turned colder every day. These refugees were fleeing the approaching front, trekking with horses and wagons loaded with their belongings. Köselitz was not on a major road, so they didn't come directly through the village. Men had to go now to the main road and shovel snow in order to help keep the traffic flowing, and they reported what was going on outside our little village. Most of the refugees were women, children, and old folks. Not everyone could sit on wagons. Many walked behind, and some had small hand-pulled carts. To provide shelter for them at night, every available hall and school was opened up. Relatives, friends, and acquaintances trickled in looking for assistance. Some moved on just needing a short rest.

Köselitz at this time was relatively peaceful. I was still going to school, but now only once a week. What incredible dedication was displayed by the few teachers who still remained. They displayed unsurpassed loyalty to their profession. They didn't waver or give up. We met in the schoolyard of the Gymnasium in Pyritz because the school building was filled with refugees. They gave us plenty of homework to return the next week. Seeing this grand old school, named the "Bismarck Gymnasium," with a large bust of Bismarck at the top of the staircase, evoked sadness. I couldn't conceive that I might never walk up these steps again.

December, usually a busy month with butchering and preserving, was subdued. Mother lamented, "There won't be any Christmas presents." Not even with bribing could we find something to buy; the stores were empty. The days were short, and sometimes it seemed real daylight never quite made it. Mother baked the usual Pfefferkuchen; Christmas without it wasn't Christmas. This special dough was prepared a few weeks before the holiday; it kept well for weeks in an earthen crock. When needed, a piece was cut off and baked. One thing we had plenty of was syrup made from sugar beets. This was substituted for honey in the Pfefferkuchen, and helped it to look golden brown. In better times honey would have been used.

Father had planted sugar beets in the last few years specifically to make this syrup. It was quite an operation. It took days, and all the help was engaged. First one had to brush and clean the beets in big tubs of water. Then, a hand-operated slicing machine and a press were used to get all the juice out. This was boiled in a large copper kettle in the washhouse. It had to cook a long time before it had the consistency of syrup. It had an earthy taste and was quite dark. We spread it on bread instead of jam, and sometimes it was used in place of sugar. Sugar beets were planted and sold to factories for making sugar. Not far from Pyritz was a sugar factory. Who would have thought a few years ago that we would be making syrup from beets and using it as a staple in the household?

Christmas was still our biggest holiday, and despite circumstances, we wanted it to be as traditional as possible. Father soon set out to get the Christmas tree. This was always a wonderful, especially exciting moment when we were younger. As usual, he took it into the washhouse and went to work to make it into a perfect tree. He drilled holes into the trunk where the tree needed another branch or two, and glued them in. He had as much fun as we had watching him.

Then came the moment when he carried it into the house, usually the day before Christmas. Mother had the ornaments ready, and we all decorated the tree. The fragrance of this fresh, just-cut tree brought the Christmas spirit right into our living room, and helped to make it seem more like a traditional Christmas. In previous years, mother had bought cookies in the shape of bells and stars which were hung on the tree. We could always pick one; they were there for us. The lights were real candles which were held on the branches with little metal snap-on candleholders.

Everyone finished work early on Christmas Eve. This was very special, and the start of the holidays. Mother made up plates with cookies and candies for the help. She used to buy them clothing for gifts, but now she had to fall back on the stored clothing in the attic, such as grandmother's skirts and blouses.

We went to church on Christmas Eve to celebrate the birth of Christ. In past years, Santa would come while we were in church. Our excitement grew as we walked home. What did Santa leave under the Christmas tree? It was always a total surprise. But this was Christmas 1944; there were no gifts under the tree for us.

The Europeans celebrate the first and second Christmas day. The roasted goose stuffed with apples and red cabbage was the big dinner on this occasion. We had two days of great feasting. Mother had saved a goose for Christmas, and we had wonderful meals.

On a Christmas Eve when we were younger, a neighbor dressed up as Santa in father's fur coat turned inside out, would come to the door with a sack, sled, and bell. We trembled when we heard the knock on the door and the bell. Santa looked like he had really traveled far. He put his sack down, and asked us if we had been good children. He made us recite our Christmas poem; we were so anxious that sometimes we were in tears before we could finish. Mother lit the candles on the tree and turned off the light. Our faces glowed in the flickering candlelight; the room was filled with the scent of the freshly cut tree. These are unforgettable Christmas memories.

Aunt Lydia was expecting a baby around Christmas, and mother had promised her she would come and stay. Ewald, her husband, had been home most of the war years, but was now drafted. They had two young boys, Arno and Lothar, and Uncle Ewald's elderly mother also lived with them. Baby Theo arrived on Christmas Eve. We had little communication, but the telephone must have still been working. Mother prepared to leave. Rumors circulated that the Russian front was very close. All our begging her not to travel to Seefeld was in vain. Mother left right after the holidays. I went to the Post Office every day, and put a call through for mother to come home. Finally, I told her that I would meet her on the next day at the train station in Stargard, a station where she had to change trains. I think we were never more worried about our mother than at this time. The train station was overwhelmed with refugees and soldiers, trains with wounded soldiers, and trains with guns and tanks. By this time, we were never sure the trains ran at all. Rumors changed from day to day. Was I glad when I met mother there!

Some people ventured into the surrounding villages, and brought back shocking and sad stories about the difficulties refugees experienced on the roads. The winter was exceptionally cold with much snow. High snow banks lined the roads and made traveling difficult. When people died, there was no place to bury them; they were left alongside the roads. Pushing ahead from one little town to another was all anyone could concentrate on. There was no time for grieving.

One late afternoon, a column of cavalrymen came through our village. They were so tired and hungry they could hardly stand on their feet. Father, of course, having been a cavalry soldier during the First World War, knew just what to do. The horses were fed, and mother quickly cooked a large pot of soup. It was milk soup with noodles, as I remember; something that could be prepared very quickly. The soldiers were thankful, and practically fell asleep standing up. Wherever they found a place to lie down they did. It was only for a few hours before they had to move on. I had a gripping feeling that we were close to the front and the fighting. How could these poor worn-out soldiers fight or hold back the Russian army? Father must have realized that there was no chance for us unless we left. I wonder what was in his heart. The talk of leaving was like a mountainous guilt feeling. A farmer just can't pick up and leave. Who would take care of the livestock? We had a wagon in the barn ready to pack and leave, but I couldn't think of climbing on this wagon and leaving home—where would we go? We knew we were very lucky that father was with us when many families had lost their fathers at the front.

Several times the men rallied together at one of the pubs to decide what chances they had and what to do. Groping for ideas and input from the group only led to the decision to stay. There didn't seem to be an alternative; someone had to take care of the livestock. Bracing for the Russian forces was the chance they had to take.

One time, father came home from the gathering in the pub and was a little tipsy, the first time in my life that I saw him like that. He excused himself, and explained that they didn't want the Russians to find the liquor, so they drank it. I can only guess how hard it was for these men to know what might befall us in a few weeks, or perhaps even days. Father, with his WWI experience, knew the character of Russian soldiers and the awful possibilities.

Paul Buchholz in his WWI calvary uniform.

chapter seven

LEAVING KÖSELITZ IN 1945

Winter held us in a tight grip, and even a clear sunny day now and then didn't change the bitter cold temperatures. The new year brought more apprehension, worries, and fear. We knew by now that it would only be a matter of days, perhaps hours, before the Russian forces would come; no one could tell us how much time we had left. Communication had come to a standstill; newspapers stopped before Christmas, but the radio lasted a little longer.

People didn't dare leave home; families wanted to stay together. By now, most farmers had a wagon ready in the barn. Father had prepared one, too. Christa and I packed a suitcase with our best clothes, pictures, and things that were dear to us.

Silently, more snow fell, and added layer upon layer to what had fallen a month ago, a week ago. A white blanket covered field and roads. How we wished it would protect us from what was to come. The narrow cobblestone road to Pyritz had to be kept open. It was our connection to the main road. The men in the village had decided to shovel the road by hand in addition to the plowing with horses. Every morning a group of them, with shovels over their shoulders, headed out to the road.

The snow had always been welcomed. It was the great protector of the fields and the seeds that had been planted in the fall. But now snow was the enemy, hampering the movement of soldiers and the many refugees who were heading to safer areas.

Father worried about the foreign help. For them, the day of reckoning was approaching. The Russians were their liberators. No one knew how many of the help craved revenge, especially the men who felt they hadn't been treated right. Father questioned himself and whether he had been kind enough to our help. He knew their retribution could mean his death.

Around the middle of January, two cars drove up to our house. They were friends of father's brother, who lived farther east closer to the border with Poland. We didn't know these people, but they asked if they could stay with us. They had left their hometown just before the Russians came. We were stunned that they had their own cars when everyone else had to turn theirs in. How did they make it all the way to us? They told us how terrible it was getting through crowded roads and the ice and snow. They were totally exhausted, and decided not go any farther. How could one at this point turn away anyone? Mother looked around saying, "Where will all these people sleep, seven of them?" Our house was not large. One family had two daughters and the husband was a soldier on furlough. He was in his uniform and had weapons. The other couple was middle-aged, and the man was crippled with childhood polio. His secretary, a young woman, was with them, too.

Father was quick to announce, "The cars have to be hidden." Everyone went to work to hide the cars in the barn, covering them with bundles of straw. Then father had a long talk with the soldier. He knew if the Russians found a soldier in our house, it would incriminate all of us. The outcome would be unthinkable. They decided the man needed to put on civilian clothes and try to walk to Pyritz. We had no way of knowing if Pyritz was taken by the enemy; however, it seemed a sensible plan. It looked quiet in that direction, and he might meet up with other German soldiers. Father described a road that led though fields and would bring him to Pyritz. It was a heartbreaking decision for the man to leave his wife and daughters not knowing what he might walk into. They hacked a hole in the ice of the Bruchgraben, the little creek behind our property, and submerged his uniform and weapons.

One night, we woke up and heard faint noises in the street. We quietly tiptoed to the front door and took turns looking through the mail slot. Mother whispered, "Let's listen to the language." We didn't hear a word, only the clop, clop of horses broke the silence. It was a column of German soldiers on horseback. I thought that these boys, with their heads bowing low, couldn't be much older than I. Their legs were wrapped with straw to keep warm, and the horses trotted almost mechanically. We would have liked to offer them something warm to drink, but they pushed on and didn't stop.

Now and then airplanes flew over. Most of the time we didn't know if they were friend or foe. One bomb was dropped not far from us; it hit a barn but never exploded. How thankful we were. Surely our windows would have been blown out, and where could we have gotten glass to repair them? We were told not to go near the barn, but curiosity got the better of us. We had to see what a bomb looked like.

Father came home one day and said, "The men decided that we should take turns at night to check the outskirts of the village. At least we can warn the people of danger and determine if anything is moving out there." The flat land and the snow cover certainly couldn't hide very much. And then came that morning when father arrived home from his watch, and said, "I saw something moving in the direction of the village, but it turned around and went back." He wasn't sure what it was, but he thought it looked like two vehicles.

We children had given up our bedrooms to the visitors; we slept on the living room floor closer to our parents. In the daytime we kept busy and helped mother with the cooking. People were almost bumping into each other wanting to help, or looking for a place to stow away the baggage which was piled in corners. Someone was busy washing dishes all day long. Then there were the chores for the maids. The cows had to be milked twice a day, and the pigs had to be fed. But the nights were full of fear; our senses were lying in wait of any sounds outside.

It was a few days before the end of January when suddenly Aunt Adelheid, Uncle Hans, and Cousin Sigismund, our relatives from Naulin, burst into the house. They had walked across fields to get to us, and were astounded to find us all still peaceful, though crowded, at home. Aunt Adelheid was beside herself. With terror written all over our faces, we listened to her emotional outburst as she tearfully described their ordeal with the Russian troops. "How can you just sit here and not realize what is going on?" But how could we know? No one dared to leave the home, let alone the village.

Their story was chilling; the Russians had already been in Naulin for three days, only four kilometers from Köselitz. Soldiers had threatened Uncle Hans. He had been stood against the wall to be shot, but luckily there was a moment he could escape and hide. They ventured on a back road to come to Köselitz.

We now had first-hand information of the enormous brutality that awaited us, and we knew it could be a matter of hours until we might have the same situation. It stunned us all. The three of them turned around and went back. No begging from mother could persuade them to stay. Father, after hearing what they had gone through, brought up many reasons not to go back. He kept telling them over and over again how lucky they were to have escaped, mentioning that Uncle Hans might not be so lucky the next time. They had made up their minds to go back. Being also farmers, the responsibility of the livestock seemed more important than their lives. Home had always been a safe place, and that was where they wanted to be.

No one at this stage was able to judge the scope of the situation. Would the Russians just stay a few days and move on? This was the advancing front, the fighting troops. Perhaps if we had at this point taken the wagon and left, we might have still had a chance to get away, just getting ahead of the Russians. Father kept saying, "We have to prepare for the worst." He knew what the Russian soldier was capable of from his experience in World War I. The shooting was getting closer, and we kept guessing where it could be. I heard father say, "They can take everything from us, but they can't take our land," but later the unimaginable happened: they took our land.

Aunt Lydia's Trek

Aunt Lydia in Seefeld knew that if she stayed at home when the Russians came, she and her family would have no chance of surviving. Since her husband Ewald was a member of the National Socialists Party and everyone knew, she believed someone in town would denounce them. Her husband had finally been drafted as the front came closer to the homeland. Aunt Lydia rigged up a covered wagon to escape, and her French prisoner of war, who worked for them, went with her. For him it was a few steps closer to his homeland, and he did not want to get mixed up with the Russian Army either. Only three weeks after Aunt Lydia gave birth to Theo, they started on their journey. Clogged roads and deep snow hampered their progress. 1944-45 was one of the worst winters; more snow fell than anyone could remember, and temperatures were extremely cold. Grandmother, holding the baby, sat on the wagon near a makeshift wood stove. Aunt Lydia and her young boys Arno and Lothar walked so as not to make it any harder on the horses. In little villages, she went to people's homes and begged for milk for the infant. She couldn't nurse; it was too much strain on her. She was oftentimes refused. The Frenchman was compassionate; he shared the agonies with them and stood by their side.

After days of traveling west, they had gone far enough, and reached a place where they felt safe. They stayed there until the end of the war. Eventually, Uncle Ewald returned safely from the war and they were all reunited. Little Theo had a difficult start in his life; he died when he was six months old.

The Russians Enter Köselitz

On the 27th of January 1945, the daughter of the railroad stationmaster came running through the deep snow behind the farm buildings and barns; her message made us gasp. Her father had been shot on the spot, and several soldiers were on the way into town. A Russian tank had appeared at the station and was hiding behind a large pile of straw across the street. It was a horrifying story. We knew something like this would happen.

These soldiers—there were only a few—walked brazenly down the sidewalk. Their faces were barely visible under the wooly caps they wore. Each carried multiple guns, one slung over their shoulder and one in their hands ready to shoot. We stood behind the curtain at the window and watched them go by. The soldiers already had information from the foreign workers who worked on the farms; they were quick to strike down certain people. One was the Bürgermeister (mayor); he was shot point blank and left in his farmyard. Another person was the owner of a large estate. Then the soldiers disappeared as quickly as they came. Perhaps at this time we might have had a chance to leave. A troop of German soldiers came through the next day. We might have been able to follow them, but they pacified us and told us not to worry; they would fight the Russians. They were in a hurry and didn't want to bother with civilians. So we waited and agonized.

Two days later, the main Russian force arrived. We heard the rumble of heavy vehicles coming closer. What we saw was overwhelming. Soldiers were huddled on tanks in their quilted uniforms with all kinds of guns pointing. For three days and nights, the Russian troops on tanks and trucks drove slowly through our little village. Enormous guns labored on the cobblestone street; the house was trembling. We wondered when this would come to an end. How could our depleted military force, including those young boys on horseback who we saw just a few days ago, hold back this Russian onslaught?

The first night, father made us all go into the potato cellar, which was under one side of the barn and offered a good place to hide. The door was almost hidden. He thought they might not look there right away if they should stop and storm into the houses. We took blankets and crouched on top of the potatoes and stayed there all night, listening and waiting.

Father was very concerned about our safety. He knew that the Russian soldiers would rape the women and young girls, and he wanted us to be safely hidden. He had figured out a unique way of hiding us in a hard-to-find area in one of the haylofts. Over the stables that housed the calves and other smaller animals was a large hayloft. This loft had a division; a wall that was half brick and half boards. On one side of the wall was the grain storage, and on the other side was the hay. It was like a second floor. This long building also had the carriage house in it. From the carriage house, a stairway led up to the grain storage. He arranged a place in the hayloft next to the wall for us. Then he took out a few boards on top of the wall. From the grain storage side we climbed up a ladder; slipped through the opening, and then pulled up the ladder and replaced the boards. All the other ladders on the property were hidden in the barn under the straw so that no one could get the idea to climb up into the hayloft from the outside. Soldiers were everywhere looking for places to sleep, and a hayloft provided a great sleeping place. It was still February and very cold.

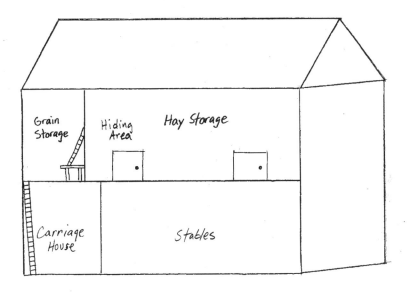

Diagram of the Buchholz barn showing Ingrid's hiding area when the Russians first arrived in Köselitz.

We quickly packed a few things, including some food, warm clothing, pillows, and blankets, and took our suitcases with us. This all happened the second day of the invasion. Christa collected pictures of movie stars, and she took those with her, as well as many family photographs. We must have looked at them a hundred times. The carriage house had a large door with a big padlock. So far we had not had any contact with the soldiers. They were still rumbling through the village. The two young girls from the family in the house, and the wife of the man who had polio, were with us, too. The daughter of a neighbor joined us for a few days. Several days later, the young secretary of the crippled man joined us. People opened their homes and took in strangers because it felt safer to have more people around.

The young secretary had a horrifying story to tell. The family she had stayed with had all been killed: three young children, mother, father, and grandparents. The husband was denounced by some of the foreign workers, and the Russians had threatened to shoot him several times. The ordeal was too much for his wife, and she begged him to bring an end to this, to shoot all of them. First he set fire to the barn, and then shot his wife, his three little children, and mother. His father had a change of heart and walked away. The man then took his own life. The secretary, who had been taken in by this family, was hiding in the barn, and was unaware of what was going to happen when the family walked in. She witnessed this tragedy.

Many years later, I met Meta and Carl Heinz Birk who had immigrated to Canada. Meta was the sister of the young mother from this tragic incident, and I heard Meta's account of this, too.

On the third day, the columns stopped and the soldiers burst into the homes. They drove their vehicles into every space they could find. Some people had to get out of their houses, which meant people crowded even more together. We, in the hayloft, had no idea what was

A view of the approximately 200 year old Buchholz barn that contained the "hiding area," 64 years after the Russian invasion, showing its age and several alterations made by the Polish inhabitants since that time.

happening in the house. We also didn't know how long we would have to hide there. We heard noises; shooting and shouting, the clanking of metal, loud motor noises. We were bewildered. What was going on? Werner, my brother, was our liaison. He took a basket and pretended to get wood for the stove, but he had stashed food for us in the basket. He had to wait for the right moment when he could unlock the carriage house door and come up to the grain storage. A soft whistle let us know that he was there. We were training our senses to the noises around us, especially when we heard someone coming up the stairs to the grain loft. We let down the ladder so he could climb up and hand us the food. It all had to be done quietly and swiftly. We bombarded him with questions. He gave us a quick rundown of what was happening in the house.

It became harder and harder to bring food to us. There was so much activity in the farmyard. Sometimes the soldiers made a game of shooting chickens, which mother and the women had to cook for them. Mother could save some for Werner to bring to us in the hiding place, so we had chicken soup most of the first days. Every pigeon on the rooftops and every dog was a practice target for the soldiers. Soldiers were also repairing vehicles in the barn, and that's why we heard those clanking noises. The door to the carriage house below our hiding area was very much in the open. Mother told us later that several times she saw a soldier fingering the heavy padlock, but no one broke it open. So far we hadn't had any encounter with the soldiers; we hadn't even seen any, except when they were driving through sitting on their tanks on the first day.

We passed the days with reminiscing and listening to stories the secretary and the wife of the crippled man, who had joined us, told us. I don't think we ever stood up. It was amazing how warm we kept in the hay. Each of us had a little nest with a pillow and blanket.

Then came the terrible news that the Russians had come and taken my father with them. The date was the 7th of February, about a week after they had marched in. Our uncertain and fragile world collapsed. It was unthinkable not to have our father to take care of us. What was going to happen from now on? That night, mother and

Paul Buchholz.

Werner came to us. She made us climb down of our hiding place, and we sat on the grain piles hugging each other, our bodies shivering from the cold. We cried our hearts out. Mother didn't want to go on and she wanted us to take our lives. She knew where father had hidden his gun.

It took all night to persuade her that we wanted to go on living. We hoped that he might just be taken for interrogation. I think it broke my mother's spirit; she was never the same after that. Finally, in the morning, she and Werner left and we climbed back into our hiding place. The next time Werner came, he reported to us that all the men and young boys who were still around had been taken into a makeshift prison that was a farmhouse near the end of the village. They were held there for a while; no one knows for how long. All these older men, too old to fight in the war, now faced an awful ordeal. Some didn't even have shoes on, so the rumor went. They were taken the way they were dressed in their homes.

Days went by when we didn't see anyone, and Werner didn't bring us food. He had to wait for the right moment to open the door; too many soldiers were about all day long. He couldn't give away his mission. Then one day, we heard commotion on the other side of the building; the neighbor's side. The Russians had placed a huge cannon there. It was the "Stalinorgel," so named by us Germans. I think it was a forerunner of the missile. The noise was earsplitting, unbearable, a sound we had never heard before. We covered our ears with our hands, but it didn't help because we were too close; there was just a brick wall between us and this monster of a gun. What was their target? Were they shooting at the little airport? We had no idea that they were shooting at Pyritz, our little town with the ancient wall and the well-preserved towers. When they finally stopped, our ears felt very strange. We had to endure this a few more times. Werner was always bombarded with questions when he came to bring us food. We actually didn't realize how dangerous it was for him to come, and in turn, for us, too. We had no idea what was going on outside and in the house, but he couldn't take the time to tell us. There was the constant fear that someone had seen him. He told us only bits and pieces, how mother worried about us and that the soldiers were everywhere in the house. We asked him about the cannon next door. He had found out that Pyritz had decided not to surrender. It stopped the advancement of the Russian troops. What we didn't know until later was that all the civilians had been evacuated at the last minute. There was still one opening in a direction where a train ran. It was hard to believe that this had been accomplished. Pyritz was now a fort, surrounded by the enemy. We found out much later that a small group of German soldiers, many of them young boys, fought to the last man. The town was totally demolished. The bombardment took almost four weeks. It was a last effort in our area to hold back the enemy, and we were in the middle of it.

During these weeks the Russian troops lived like kings with all the good food they found in the farmers' pantries. Father had just butchered before Christmas. The raping and killing did not stop. Girls and women searched for hiding places. Young mothers had their children sleep on top of them. Ruth, our neighbor, stayed in bed pretending that she had a terrible disease. Whenever the soldiers came around looking for women, mother slipped out and hid in the cow stable; she often stayed there all night. Young girls were raped by ten or more soldiers at a time and left for dead, or were killed.

Our Ukrainian maid, Sofia, disappeared the first day the troops stopped in the town, but Maria, the Polish maid, was just as afraid as we were, and stuck close to the family. But a few days later she disappeared, too. Our farm help were foreign workers, and they organized themselves very quickly. They took wagons and horses from the farmers and escaped. Maria left with them. But we still had Franz, the man who took care of the horses. He was frightened by what had happened, and he had no place else to go to. His roommate had run away, probably going home to Poland. Franz stayed near the empty stable, and walked around with a kerosene lantern under his jacket; he had to hold on to something. I found him a few weeks later after we had to move to Marienwerder, dying on the floor in someone's stable. I searched for a little bit of soup to give to him, but he couldn't eat. Later that day, I looked in on him and he had died. This was the fate of so many old people: the cold, fear, and hunger were more than they could endure.

Father

I wished with all my heart that I could have had my father a little longer. I was a teenager, and spent most of the time in school. At fifteen, father and I had never had profound conversations. I never found out what he was really thinking. He was my father, and he was always there for me. I was happy he didn't have to go to war.

Marrying my mother and having his own farm was, I think, the fulfillment of his dream. The farm had been in good shape although it was run by women. Grandfather died during World War I when he was only in his fifties. Grandmother had to run the farm by herself, and had become quite proficient and independent. She held the reins tightly in her hands. It was difficult for her to turn them over to her new son-in-law and let him make decisions. Father wanted to modernize the farm equipment. Grandmother felt it was good enough for her; why change things? Many long discussions took place. Father was a hardworking man and gradually proved his abilities. Fears of relationships not working out disappeared. Slowly he bought new farm equipment and electrified some machinery that had only been manually operated before. Life on the farm was good.

He had been a cavalryman during his military services in World War I and loved horses. He saw to it that there were good horses in the stable, and his pleasure was to always keep a riding horse.

Now and then on long winter evenings, he got together with acquaintances, farmers like himself, and played cards. This gave them

Martha and Paul Buchholz wedding photo.

a chance to talk about plans for the next year. Christa and I always looked forward to the times when the card games came to our house. Mother had delicious snacks ready. Father smoked cigars and also a pipe. One winter, he made little furniture for our dollhouse from cigar boxes that we had saved. We never expected him to take time out to make toys for us. Eagerly, Christa and I sat around the table watching. We couldn't wait for the glue to dry so we could put those little stools and benches into our dollhouse.

Father's homeland was West Prussia, also called the "Corridor." It was a somewhat narrow province running from the south to the Baltic Sea, between East Prussia and the motherland. West Prussia was annexed to Poland after Germany lost the First World War in 1918. This had given Poland an important opening to the Baltic Sea.

It was especially bitter for father and his brothers to pull up their roots and leave everything behind. His brother Wilhelm and wife Emily lived in Pyritz, and were already established farmers. They asked father to stay with them. Since Wilhelm and Emily had no children, they made offers to other family members to come and live with them so they could later inherit the farm.

Now that we were at war again with the Russians, father was

reminded of his wartime experiences. He talked of the cold winters he had endured fighting in Russia. We prayed that he wouldn't have to go to war, but sadly, the war caught up with him at home.

On special occasions when he put on tails and a top hat, I thought he was the most handsome man in the world. I loved my father. He was fair and encouraging. He respected us and never put us down. I sometimes wonder what my life would have been like if he had been with us longer—to be on an adult level with him, to debate politics with him, or argue about some silly idea.

Years later, mother received two letters, independently, from men who knew my father in the Russian camps. They had survived, and could tell my mother about his death and when he had died. Father survived until September of 1945.

Much later, listening to a eulogy a son wrote for his father deeply touched me. The loss of my father rushed to my mind as I tried to picture the camp deep in Russia. Did someone say a prayer when he died? Was he alone? Did he have a proper grave? These questions will never be answered.

We didn't mourn our father the way one would normally mourn a loved one. We kept up our hope of being reunited with him again, even though deep in our hearts we knew that he couldn't have survived the ordeal of being transported to Russia and living and working there under the worst conditions. But a little flicker of hope remained, and we held on to that. Our lives had to go on. A year went by, and another one. There was no communication. Gradually, we accepted the inevitable. Each of us had to learn to survive on our own without the backbone of our family.

In 2002, I wrote to the German Red Cross in Munich after I learned that the Russian archives were available for research. The German Red Cross had searched the Russian archives looking for information regarding the German civilians who died in the former Soviet Union. I received in response to my inquiry the following:

Paul Buchholz died on September 17, 1945 in the USSR. No information has been found regarding where he died or where he might be buried. We hope this information will be helpful after all these years.

Deutsches Rotes Kreuz
Generalsekretariat

SUCHDIENST MÜNCHEN
Zentrale Auskunfts- und Dokumentationsstelle

DRK-Suchdienst · Chiemgaustr. 109 · D-81549 München

Frau
Ingrid Stabins
3 Catherine Rose Rd.

USA- Harwich, MA 02645

bitte, geben sie stets unser Aktenzeichen an:
II/42-db-DT 28.10.2002

Betr.: BUCHHOLZ, Paul, geb.: 19.02.1889

Sehr geehrte Frau Stabins,

der Suchdienst des Deutschen Roten Kreuzes hat aus den Archivbeständen der Gemeinschaft Unabhängiger Staaten (GUS) Meldungen mit den Namen deutscher Zivilgefangener erhalten, die auf dem Gebiet der früheren Sowjetunion verstorben sind.

In diesen Unterlagen ist Ihr Angehöriger

Paul BUCHHOLZ aufgeführt, der am 17.09.1945 auf dem Gebiet der ehem. UdSSR verstorben ist.

Nähere Angaben zum Todesort und der Grablage liegen uns ebensowenig vor wie Angaben zur Todesursache.

Wir bedauern, diese Nachricht, die auch nach so vielen Jahren für Sie schmerzlich sein wird, übermitteln zu müssen. Wir sind jedoch sicher, daß sie von Ihnen als Befreiung von einer langjährigen Ungewißheit empfunden wird.

Mit freundlichem Gruß
i.A.

Dr. H. Kalcyk, Abt. Leiter

German Red Cross letter received by Ingrid, dated October 28, 2002, in response to her inquiry that same year. "The German Red Cross has searched the archives looking for information regarding the German civilians who died in the former Soviet Union. In these records is an item: Paul Buchholz died on September 17, 1945 in the USSR. No information has been found regarding where he died or where he might be buried. We hope this information will be helpful after all these years."

Leaving the Hideaway

After three long weeks, we had to give up our hiding place. On February 21ˢᵗ, Werner came to us in the evening and told us that we had to be ready the next morning; the village was to be evacuated. This was stunning news; that's all he told us. We started asking ourselves, "Where will we go?" thinking that we might have to find a place somewhere in a neighboring town. Why did the Russians want us all to leave? Why the whole town? Christa and I hadn't had any contact with the soldiers except seeing them the day they initially moved through the village.

What will happen to the livestock, we wondered? Not knowing what was really going on in the village, we did not know if this would be permanent or temporary. Christa had more common sense than I had, because she put layers of clothes on, and tucked all the pictures she had taken with her between her stockings and knee socks, which she pulled over her stockings. We climbed down the ladder the next morning and waited for Werner to come and get us. Mother had instructed him to tell us to mingle with the people and to be inconspicuous. She didn't want us to come into the house. Seeing mother again was wonderful, but we had no time to savor the moment.

People had assembled in the farmyard, and were running back and forth with bundles. Some of it looked like food. Wide-eyed and astounded, we watched and joined them. The decision to vacate the village came unexpectedly. Everyone was rushing to take with them as much as they could. Mother had quickly gathered warm clothing and blankets.

Now that we had abandoned our hiding place, there was no reason to lock the door to the carriage house. Before we knew it, someone had pulled out the carriage. The horses were gone, but we still had the pair of oxen. One of the people brought out an ox and tried to harness him to the carriage. When mother saw that, she went into the smoke chamber in the attic, one place the soldiers hadn't discovered, and took out what she could find—ham, salamis, and bacon, and put it on the carriage.

The ox was used to working with another ox, and became so

nervous and confused with all the commotion around him that he just took off. He ran into the backyard with the carriage bouncing behind him. A little old lady was already on it, and it was sheer luck that the whole thing didn't tip over. More people wanted to store their bundles on the carriage, but there was only so much space. We couldn't sit on the carriage, and we still didn't know where we had to go. The order was to assemble at the end of the village.

I had held on to my suitcase with all my favorite things. I didn't want to part with it. Finally, with the ox all harnessed to the carriage, we were heading out of the farmyard, followed by an entourage of people who had placed things on the carriage. We walked with the rest of the folks to the end of the village. At this point, nothing seemed to matter. Everyone tried to carry as much as they could. Soon, other townspeople took over the carriage, and it just disappeared. We didn't know where we were heading. Soldiers walked along with us.

This day changed our lives forever. Our struggle began immediately; we all had taken too much to carry. A friend walked alongside of me, and offered to carry my suitcase. She was older and bigger, but also could only carry it for so long before putting it down. She apologized, and I knew I couldn't carry it anymore. I took a long look at it, and said a quiet goodbye to my favorite things. I just left it there for someone else to pick up. Some people carried smoked hams and sausages in pillowcases on their backs. We soon saw these and many other things hanging on trees alongside the road. I remember on one stretch we had to make way for Russian trucks. We walked on plowed fields that had turned very muddy, since snow melted during the day. I became stuck, my foot came out of my boot, and I nearly fell down into the mud.

All this time we heard off-and-on shooting. Word came around that Pyritz was still under fire and that it hadn't surrendered. We were puzzled. It seemed impossible that Pyritz was still resisting three weeks after the Russians had surrounded it. What was happening in the town? What about the people?

We had walked a good part of the day, stopping and resting to the dismay of the soldiers who were leading us. Finally, we reached the village Pitzerwitz. The soldiers just walked us into town and left us to our own misery. Mother urged us to find a safe place and to keep out of sight of the soldiers; that was difficult because they started to mingle with the people. We had no experience, and had not been face to face with the soldiers. We found a place in a washhouse where older men had settled in. In the back in the corner was the big stove that heated the water on washdays. Here Christa and I tried to hide; the space was so small I had to stick my legs into the ash opening on the stove. Loud shouts from the soldiers soon interrupted our rest. We all had to come out, and were marched on a dirt road into the fields. Here they had tanks and cannons stationed which were shooting into Pyritz. Here the war was still going on.

The Russians had problems with the weather. In the daytime, the plowed fields were soft and the tanks became stuck in deep ruts. We had to carry bundles of straw from a nearby barn and put that in the tracks. In the barn were also small bundles of flax, so we grabbed those first since they were smaller and not so heavy, and discovered that we actually did more harm than good. The flax fibers mixed with the wet dirt and became very tough. They wrapped around the chains of the tanks until they couldn't roll anymore. At night we had to go out in the freezing cold with picks and spades to fix the deep ruts the tanks and guns had made in the daytime. One night, it was so cold that I thought my brother, who was standing in a hollow tree, would freeze. I sat on our bundle to keep an eye on our belongings. We had to take them with us wherever we went, and one of us had to guard it. A little baby goat kept climbing on me for warmth or help; it was shivering so much that it couldn't hold still. The animals also suffered. If they were not killed for food, or shot for fun, they had to fend for themselves, and they just walked about. There was no food for them in the fields during the winter.

After a few more days, the fighting stopped. Pyritz had fallen. We were ordered to gather our few belongings and move on. This time we were herded to the village of Marienwerder. The village was already crowded with people from surrounding villages. The first few nights, we slept in a barn with only half a roof. We buried ourselves in the straw to keep warm. The worst was that we had nothing to eat. Father had butchered a large, fat pig in December about two months earlier, and here we were now begging for food. A family who was also in the barn, likely longer than we, had a large pot of boiled potatoes and a stoneware pot of plum marmalade. Is this what they had carried with them, or did they find it in one of the houses? This is what they shared with us. Soon the sweet marmalade with potatoes didn't taste all that bad, though who would have ever thought of eating the two foods together?

We searched around for friends and neighbors, and finally found space in a big farmhouse. We were lucky our hometown neighbors were there, too, and invited us to share the room with them. It was nice for us children; we had played together all our short lives. And now in this turmoil, we stuck together and looked out for each other. Christa was the same age as the neighbor's daughter Ruth, and our mothers were good friends. The Russians had taken our fathers at the same time, and we shared this painful grief. Each room seemed to have a whole family in it. Toddlers were running around playing happily—they didn't have a worry in the world. There was no privacy; people had to go through other peoples' rooms.

We all thought that this would be over soon, and that we could return to our village and homes. How long could we last? Food became a big problem. The owner of the house was there too, but what could she do, because people had just taken over her property.

We all foraged for food. The farmer kept grain in one of the lofts in the barn, and this was now a welcome resource. The mothers took turns grinding grain with an old-fashioned coffee grinder. Besides potatoes, this was about all they could prepare. The kitchen was a busy place; people had to take turns cooking, which went on practically all day.

At night, we spread straw on the floor, and everyone slept close together in one room. The constant fear of being raped kept us on guard day and night. But there was safety in numbers. Christa and I always looked for a safe place, and huddled in a corner or a back row. The soldiers roamed around at night, demanding to get into the houses, searching for women and girls. They came to this house, too. One time a soldier lit a piece of paper so that he could see since we had no lights. He almost set the straw on fire. After incidences like this, the adults finally came to the conclusion that something had to be done; they had to make it safer for us. The room had a heavy solid door, and they barricaded it with broomsticks and ropes.

On the first night, everyone was lying in wait for the rattle on the door. The test had yet to come. What will happen, will the ropes hold? Will the soldier go away if he can't get in, or would he shoot through the door? We were waiting; then there came the heavy footsteps and the fumbling and rattling on the door, with much cursing. In our panic we started to scream. We screamed so loud we couldn't even hear him leave. We had found our defense. The earsplitting noise of twenty or so people screaming was too much for any amorous soldier.

We felt a little safer moving around in the daytime. We talked about our predicament with other people, and asked what they did to defend themselves at night. It turned out that the simple method of screaming was the solution. This idea was quickly picked up in other houses. We heard screaming off and on during the night.

When the first troops came, they rampaged through the villages, and everything in the houses were thrown about. Now that they wanted to occupy the houses themselves, they came around and made us clean them up. Soldiers just burst into the houses, and went from room to room, selecting the young and able people. They stood there – "paschli, paschli" they would say – "hurry up." Christa and I had to go. Usually a group of people were already waiting in the street. We didn't want our mother to work, too; she had enough distress trying to provide a meal for us. Werner helped mother to hide when we saw them come around. It was a challenge every time. If she were found in an isolated place, she took the chance of being raped, so she had to stay near other people. Sliding under a bed or kneeling in the back of a wardrobe were quick hiding places.

And then came that fateful day when our mother couldn't get into her hiding place in time. The soldier pointed his finger at her and flung his arm to the door indicating she had to go with us, too. We were sorry that this happened, but she consoled us: "Don't worry, we will be all together in the evening again." Werner walked with us to the door, but stayed behind.

We joined the people outside. It was a much larger group this time, and before we knew it, they split us up; Christa and mother were sent in a different direction. I wasn't alarmed; there were many areas to clean up, and we would certainly all come back in the evening. Mother and Christa didn't come back. I feared the worst. What if something happened to them and they don't come back? I couldn't even finish the thought. I lay on my straw bed that night praying for their safe return.

We had to find out, and went around in the village to ask if other people were also missing. Someone had heard that a group of people had been sent to the little airfield between Köselitz and Pyritz. The Russians apparently wanted to use these facilities even though they were badly damaged.

Werner and I were glad to know at least where they were. We were very much on our own now. To get food was a dilemma. Our neighbors, who had been cooking together with mother, gave us food. It was a daily struggle to get a meal together with only potatoes and grains. I helped to roast barley outside on a makeshift fireplace made of a circle of stones topped with an old cookie sheet. With an old spoon, I kept moving the grains around until they had a dark brown color. This was later ground for "Coffee Ersatz." This had been done and used in every home even before the war. Real coffee was expensive and unattainable during the war. Most households had a special pan for roasting grain. It had a handle on top that was turned, moving the grain in the pan. Here the mothers were busy all day taking turns grinding grain with an old-fashioned coffee grinder. The grain was used to make soups and porridge.

Finding Our Ox

One day in early March started with an unexpected surprise. Werner had bumped into his best friend Herbert; he lived just across the street in Köselitz, and they had been inseparable. Herbert knew who had taken our carriage and the ox, and where they were. This was the best news anyone could have given Werner. Hometown people had managed to hang on to the carriage, and were now living in a little hunting hut in the woods. There was no holding Werner back. "We have to go and check this out and bring back the ox," he declared.

I was hesitant to believe this. Who could these people be? We had lost track of the people who took over the carriage when we left Köselitz. "Was Herbert sure the ox was still alive when he last heard about it?" I asked.

Werner stood in front of me with clenched fists as if he already held the reins. I saw a determined look in his eyes, not of a thirteen-year-old boy, but of a man. At this moment he didn't seem like my little brother anymore. He was tall for his age, and I realized that he had grown up fast.

His excitement was contagious. I thought about it, and reasoned that perhaps we should give it a try. "But let's first find out where these woods are and how far it is," I said. We started plotting how to go about it.

Mother and Christa were still away; no one kept an eye on us and held us back from undertaking this venture. We didn't know much about this town, and certainly didn't know the nearby woods. Werner's mind was set—he wanted to go there and bring back the ox. I needed more information, and asked the owner of the house about the hut. She knew about it and gave me directions. She could have warned us just from an adult's point of view, but nobody did. The ox was the most important thing for Werner right now; he was ours and he wanted him back.

I brushed away the thoughts that we might be doing something dangerous. Perhaps we should ask Herbert again. Not knowing how our undertaking would unfold and how long it would take us, we decided to leave mid-morning. The narrow path she had described was easy to find. Frost was still on the ground, and a thin dusting of snow covered a carpet of dry leaves, a sign that the sun hadn't warmed the forest floor. The stillness struck us; not even a bird chattered. It was amazing how quiet a forest can be. I wanted to whisper.

The crackling sound of our footsteps was the only sound. Could that be a give-away if anyone was around? I felt like tiptoeing. This was a new experience. The path wound through gray trunks of leafless trees. I began to feel uneasy, my throat was dry. I should have known better and not given in to Werner's begging. We were taking a great risk with our lives.

Werner led the way, walking ahead with big strides. Every so often he turned his head. I tried to read his emotions; did he look scared? "Let's go back," I whispered. He threw his head around and all he said was, "NO!"

Suddenly a German soldier stepped out from behind a tree. I felt an electric surge go right through my body; my hands went up to my throat. Was this a mirage, or really a live German soldier, or was he a Russian disguised as a German soldier? Should I run or should I stay? My body was shaking, my legs felt like rubber. I couldn't have run even if I wanted to. He raised his hand like a peace offering.

"Are you coming from the village?" He spoke German, thank God. My trembling arms dropped to my sides. I took a deep breath; my body continued trembling. The scare was too much. What was he doing here, were there more of them? My eyes scanned the woods behind him. An instant flash went through my mind; what if this had been a Russian soldier? I didn't want to think what could have happened to me.

He wanted to know what was going on in the village. We told him that the Russians had occupied a section of the village and had forced the people into the rest of the homes, that every place was very crowded, and that we had little food.

My heart ached for him—he looked cold and haggard and unshaven. His long coat was dirty, and so were his Knobelbecher—the short army boots. He had wrapped a gray scarf around his neck, and had pulled a wool hat over his ears and all the way down to his eyes. How and where was he surviving in this weather? We couldn't help him. As we pushed on, now more carefully, we saw another soldier in the distance, but he avoided us.

It was hard to believe that after weeks of Russian occupation, German soldiers were still hiding, practically amongst the Russians. I couldn't shake off this frightening encounter, and wanted to go back, but Werner was pushing on. He had only one mindset: getting the ox.

The path led us directly to the hut, and there tethered to a nearby tree was the ox. Werner ran ahead, kicking up mushy dead leaves. It was really true; the ox was still alive. I started running, too. We looked him over, stroked his back, and saw that the poor animal was very thin. His hipbones protruded; it seemed they were just holding up a skeleton. We talked to him like we had found a lost friend. He turned his head to us. Werner threw his arms around his neck; his sad eyes begged for help. There was nothing for him to eat in the woods. He had chewed a big wedge into the tree. All of a sudden we heard, "Oh my Lord, where are you coming from?" The people in the hut were our next-door neighbors, the Holzhueters, from Köselitz. They asked us in and explained how they had held on to the carriage and the ox. It all seemed so incredible. It was the food that mother had put in the carriage that helped sustain them. They were astounded about the risk we had taken. Werner went to take a look at the carriage, which they had pushed behind the hut.

"Oh no, not the carriage, too," went through my mind. He was standing on top of it holding a small object in his hand: mother's handbag. It was puzzling—why was it still there? Why did she put it in the carriage in the first place? Did she have money in it or papers, or was it just a habit to take the handbag along? Sure, we had been on an outing, the most tragic outing of our lives. We checked the bag; my heart took a leap—it still had scissors and a comb in it, something we badly needed. What a surprise we will have for mother, I thought.

Nearby was a dugout in the ground someone must have been using for a sleeping place. The hole was covered with the leather lap covers from the carriage. The people gave us something to eat, and mentioned that German soldiers came by for a quick meal. We informed them about the situation in the village. They somehow survived here in this hut, but we never saw them again.

Since the ox was ours, there was no question that we take him back. The poor ox was terribly weak; we had to pull hard to make him walk at all, and then had to stop often. We came to a little creek that contained some frozen snow. A narrow board led across it. The ox refused to step on the board. We had come so far; we had to get him across. Werner kept saying, "Look for something for him to eat, we might tease him with that." But there was nothing.

I grabbed dead grass and leaves, and held it out to him, but he was not moving. We were at our wits' end. But leaving him there was far from our minds. We finally decided to both go behind him and just push with all our might. He would have to take a step or fall over. That did it. The push made him take the first step on the board, and after that he kept on going across. Slowly we made it back to Marienwerder. I was scared all the way, but we couldn't make the animal walk any faster.

We headed straight for the barn at the farmyard. Werner looked around, "Wouldn't it be better if we hid him?" he asked. The barn was large, and there was plenty of room and straw everywhere; it seemed easy to fix up a place for him in a corner. Werner was so happy to have the ox, he kept saying, "You wait and see, he'll be back on his feet in no time. I'll fatten him up." I was wondering what we would do with this ox. Perhaps if we had the carriage, it would be a start. After a few more days, mother and Christa came back exhausted and hungry; they had walked all the way from Pyritz. We hugged and cried and promised never to separate again. They had to clean up the former little airport under terrible conditions, and slept on a cement floor with nothing to keep them warm. They, too, had expected to be back that first evening.

What a surprise we had for them—we all walked to the barn and there he was, our ox. It was touching to see the smiles on everyone's faces. We told the story of how we found him, but that didn't go over well. Mother couldn't believe that we put ourselves in so much danger. However, she didn't want to spoil Werner's enthusiasm. She couldn't bear having lost everything; tears glistened in her eyes, and now here we were so excited about the ox—the only thing that belonged to us now and something we had risked our lives for.

Russian soldiers were roaming around everywhere, and after a short time they discovered the ox hidden in the barn and took him away. Werner was heartbroken, "What will they do with one ox?" I was thinking that, too. He probably didn't make it very far, and ended up in the soup kitchen.

chapter eight

MY ORDEAL

My whole body ached and felt stiff. Sleeping on the floor was uncomfortable, even on a layer of straw; but nobody complained. We were all glad to have a place to lie down at night. As I knelt and stretched my arms, I craned my neck to look out of the window. What would it be today? went through my mind. Little rivulets of raindrops ran down the windowpanes; another nasty morning. A blanket of gray clouds hung low as far as I could see.

I didn't want to go out and work in this weather. Looking for a good hiding place was the first thing that popped into my mind. The Russians would probably come around again searching for workers no matter what kind of weather we had. Just as I was contemplating this, Christa came and asked, "Feel my head, I think I have a fever." Indeed she did—her face was flushed and she said she felt sick. "You definitely can't go out in this weather today," was mother's decision. I saw her worried look; getting sick was the worst thing that could happen to us now. Up to now we had been concerned with survival, finding food, and being safe. Becoming sick was something we didn't consider. "I'll go alone," I decided, and I put on an extra jacket under my coat because it was such a raw day. I was hoping that some sympathetic Russian would have pity on us and not make us work outside.

At this time, we were working on a field that the Russians were preparing for an airstrip. It was March; in the daytime the snow melted. Stomping around on the field where the winter rye was already sprouting was cumbersome. The rich, black earth clung to our shoes and clothes. It was sinful to ruin the crops that were so necessary to keep people alive. The last five years of war had taught us that every kernel of grain was important.

Mother kept saying, "Let me find something that will protect you from the rain." She went to the barn and came back with a burlap potato sack. "Look what I found." I could tell by her expression that she was relieved. She held it up, "It looks pretty clean." She stuck one corner into the other and that formed a hood-like protection that also covered part of my back. When the soldiers came around, we had to insist that Christa couldn't go. I grabbed my tin can and my spoon and walked out to join the others in the street. Mother's warning, "Be very careful," which she never forgot to remind us, were the last words I heard.

People were already standing in line. However, this time it was different; there were more soldiers. One of them with an interpreter came to each of us asking our age. I was always cautious, so I decided to make myself younger. I had braided my hair into two little pigtails and wore a headscarf. I thought I could get away with telling them I was fourteen. They formed two groups. All the younger people were separated from the much older ones. The girl next to me thought she knew why: "They probably want us to work at another place. I hope it is inside," she added.

The older group was marched off, and then came our turn. Soldiers with bayonets on their rifles escorted us; that seemed strange, since they had never done that before. I put my spoon in my coat pocket and hugged my tin can close to my body. The soldiers led us out of the village in a different direction, away from all the workplaces we had been. Rain kept drizzling; my burlap sack became soaked and heavy. We walked on a narrow path along a dirt road, avoiding puddles on the uneven path. I was concerned because no one knew where we were going, and the soldiers were guarding us very seriously. That had never been the case when they marched us to a workplace. I was worried about what they had in mind. We walked on with our heads down. No one talked; there was a sense of uneasiness and apprehension among the group.

Finally, we reached a village. They ushered us into a house, and everyone was glad to be out of the bad weather. Our feet and shoes were wet, and our clothes were not any better. We sat down on the floor. All the rooms were empty. After a while, more young people joined us. They had been picked up in the neighboring village; no one knew what to make of it.

Now our group had grown much larger, and soon we were ordered to line up again and ordered to walk again. It didn't seem that we were going back. Nothing looked familiar. The rain had let up a bit, and I rolled up my wet sack and carried it. My instinct told me to hang on to the sack.

We shuffled along on another dirt road. I was cold in my wet clothes, and tried to estimate how far we were from Marienwerder considering the time we had walked. It didn't seem very far. In late afternoon, we arrived at Augustinenhof, a farming estate. Someone knew this place. There were several of these large estates in this area; I had heard the name of this place, too. The place had been cleaned up, which made me wonder why we were there. Even the pigsties were clean, and this is where they put us; a few girls in each little stall.

By this time it was evening, and we still didn't have a clue why we were there. Even though we had not eaten all day, no one was concerned about food. It was now dark, and the unknown was frightening. Someone whispered, "What will happen to us?" No one answered. After some time, a soldier came and took out one girl at a time. Since no one came back, this greatly added to our worries. I told my companions in the stall that I had a little pocket calendar, which I was using as a diary. I didn't want the soldiers to see it in case they searched us. My companion urged me, "You have to get rid of it," but where and how? We could hear a guard walking back and forth outside. Up high was a small window, but I was afraid to throw it out. I quickly tore out the pages and ripped them into small pieces, and when I didn't hear the guard, I tossed them out of the window a few pieces at a time. I was relieved to be rid of it, but was sorry to have lost my notes. I also had a little comb in my pocket, and stuck this into a ripped seam in my jacket sleeve. That was all I had with me, in addition of course to my little tin can and spoon.

When my turn came, I was escorted to a house nearby where a woman sat behind a table with pen and paper in front of her; dim light spread from a kerosene lantern on the edge of the table. A Russian officer was sprawled on a bed in one corner. My first thought was that he would rape me. By now it must have been the middle of the night. The woman was in civilian clothes. She could have been Polish, but she spoke Russian and German. After taking down all my personal data, it came down to whether I was a member of the Youth Movement or not. JM (Jungmädel) was the ten- to fourteen-year-old group, and the older ones belonged to the BDM (Bund Deutcher Mädchen). I had told her my age, but I shouldn't have been so honest. She figured that I must belong to the older group, which I didn't. I was a sports coach for the younger group. I insisted that I didn't belong to the older group, but I didn't want to tell her that I was a coach. Sports certainly weren't political, but that probably wouldn't have made any difference to her; we kept arguing about this. I became very angry because she didn't want to believe me, and I finally told her, "You write what you want to." I will never know what she wrote down. I should have persisted like some of the others who were let go.

After a few minutes, she mentioned to the Russian that she was finished with me, and he rose and grabbed the lantern and motioned to follow him. I wasn't sure I should because rape was always on my mind, and I didn't know what happened to the others. She pointed out that I had to go with him. We stepped into a hallway. He walked ahead and opened a door that led into a basement. I stared down into total darkness; it looked like a deep black hole. "I am not going in there." With a grim look he pointed and I knew I had to go down there. "Is anybody down there," I called. A weak voice answered, "Yes," and I carefully picked my way down, step by step, holding on to the stone wall of the stairway, not knowing what to expect. Once down, I couldn't see where I was stepping. I didn't know who was there or how many. Someone said, "Just sit down." Getting down on my knees, I knew it was a potato cellar, and we had to sit on the potatoes. I was tired and exhausted; I crawled to a free spot and sat down. We had to keep moving to make room for the next person. Not to be able to see anything was terrible. The interrogation went on all night. We talked quietly, and everyone was worried about what would happen next.

There was no way to escape, but I was still positive that they would let us go back to our towns the next day.

I looked around as we emerged from the cellar the next morning to see if there was a familiar face. Some were familiar from the day before, and I noticed some new people had joined us. How can I find someone to take a message to my mother? was all I could think about, but we were kept in a group, and there weren't any people around who we could talk with. I still hoped they would let us go back home. I wondered how far we were from Marienwerder. I also worried about Christa and her fever; people talked about cases of typhoid. It was the first time I had heard about it, and I was alarmed. What if Christa was getting sick with typhoid? Wasn't that very contagious? Could I have been infected, too? My mind raced from one thing to another.

As we waited outside, a truck pulled up and we all had to climb in; we were not going home. Some of the towns we drove through I knew by name, though I had never been there. I tried to figure out how far we might have gone and in which direction. In places, the road was bumpy and broken up from the Russian's heavy equipment. We were shivering standing in the back of the truck; I was thankful that it didn't rain.

The villages looked bleak and desolate, and showed the wounds of war. Dead animals were decaying on the wayside, and one could see burned-out houses and barns. This contrasted with the fields looking like green carpets. Wheat that had been planted in the fall was now welcoming the new season.

Where have all the people gone? There had been fighting in this area, and perhaps the inhabitants were forced out like we were. I wondered if all the land the Russians had gone through looked like this. Köselitz certainly did—many houses and barns had been burned down, even the schoolhouse.

We must have been about twenty-five in this group of all young women and girls; I was the youngest at sixteen. We were taken to another farming estate. Here the Russians had set up headquarters, as I found out at my interrogation. Several of us spent the first night in the washhouse. I remember we begged for coal so we could build a fire under the kettle that was used to heat water on washdays. Finally, a woman came and brought us burning coal on a dust-pan, but nothing else to keep a fire going. We started to break up whatever we could to keep the fire going. The hardest test was a bench; we had no tools. We worked with our hands, smashing it on the cement floor, letting our anger and frustration out.

I became sick with diarrhea. One of the women suggested eating charcoal. I took little charred pieces of wood out of the fire, scraped off some black powdery substance, and ate it; but this did not work.

The next day we were moved from the washhouse to an attic, where they had put down straw for us. A soldier brought us cabbage soup. I was afraid to eat anything, since my diarrhea was getting worse and there was no bathroom. Most likely there was an outhouse somewhere, but we weren't allowed to leave the attic. Every so often, a soldier came and led us outside, and we had to squat down right in front of him in the middle of the farmyard; it was humiliating beyond words. I became very frightened about my condition, and there was nothing I could do. We stayed there several days, and all we had to eat was cabbage soup brought to us in a bucket.

It seemed they had split up the group; we had no idea where the others were. Each night, some of us were brought to the main house for interrogation. This was the Russian way; they interrogated at night when the resistance of their victims was at the lowest point. By this time I was really sick; I just hung on to the chair. The interrogator asked me if I was sick, and I told him that I was weak and had diarrhea, but it didn't make any difference.

I was perplexed to hear what these people already knew about my family. Where could they have obtained the information? Could these have been the same people who had interrogated my father? But that was weeks ago. I couldn't believe that the Russians were such great record keepers, but how and where could they have obtained the information?

The soldiers in this room were all in an exhilarated mood. A radio was blaring, and one could sense the announcer had great news. The interrogator told me that Königsberg had fallen; this was the provincial city in East Prussia, and a German stronghold. Because it was on the Baltic Sea with an important harbor and supply depot, it was a strategic victory for the Russians. Many refugees boarded ships there, and escaped through the Baltic Sea to the Scandinavian countries. The biggest tragedy was the Russians' torpedoing of the "Wilhelm Gustloff," a pleasure ship, which had over ten thousand refugees on board. Only a fraction of them survived.

Overcoming Typhoid in Camp Schwiebus

After having spent several days in the attic, we were told to get ready for transport. Again we had to climb on a truck. This time the group was larger; including a few old men. I was so sick that my only thought was how I could get away from here. No one knew what was going on or where they were taking us. I thought of my mother and how worried she must be. If there could only be a way to let her know.

The back of the truck had no cover, so we huddled together to keep warm. We passed many towns and villages with unfamiliar names. It took a good part of the day before we arrived at our destination in Schwiebus, in the province of Selesia.

Spread out before us was a large camp, all fenced in with many wooden barracks. It was a long way from home. I had never heard of Schwiebus. It was just a little city like many others, and it was farther south from where we were. I was cold and sick, and could hardly stand up. I waited in line, crying quietly, for my turn for registration. No one gave us any information. "What is the reason for holding us?" everyone asked.

When I look back, I must admit, the thought of being shipped to Russia had never entered my mind. I don't know what I would have done. Many people thought that this detention would only last until the end of the war. Was the war still raging on? How could we tell, since we had no information? Finally, we were all registered and led into barracks. I later found out this place had previously been a camp for Russian prisoners of war. The windows were covered with wire, and the barrack had nothing in it except lower and upper bunks of just planks; no straw here like we had in the attic a day ago. We were all lying next to each other with no divisions. I had held on to my potato sack, and used it now to lie on. Most of us had nothing else but the clothes on our backs. My condition had worsened; my diarrhea was so bad I couldn't keep anything in my body. Finally I was placed in the "Sick Barrack." It had upper and lower bunks just like the other barrack. I was ill, terrified, and homesick—will I ever make it out of here alive? —was my constant thought. My throat was so tight I couldn't swallow. When the two women who were doling out the soup noticed I wasn't eating it, they came back and persisted that I had to eat this awful soup. Up to now, the Russians had given us cabbage soup; it had a little more substance, even though I hardly ate any. But this soup was just grain and water; it had so much sand in it that it made a crunching sound in my mouth. The women didn't give up. I can still hear their encouraging words, "Take one more bite, you want to get better and go home." Each spoonful I washed down with a swallow of coffee, *Coffee Ersatz*, which they had brought in; it was the only way I could swallow the soup.

Next to me was a girl about my age; we were in the upper bunks and found out that we came from the same area. But we were too weak and ill to engage in conversations. A few days later she died during the night. I cried all morning. Will her mother ever find out what happened to her? Will that be my fate too? Death was all around me. I watched a narrow band of blood on the uneven floor, like a little red river, stretching longer and longer, coming from the bunk of a young woman. I wanted to see my mother again. I didn't want to die. I knew if I died here, no one would ever know what happened to me.

On the other side of me was a woman who was about my mother's age. She didn't seem very sick, but she died, too, within a few days. Nearly everyone in this room died. I was terrified. I had already seen dying and dead people along the roadside, but this was different. Here were people who slept right next to me and died. All I could think of was, will I be next?

My stay in this barrack was not long. I was transferred to a quarantine barrack. Here were the very sick, and I was one of them. The situation was the same: bunk beds with no divisions. A woman was in charge; she could have been a nurse, but there were no doctors and no medicines. A large milk can was placed in the room; that was our toilet. None of us could go outside to the latrines. A bowl of water was handed to us in the morning to wash our faces. It took a long time to get your turn. Some women who were less sick helped the very sick.

I only remember the black coffee in the morning, (of course it wasn't real coffee). By the time it was distributed, it was cold. I still had my tin can, but it was small and didn't hold much. I gulped it down the moment I received it; I was so terribly thirsty. By now, I had typhoid with a raging fever. All I remember is that I was so thirsty and didn't have much to drink. I wanted to drink my wash water. How did I survive? I don't know; I must have been given some water.

We were all lying in rows very close together on planks, and I saw that the girl next to me had lice crawling all over her head. But what could I do? I thought that perhaps if I hold my head real still, they wouldn't crawl on me. I couldn't even hold up my head, and it didn't seem to matter after a while. I remember a very kind, tall, young woman in a red dress who wore her blond hair in a thick ponytail. She brought us our food, helped us up, and brought the washbowl around in the morning. She is the one I remember most. Her gentle voice encouraged me to fight for my life. The one thought, "I have to get well and go home," never left me.

My illness had advanced to a delirious state, and I was told later that I talked mindlessly. How long this went on I don't know. They had moved me to the end of the planks where they put the dying. I had reached the crisis stage. The gates of heaven opened up before me, and a brilliant light shone; the color unforgettable. My senses and body felt suspended and wanted to follow the light. It was a very peaceful moment. The light faded and I don't know how much time passed before I woke up. I had passed the crisis and defied death.

Was this real; was I alive? My clothes were wet from perspiration. I was cold and shivering, but my mind became clear and I tried to move my arms and then my body. How many days had passed? I'll never know. A feeling of hope came over me. I came back. I was alive. "I will get well and go home," I prayed every day.

Recovery was slow. I was weak and couldn't stand up. But there wasn't any place I could go anyway. If I had to, I crawled. Soon after, my ears began to hurt, and I found out that I had ear infections on both sides. A woman flushed my ears every morning. I crawled to her because I was so weak I couldn't walk. After a while, I was deaf, and I couldn't understand anyone.

Now I had another worry: will I lose my hearing? The woman kept telling me that I had to wait. There was no one else who had any experience with ear infections. I have no recollection about the food, but it must have sustained me. I became a little stronger and could walk again. The weather was becoming warmer; it must have been late April. I ventured to stand by the door and look around. Next to one side was a barrack with Ukrainian men. One day, a man motioned to me to come to the window. He pushed a plate with soup under the wiring, and asked me to eat it quickly. This to me was the most wonderful potato soup. Apparently these men were not actual prisoners; perhaps they had to wait for transportation to their homeland. They seemed to be treated much better. On one of these meetings, he pointed to my pants, which had a tear. He gave me a needle and thread so I could fix it; and that's when I discovered that I couldn't see very well. Another worry. These little rendezvous didn't last very long; I was sorry when the men left.

Next to our sick barrack was also a men's ward. My thoughts went to my father; perhaps he had been in this camp, too. I asked the woman who came around collecting our eating utensils if I could help; she also washed the ones from the men. This gave me a little more freedom to look around. "Yes, you can," she answered. "You can take the clean cans back to the men."

I remember a young boy stumbling about. He was tall and thin, and I overheard the dish washer woman say to him, "You better wash your dirty neck—if your mother ever saw you like this…." He was so ashamed he went to an outside faucet and scrubbed his neck until it was red. Then he came and asked if it was clean. She praised him, and I watched him go back into the barrack. Seeing him unstable on his feet, she urged him to take a rest. The next day when I asked if I could help again taking the cleaned cans back, I noticed the boy lying very still on his bed, with flies all over his face. He was dead. My heart ached for him. He was still around the day before; how quickly death can come. He was tall and lanky, and probably not older than fifteen. Will his family ever find out what happened to him? Perhaps his mother waited years for his return. Outside was a flat cart. First I wondered what it was used for, but I soon found out; this was how they transported the dead.

No one was allowed to walk outside, but whenever a new person came into the barrack, everyone had questions about family members or hometown people. We were mostly from Pomerania, and there was always a chance to meet someone or hear of someone. Despite the isolation, people were quite resourceful and found ways to communicate. It was the number-one challenge. We all had the same thought: to let the family know where we were. But I never made contact with anyone I knew.

During the time I was very ill, a burning plane had fallen onto the complex. All I remember was the loud noise of the crash. It had fallen on the women's side of the camp, and several were killed. The injured had mainly facial and eye injuries. They had rushed to the windows when they heard the loud noise of the plane, and the glass burst at the impact, cutting their faces. It seemed the war wasn't over or this wouldn't have happened.

Spring brought warm sunshine and longer days. It felt good to stand by the door and hold my face towards the sun, and I was thankful to be alive. The kind young woman in the red dress made a skirt for me. I remember it was black and looked so little; I had grown so thin that it kept slipping down. The safety pin that I had to hold up my pants came to my rescue.

I really wished I could see myself, but we didn't have the luxury of a mirror. My loss of hearing worried me. I couldn't participate in any conversation. If I asked someone to repeat something, the reply often wasn't a kind one. Little by little I withdrew. But my dear friend in the red dress encouraged me not to despair. I was still in quarantine, but had become a little stronger, and I knew that I would have to leave soon to join the others in the barracks.

My most treasured possession was the little comb which I had hidden in the seam of my jacket sleeve. It was just an inexpensive comb that had come with my mother's handbag, I think, but it served me well. I had teamed up with another woman to check our heads for lice every day.

After the typhoid, my hair started to fall out, leaving the temples and front all bare. The older women seemed to know that this happens after an illness like that and consoled me, "Give it time, it will grow back."

I have no recollection of actual dates; one day was like the other. No one had a watch. We judged the time by the arrival of the food, like morning, noon, and evening. The only news we had was rumors. The day came when I was considered well enough to leave the sick barrack. I rolled up my meager belongings in my burlap sack and said, "Good-bye" to my friend in the red dress. I gave her a big hug, and tears rolled down my cheeks because I owed her so much, but sadly, I never saw her again.

A woman came around to pick up those who were ready to join the others in the women's barracks. Once outside, I looked around; it was an amazing place. I saw barracks lined up and windows covered with wire; the place seemed very quiet. Not a soul was outside, which was odd, considering the many people who were detained here. I was more aware now of the situation than when I had first arrived. Human nature is extraordinary; it adapts or arranges itself and stores experiences in the far corners of the mind. Survival moves into the forefront and adds another dimension to our existence.

I felt the warm sun on my body as the woman walked me to a barrack, and wished I could just go home, that all the misery was a bad dream. We passed the short water pipe sticking up just about a foot above the ground. I thought of my terrible thirst when I was so feverish, and the boy who came here to scrub his neck before he died. My thoughts lingered with the boy. A big sign read, "Not for Drinking." The ground wasn't paved, but it was a hard surface; many feet had walked over it and packed it down.

When we arrived at a barrack, the person who led me there opened the door and shouted, "Make room for another one." That was it. I looked around at the same bunks without separations so that you could always squeeze in one more person. Here were again women of all ages. Small groups sat together talking. I told them that I had been ill, and again felt left out because my hearing was so bad.

Leaving the Schwiebus Camp

Just as I was settled in, an order came to get ready to leave the camp; we weren't told anything else. Rumors were the order of the day, but none went so far as to have us all being shipped to Russia. It was something we blocked out of our minds; it was too terrible a thought. I was praying that this was our release and they would let us go home. I realized I was far away from home, but I felt an inner strength that somehow, despite my physical weakness, I would make it. I had to make it. I clung to this hope. I often pictured our family reunion, thinking that by now they must be back in Köselitz. My thoughts turned to my father—was he really taken to Russia, or could he be in a camp like this? Was he still alive? I felt if he had been as sick as I had been, he wouldn't have survived. I was young and healthy, and barely made it.

Then I wondered what Köselitz might look like. Would the Russians let people get back into their houses? All these thoughts tumbled in my mind. Perhaps mother had come back early enough to plant some things in the garden. I caught myself; what an absurd thought. There was nothing left; what could she be planting? I just couldn't bring myself to the point of thinking that everything was lost and that we had nothing to come back to. Six months ago, I had still been going to school; I had enough to eat and our family was together. I will never forget my father's words, "They can take everything, but they can't take our land." This gave me hope. Perhaps there wouldn't be anything to eat, but we were young and had our land where we could start anew. I knew the livestock were gone, and perhaps we would have to start with just one cow.

We had no communication with the outside during these

weeks, and now the news of leaving this place filled us all with hope. Once again, the Russians came with lists and called off our names. We had to line up outside, a sad and bedraggled group of women. Every person carried a little bundle of their meager belongings under her arm. We walked in columns to the train station. What did this mean; are we going home by train? It was a cumbersome walk for me as I was still very weak. A freight train awaited us. A shiver ran down my spine; I knew we weren't going home. The Russians wouldn't take us back on trains. Something terrifying was brewing in the air. Here and there the word "Russia" was whispered. Schwiebus was already far enough away from home, but it was still Germany. It was an inconceivable thought to perhaps be shipped to Russia. I was frightened, and felt that in my frail condition I would never see my family again.

Soldiers were busy sectioning off groups, and then finally we had to board the cars. I can't remember if we were given food and water, but they did give us a milk can for our personal needs. Then we heard the clanking of the metal bars as they locked the door from the outside. Everyone looked for a place to sit. After the first shock, the grim reality set in and I wept quietly.

After a long wait, the train finally started to move. It was not possible to determine which direction we were going. The little slots in the corners were too high to look out. All night the train rattled along, with many long stops; we traveled part of the next day, too. Some women were hysterical, and then there were the brave and empathetic souls who tried to help and encourage. Others prayed, and in the end, we all suffered in our own way. We had no way out of here.

Finally, the train stopped, and this time we heard loud shouts and a lot of commotion; the doors were unlocked and we were ordered out. We anxiously left our confinement, not knowing what was going to happen next and where we were. It was at least comforting to be in such a large group.

We had been traveling east, and it seemed that we must have gone a long way. But the train stopped so often that we lost track of the distance. Actually, we hadn't traveled very far, but it seemed that we must be halfway to Russia. Thinking of Russia was an ominous cloud hanging over our heads. We would only whisper the name. Were we on the threshold of the unimaginable—Siberia?

Camp Posen in Poland

We learned that we were in Poland, in the city of Posen. This part of Poland had been annexed by Germany after Poland had lost the war in 1939. It was puzzling that we were taken to another camp. Posen was a huge complex. Someone mentioned that it had been built by the Germans for the Abeitsdienst (youth workforce which was established by Hitler). Tall wire fences surrounded the compounds, even between sections of barracks. Rows and rows of barracks stood neatly in line with gravel paths on the sides. Dandelions dotted the narrow grass strips between the buildings; it seemed they wanted to cheer us up with their sunshine colors. Was this to be our next detainment? Our columns were escorted to vacant barracks, and a certain number of people were assigned to each barrack.

Are we really on our way to Russia? If we were, why stop here? The war must be over by now, so why couldn't we go home? No one answered our questions.

All this looked so orderly; no broken glass windows. Unlike in the previous camp, the windows were not covered with wire. On one side of the road was a large fenced-in strawberry patch. It looked nice and neat, and judging by the abundance of blossoms it would soon be bearing loads of fruit. One could guess who would be picking the berries. It turned out later that we couldn't even get near the fence even though it was in sight. Maybe that was good, since our mouths would have been watering seeing all the luscious berries.

I was anxious to see the inside when my turn came; nothing could be worse than what we had before. What a pleasant surprise. These barracks were clean, and had small rooms with a hallway in the middle. Some rooms had bunks and some were bare. The lucky ones with bunks could only have as many people as there were bunks; it gave them a little more privacy. But most rooms were bare, and we had to settle on the floor. The walls were wooden panels and the rooms had wooden floors.

While exploring our new home, we discovered real toilets located in the middle of the building. No more outside latrines and wiggly boards over a hole in the ground. Of course, no showers and only cold water; it sufficed, and was more than we had had before. To think we could go there any time day or night seemed too good to be true. It certainly was a boost to our morale, but what was the reason behind this? It was mind-boggling; it just didn't add up. And in back of our minds was always, "Is this a way station to Russia?"

The place was buzzing with activity; everyone searched for a room, and some women talked about staying together. They had formed friendships or had known each other before. I felt lost, as I was so much younger than the rest and hadn't made any friends since I hadn't stayed long enough in the barracks after my illness. So it didn't make much difference which room I chose. I still had my hearing problem, and was glad to have a place where I could put down my burlap sack. Unfortunately, this was a room without bunks. I would have loved to climb onto an upper bunk and be in my own little world.

Most of the women came from Pomerania. Of course, this was the first province the Russian front spearheaded into the motherland. With all these people, I was hoping I might meet a familiar face. As I walked down the hallway peeking into the rooms, Erika Krause stood suddenly in front of me. For a second we looked at each other. "I can't believe you are here, too," she burst out. We hugged, and I wanted to pinch myself to make sure this was real. This time my tears were of gladness. Her mother and sister were in the camp, too, but in another barrack. They had been lucky and were able to stay together until they came to this camp, but each knew where the others were. They were only separated by barracks.

This unexpected meeting with Erika lifted my spirits. I had known her all my life. Her family ran the post office in Köselitz, and until the last two years of the war, they lived across the street from us. I used to see her every day. She was older than I and already engaged; her fiancé was, of course, in the war. After we were all settled, we exchanged our stories. Her father had also been taken by the Russians, and they, too, had no idea what had happened to him.

The rooms were small, and became very crowded; there were more people than space. In my room there were as many people as could lie on the floor, and two had to sleep alongside our feet. I rolled up my jacket for a pillow and used my coat for a cover, and was glad I had the potato sack to lie on. I had lost so much weight my hips were just skin and bones, and after sleeping all these weeks on wooden boards, it became painful to sleep on my side. Eventually, the hip bones became so numb that the pain disappeared. The numbness lasted for a long time, and I wondered if I would ever be normal again.

The surprise meeting with Erika didn't stop here. She was chosen to be the spokesperson for this barrack; obviously she must have made an impression on whoever was in charge, or perhaps she volunteered. I saw this as a good omen.

The women in my room were all Catholics, and they started to spend hours praying fervent "Hail Mary's." I hadn't met any Catholics before and had no idea how different their faith was from mine. I joined their prayer; it wasn't hard to memorize the "Hail Mary's." We all needed prayers.

Many women had been raped by soldiers and were depressed and disturbed. All worried about their families at home, some had little children, and others had already lost their husbands in the war. But some were optimists. Thank God for them. They tried to inspire and encourage the downhearted, and painted pictures of hope and survival. Now that we all had a place where we could put our heads down, we were waiting for what came next. The Russians didn't just bring us here to sit around; there had to be a plan.

In Marienwerder I had worked on an airstrip putting down metal sheets for a runway. I cleaned houses and cut down trees. What kind of work was waiting for us here? I didn't have to wait and ponder this very long. Several Russian officers appeared with a translator who told us the daily routine and rules. No work projects were mentioned. I couldn't believe we could be kept here. Of course, the rumors of being shipped to Russia never ceased, and that worried me now more than before.

The first thing early in the morning, we lined up outside for roll call, rain or shine; only the very sick were allowed to stay in the rooms. The place had to be kept clean and orderly. That wasn't hard, since we had no furniture to dust and polish. Next, we spent a good part of the day outside. Of course, we preferred that to sitting on the floor inside. We also were told to keep the outside neat and clean. We wouldn't have any problem with that either, since there weren't any papers or cigarette butts to pick up. The last rule was harsh—to stick close to the barrack, and no visiting other barracks. That hit us hard, since we all looked for friends and people like Erika looked for family members. Mostly we thought about food; it became our priority. We soon found out there wasn't much food, and it was not appealing at all, especially the morning soup.

We were already up early for the roll call, and with gnawing hunger pangs waited for the breakfast soup. Men brought it in milk cans. Erika was in charge, ladling out the soup room by room; one ladle per person. The lukewarm bluish-looking soup was only barley and water with a little salt. It had no flavor, but it filled the stomach for a little while and quieted the hunger pangs.

This soup never changed. Waiting for the bread, the most precious item, was a test of patience. Breads were baked in forms so they were all the same size. It was dark rye, and often sticky inside (probably undercooked sourdough). The bread was apportioned to each room according to how many women shared it. It came down to one slice per person not wider than an inch. But first we had to wait for the bread knife to make the rounds. Usually there was one brave person in each room who volunteered to divide the bread. This wasn't an easy task, with all of us standing around watching to see that all slices were equal. That one slice of bread was like a jewel; it meant so much. I only nibbled on my slice and then wrapped the rest in a piece of cloth to save it for later.

I used to be a picky eater, and mother often made something special for me because I missed the main meal at noontime since I was at school in Pyritz. Now I wished I had some of the dishes I didn't even like. I swore that if I came out of here alive, I would never complain about food. But here I was breaking my promise so soon. One day the bread arrived smelling oily; they must have greased the forms with motor oil—that's just how it smelled. The taste was disgusting to me. I tried, but couldn't eat it; I gave my bread away. Thank God it didn't happen very often. My little tin can was small and didn't hold much, but it was big enough for the portions we received every day; we were given only one ladle of food.

The evening meal was a so-called potato soup. In the beginning, it was made with potato flakes. These were flakes the farmers bought to feed their animals, and were made from potatoes that couldn't be used for anything else, the small or broken ones. I knew all about this since father had bought them too. These flakes must have been scooped up outside, or perhaps they had been stored on the floor of a barn. It made me shudder to see pieces of straw floating on top; sand settled on the bottom of my tin can.

Luckily, this didn't last too long. Probably the flakes were used up. Afterward, we received real potatoes in our soup, and occasionally we even found little pieces of meat. Though it was still a watery soup with not many potatoes, it looked so much nicer and more appetizing until we figured out what kind of meat it was. They had cooked the cow heads for us, and didn't bother to take out the teeth. The teeth looked sickening; they came in all shapes and colors. But we ate the soup because we needed it for our subsistence. We picked out the teeth, and some women saved them and tied them together and hung them around their necks like a trophy.

Being picked to go to the kitchen to peel potatoes was the only break in the monotony of the daily routine. But that wasn't as easy as it sounds. Everyone wanted to go; it made Erika very popular. She was the one to choose the women when our barrack had its turn. This was a great opportunity to quickly exchange names and messages with women from other barracks. Many were anxious to find out about family members and friends, and of course more rumors were spread. The biggest attraction, the reason why everyone really wanted to go, was additional soup they brought back in their tins. It meant so much to have that extra ladle of soup. If you knew someone a little better and she was in the group to peel potatoes, you asked her to bring back a raw one for you. She smuggled it in her clothing; they all did. I was always glad if I could nibble on a raw potato; we jokingly called them a "radish." We were always hungry and waiting for the next meal.

I asked Erika to let me go, too. I tried to convince her that I could peel potatoes, but she always had an excuse. "You can hardly stand on your feet, how will you peel potatoes?" I wanted so much to at least once get the extra food. Begging Erika became my obsession, and after a while she gave in and let me go with the group. I was more excited than if I were going to the biggest amusement. It really didn't matter how many potatoes I peeled; no one checked on us, and we stayed there until the work was finished.

Meanwhile, men cleaned out the huge soup kettles, leading to the moment of our reward—we stood in line to have our tins filled to take back. It was the rest of the soup that was in the bottom of the kettles which they divided amongst us; everyone had a full tin. I was so happy and so looking forward to enjoying this special gift. I carried my tin can very carefully so as to not lose a drop, and all along the way envisioned the pleasure of having a whole tin of soup for myself. I thanked Erika again on my way in, and got ready to feast on my soup. As I took my first spoonful, I felt big kernels of salt in my mouth. I took another spoonful, and I was crushed; there was so much salt in it I couldn't eat it. I sat there in disbelief; they must have used rock salt or something like that. It had never dissolved, and settled at the bottom of the kettle. My disappointment was so painful. I kept thinking, why was this happening to me? It made me very angry, and I gave away the soup and vowed never to go there again.

By now it was June, the longest days of the year, and we had daylight until ten o'clock. Most of the time was spent outside, letting the sun warm and heal our bodies. Little groups of twos and threes walked back and forth along the barrack. It was the only place we could walk. The narrow grass strip dividing our barrack from the next one was a favorite place to sit down. Some women nibbled on blades of grass and dandelion leaves, saying that we needed vitamins and should pretend it was spinach or lettuce. Gradually, the little grass strip dried up from sitting and walking on it, and with it, so did the dandelions, our only little spot of color. Visiting people in the next barrack was forbidden.

But messages and notes found a way to their destinations.

I visited Erika often; she was my lifeline. One of her roommates became a good friend. Gertrud Goetz had worked in the vicinity of Pyritz and knew the surrounding towns, and was always very kind to me. Besides our worries about the reason for being there, we talked much about our families. Gertrud was married to a soldier who was a prisoner of war captured in North Africa. I was a compassionate listener when she talked and worried about him. They had taken their marriage vows by proxy while he was at the front in North Africa. I had never heard of a proxy marriage. To a sixteen-year-old, this was fascinating, and I wanted to know how this was done. She described that she dressed in her best outfit and went to the Justice of Peace in Pyritz, signed the marriage paper, and then turned around and went back, changed her clothes, and went to her work place. I think she had mentioned that she did have two witnesses, people from the office. I was mesmerized. No celebration or anything, except she was now a married woman. Her hope was that her husband had a chance to take his vows on the same day. I wondered whether it was really possible, or if it mattered since he was so far away?

A few years later, Gertrud Goetz crossed my path again. It was in 1947 when I lived with my cousin Brigitta in Bamberg, Bavaria. I had passed a woman several times on my way to the milk store who reminded me of Gertrud. I kept thinking that with a little fuller face and figure it could really be her. Every time I saw her I became more curious, but I didn't have the nerve to ask her. Then one day, meeting up with her at the same place at the milk store, I spontaneously stepped up to her. She gave me a puzzled look and I was already sorry to have stopped her. But the surprise was mine when she acknowledged that she was Gertrud! I watched her face light up when I told her who I was. We marveled over our unexpected meeting and could have talked for hours standing in the middle of the sidewalk. She invited me to meet her husband and new baby boy. I will never forget the sincere friendship we forged which had started in the camp, and later lasted for many years.

Camp Posen Continues into Summer

My brother's thirteenth birthday was on the thirteenth of June. I sat down and concentrated on him; I hoped that perhaps he would feel it in some way and know that I am alive. I hoped he was well. I often thought of Christa since she had become sick the day I left. I wondered where father could be.

Soon I found out that people changed rooms; we were free to do what we wanted in the barrack. I wanted very much to move in with Erika, but there was never any space. After making friends with a girl in another room, I moved in with her. I still had to sleep on the floor, but I felt I had a little more in common with this new friend. I was the youngest in our barrack, and being so thin and little, I looked like a child, and at times was treated like one.

It seemed people died of the slightest illness. Hardly anyone who went to the sick barrack came back. Consequently, more space became available. We discovered this at roll call when we lined up outside and the Russian officer and his staff walked down the line and mustered us. The officer could have been a doctor, but we never knew. He was the one who decided how sick a person was, not by examination, but just by looking at her standing in the line-up. They insisted that everyone had to come outside. But some were too sick and couldn't; this was reported to him. Then he gave permission to take these women to the sick barrack.

The window panes were our mirrors. I had been worried about my hair falling out, so I was happy to see it now slowly growing back. I could see little fuzzy curls on my temples. Would it stay that way? I wished it would since I had such straight hair. My hearing improved little by little, too. This was really my biggest worry. I had felt like an outcast not hearing well, and people didn't want to bother to repeat things for me.

I still had the little comb. By now, some teeth were missing, and I was careful using it. One of our important daily morning routines was to check our hair and clothes for lice. My partner didn't have a comb, and I constantly worried, reminding her "Be careful—don't break the comb." It was a strange sight in the morning to see everyone sitting down checking their clothes; we became such experts at finding these little beasts, no matter where they hid.

The most popular places in the barracks were the bathrooms with their cold water faucets. People were in there day and night. Though we had no soap, we washed our utensils, rinsed out our underwear, and of course washed ourselves. The floor never had a chance to dry, and it was best to go in there barefoot. I don't think anyone had a toothbrush; I didn't.

As long as we adhered to the rules, we were on our own. We visited with each other, and pencils, needles, and even scissors began to make the rounds. After awhile, I knew where I could borrow these items. The clothes from people who had died were shared, and a woman made another skirt for me. I kept the scraps, and my headscarf came in handy. It was woven with shiny colorful yarn, and all I had to do was to pull out the threads if I needed something to sew with.

One of the women who had been to the kitchen to peel potatoes found a roll of register tape. She managed to bring it with her, and now we had something to write on. She gave me a strip. It wasn't more than two inches wide, but I found many things to do with it. It was stiffer than the usual register tape. Having had fun as an eight- or nine-year-old making little doll clothes, I now was able to use the scraps of material to make little things. I had already started to make little hearts from scraps, and embroidered them with the threads from my scarf. Now I used some of the tape and cut out shapes of tiny slippers, covered them with the material, and embroidered them. From the rest of the tape, I made a small booklet, and had several of my new friends write little poems in it. I had to finally stop pulling threads out of the headscarf, or it wouldn't have held together any longer.

These little creations with paper and threads from my scarf broke the boredom and monotony for a while, especially on rainy days. What amazed me was the older women who sat together and talked most of the time about cooking and recipes; it was their favorite subject. They talked for hours. They explored and exchanged recipes, and became as excited as if they could get up and go into the kitchen to cook. I had never really cooked, and wondered how anyone could remember all these recipes. Hearing them made me yearn for all the wonderful meals my mother made. Practically every night I dreamt of the savory meals from our celebrations and holidays.

We had been there for quite a while when an order came one day to line up outside. We weren't to take anything with us. I mentally went over the possibilities of what could await us. Soldiers led us to a large building. The big puzzle always was, why have they brought us here? What is the purpose behind it? So far, we hadn't had to work, and they fed us—though just barely enough to keep us alive. Something unusual and out of our daily pattern stirred up an uneasy feeling, especially since all of us had to go.

The road wound along the men's section, and many men were standing at the fence. Suddenly, I heard a loud yell, "Ingrid." It was Karl, a boy from my hometown who was amongst them. If he hadn't waved, I wouldn't have recognized him, he was so thin. We hastily exchanged a few words, but I had to move on. I shouted to ask if he had met anyone from Köselitz, and all I could hear was, "Yes." I wished I knew who these men or boys from Köselitz were. We had to move on, and were led to a large barn-like building and into a bare room. Men came in and announced that our clothes will be deloused, and we would have to take everything off. This was an uncomfortable situation. They rolled in clothes racks, and asked us to put our clothes on the hangers. There was no place to hide, and we certainly didn't look very pretty in our nakedness. We were embarrassed, and they tried to put us at ease by telling us, "We do this every day, don't worry. The clothes will be put into a chamber to be deloused and you will get them back." And then something entirely unexpected happened. Someone opened a door, and we entered a huge washroom. We practically jumped for joy; this was so heavenly. Washbowls were sitting on long benches along the walls; a man at the door gave us a tiny piece of gray soap. I don't think they gave us towels but who cared? In the middle of the room was a huge kettle with steaming hot water. Men were ready with big ladles. We rushed and stood in line with our bowls. The expression of joy to wash ourselves with hot water and soap transformed us all into a bunch of giggly girls. We washed each other's backs, and our hair, and kept going back for more hot water. The feeling of being so clean was wonderful. After being ushered into another room, the racks with our clothes were brought in, and everyone hurried to find her things.

This trip to the washhouse was repeated once or twice, and on the last trip my clothes weren't on the racks coming back from the chamber. People got dressed, and I stood there naked; no one could help me out. Everyone just had the clothes they wore. Someone called for the men to come back and confronted them with this situation. They promised to find clothes for me; everyone denied taking my clothes. I had pinned all my clothes into my pants with the safety pin I had so nothing would become lost or mixed up. My father had had the pants made for me by a tailor from a pair of his own pants. They were still good except for the little tear that I had fixed in the previous camp. Meanwhile, the group went back to the barrack. I sat down on the floor and waited and waited. What could I do? I couldn't walk out. It seemed like an eternity, but finally a man came with clothes over his arm. I picked out what I needed and could wear. I was glad that there were pants, too, but I wished I had my own pants back.

On those warm midsummer evenings, we stayed outside as long as we could.

Our rooms had become hot and sticky. I often sat on the ground leaning against the wall of the barrack and thought of the future. What will life be like without father if he doesn't come back? Going back to school would probably be out of the question. It would take all our courage and determination to start again. But we had our land and house, and a place to come home to. My thoughts circled around the future; it looked bleak.

Unexpectedly one evening, the sound of beautiful, haunting songs drifted over to us, as only a Russian men's chorus can sing them. These must have been Ukrainians. We quietly listened and wiped tears from our eyes. We sat there long after they had finished, overcome with homesickness and fear about what was to come. They sang a few more evenings, and then there was silence again. I don't know why they were detained here; perhaps they had worked in Germany and were now waiting for transportation to their homeland.

In the middle of summer, a group of women from Berlin were moved into our place. The rooms had become less crowded because so many had died. Since all of us were from the Eastern province of Germany and were taken by the Russians before the war was over, we now learned from these women about the end of the war and the incredible experiences they had endured, not only the air raids during the war, but also the horrific fighting in Berlin. The Russians were there first, and had free reign raping women and young girls. People had no food, and slept in basements of bombed-out houses.

The women were not young; we didn't know why they were brought here. Perhaps for the same reason we were here. Many didn't have toughness and resistance to illness. The last years of the war were especially hard in the cities. Food supplies on ration cards only provided the bare minimum, and the city folks suffered most. We hadn't had any contact with the outside, and now hearing from these women about the terrible end of the war made us wonder how anyone had survived in Berlin.

The summer days went by very slowly; it was monotonous and depressing. Once in a while, if something broke down, a repairman would come with his wooden toolbox and fix it. One could think we lived a fairly good life—we sat around all day, our food was delivered, our house was repaired when it needed it, and we had a doctor's visit every morning. Why were we so anxious to leave this easy life?

The repairman was a welcome messenger; we were eager to find out if he had any news, and people always asked for names of family and friends. He moved around and had access to many places. Gradually, a little bartering business started to bloom. Some men in the workshop made primitive wooden sandals and traded them in for bread. He would smuggle them out in his toolbox. It was hard to go without the bread, but also tough not having any shoes. We became very resourceful. Whenever possible, we went barefoot to save our shoes. Footwear was an item that had already been very hard to buy in the last few years of the war, and most of the time the storekeeper had to be bribed with foodstuffs like bacon and ham. And at this stage, many women had hardly any decent footwear. If your shoe came apart, that was it. I had leather boots that laced. The laces were so worn and knotted that I wore them without the laces, making them all crooked.

Camp life hadn't changed much, but what had changed was the deteriorating health of most of the women. Many had started to develop festering sores not only on their arms and legs, but on their bodies, too. It was hard to deal with this without any medical help. Too many were affected, and it was impossible for all to go to the sick barrack because there was nothing anyone could do for them. It was painful, and in some cases fatal. I was lucky; I had been spared so far. We couldn't find out if it was the diet or a disease, or even whether it was contagious.

One day, milk cans with dark, dirty looking water were brought in. The water had pieces of pine bark and pine needles in it. We didn't know what to do with this water. Should we wash ourselves with it? Others thought we should perhaps drink it. At this point, most of us were ready to do anything to keep well—the women with the sores especially wanted to know what to do with it, and whether it could help them. Perhaps the liquid was an old Russian remedy, made by boiling pine branches and pine needles. I had no container to hold any of it, and I didn't think I should drink it. I worried every day that I might catch this affliction, since no one could tell us what it really was.

An announcement was made that Russian doctors would come to examine us. This inspired new hope; perhaps we would be going home soon. They arrived at our place in the late evening; the Russians hadn't changed their routine. Similar to our previous experiences when they timed the interrogations at night, the examinations were also at night. It was not a pleasant situation. We all had to undress and line up in the hallway. A few Russian officers, probably doctors, sat in a room and made us step in front of them. They looked at us front and back, and that was it. I don't think they even took notes. When I saw so many naked women with these terrible sores, I was scared; I had no idea how many had been affected.

I changed rooms again. Moving to another room didn't present a problem any longer, so many had died that every room had space. My main reason was to avoid contact with women who had been affected with the sores. This time it was a room with bunks—just what I had been waiting for—and I was delighted to have the top bunk, too. Now I had my own little place.

After all these weeks, no one was a stranger any longer. One either knew the person by name, or just the face. People seemed to move all the time.

Soon after my move, I found that this room was infested with bedbugs. They hid in the wood paneling that separated the rooms. I hadn't noticed it previously, since I slept on the floor. The bites were disturbing and painful enough so that I couldn't sleep. I wanted to stay in this room; I loved having the bunk. We tried to leave the light on at night to deter the bugs. But this light, a little bulb hanging on a wire from the ceiling, didn't deter these terrible pests. They came out of the cracks, and even fell from the ceiling on us. I had a terrible time. Frustrated and weary because I wasn't able to sleep, I grabbed my burlap sack and coat one night, and went into the hallway and slept alongside the wall. Even though there were bugs there, too, there were not nearly as many. Finally, I slept a little better. We were not allowed to sleep in the room in the daytime.

Pleurisy

The warm summer days gave way to the approaching cooler fall days. I thought of the clothing I had. Would I be warm enough if we had to stay into the cold season? There was no heat in the rooms. I still slept off and on in the hallway. On each end was a window which was always open, and on some nights it was quite drafty. I started to have chest and back pain and a fever that didn't go away. The little strength I had gained seemed to ebb away. I had fought weakness and fever, and for a while I had fluid in my legs, which was very painful. But this was a bad time to get sick. I must have looked terrible, because at one of the morning roll calls, I was picked out and allowed to go to the sick barrack. My worries mounted: would I get well again? Dr. Duerholt, who seemed to be in his fifties, was the only doctor in the sick barrack, and had only one nurse to help him. Both were inmates like everyone else. They had no medications, and the few medical tools they had were used over and over again.

The doctor thought that I had pleurisy, and explained to me that it could be fluid that had accumulated between the layers around the lungs. I was frightened; he knocked with his knuckles on my back and told me that he had to try to withdraw the fluid. Then he would really know what it was.

All he had was a syringe with a long needle and a tin can. I sat on a chair, wrapping my arms around the back while he extracted the fluid. He had guessed right, and he told me that I had to stay there. Of course, I didn't mind; here I received the best care that was available. I was taken to a room with only one other person in it, Arianne von Massow, who came from a neighboring town near Köselitz. The family had a large farming estate. This was a wonderful surprise. I knew her younger sister, and we were both delighted to have a connection. We felt at ease with each other right away. She and her sister had gone to boarding school somewhere else in the country, but had come home to be with their mother as the war drew closer to home. For the last few months they had gone to the same school I did, but I had never met her. She was a year older, and attended a different class.

Sharing the room with just one person was sheer luxury. We slept on upside-down wardrobes; it was wonderful. There were two in this little room, so we spent most of the time sitting on these big boxes. It didn't leave much space for anything else, but that was all right. I struggled with my illness. Just knowing the doctor was there, even though he couldn't do much for me, was reassuring.

In addition to the regular food, we received every morning a teaspoon of sugar and a teaspoon of oil. We had to save our piece of bread for the oil. I folded a little piece of cloth to hold the sugar. I didn't want to eat it all at once. We were both very thin, and Arianne had the terrible sores on her body. But what could I do? It was the thing I had tried to avoid. However, I was so glad to be in the sick barrack that I didn't want to mention it. Not having much energy, we slept a lot. Gradually, our spirits perked up again. We began to feel a little better; eventually, we worked out a daily routine, such as checking each other's hair and our clothing for lice. We soon became good friends, and we still are.

Our conversations were often about school, our hometowns, and the people we knew. But it always turned to the question, "When will they open the gates and let us out? Will we be well enough and have the strength to leave?"

I told Arianne I had heard a knock on the window one night in September. It was loud and hard. I rose to see if someone was outside. My thoughts had immediately turned to my father. Was this an omen? Did he just die? No one else in the room had heard the knock. I knew I hadn't imagined it. I thought about it for a long time.

We were thankful for every day Dr. Duerholt kept us there. Perhaps we were so young that he made an exception. The nights began to be cooler; Arianne had a quilt, and we now huddled together on one of the narrow wardrobes sharing it.

Release from Camp

Rumors never ceased in the barrack. In October, another excitement rippled through the barrack. Someone knew that the Russians had set up tables on a grassy place; something was going to happen. Of course, all we wanted to think of was going home. Bits of information started to trickle through; Arianne and I pestered the nurse to give us information. The word had leaked out that groups of people had been seen at the tables, and that we were getting out of camp. Arianne and I were still in the sick barrack; we pleaded with the Doctor to let us go to the tables when our turn would come. There was absolutely no way we would miss our turn even if we had to crawl.

Finally, our day came. We and many others were led to the knoll, where several officers were sitting at tables with ledgers in front of them. They were taking inventory of us while we sat quietly on the ground. We soon realized that the little piece of paper they handed out to each individual was a handwritten release. I never expected them to be so thorough. All the earlier interrogations had been recorded. I was surprised how much they knew about me, a sixteen-year-old. We had a different image of them; we only saw the Russian soldier as an inhumane individual, tearing through towns and countryside, obliterating anything that was in their way, killing and raping women and children. Their record-keeping surprised me.

Russian camp release document, 1945.

My feelings overwhelmed me when I was called and stood at the table watching the officer filling out my release slip. I wanted to jump up and down, waving my paper like a flag over my head. Finally, I would be going home, and I pressed the paper to my heart. At this moment, it was the most precious treasure. Having seen their thorough recordkeeping, I suspect they had originally planned to send us to Russia.

Having the release slip in our hands didn't mean we were leaving the next day. Camp life continued the same way. Arianne and I went back to the sick barrack hoping that we could stay there until we were ordered to leave. Everything seemed brighter; even the dreary November day couldn't hold down our enthusiasm. We sat curled up under the quilt making plans. Most of our conversations now were about how we would return to our families or where we should go. My mind was made up right from the beginning: I planned to go home to Köselitz.

Cold and rainy days set in. Arianne and I had become a team; we planned to stay together. Doctor Duerhold was wonderful; I owed him my life. He kept us in the sick barrack and reassured us, telling us not to worry; that we would be going home, too. We asked the nurse every day if there were any news about the release. Finally, one day she dashed in with the big news: the first groups had left. We could hardly contain our excitement. She also had information about how the release was handled. She told us that because of the great number of people, they let only fifty out at one time. They had to stagger the process or there would be too many people on the roads. The people were given a can of some sort of meat and a loaf of bread. They opened the gate and let them go, but we thought it must have been done in an organized way, since we knew how well records were kept.

All of us had been separated from our families, and had no knowledge about where they might be. People were uncertain where to go. It was unsafe to be alone on the road. As I found out later, many were grabbed by the occupation troops and put to work.

Gradually it became quiet; the always-busy area at the fences on the men's section was nearly empty. It took many days before they started the release around our barracks. Dr. Duerhold and the nurse were still occupied with many very sick people. The news was that the sick and the ones who couldn't walk would be taken by train. Arianne and I were scheduled to join this group. This was more than we prayed for, and we were elated; we knew we had the doctor to thank for this.

My mind was set to go home. I couldn't imagine that mother and my sister and brother wouldn't be there. Our house had still been there when we left; we had a place to go back to. Father was often on my mind, especially after the strange experience, the knock on the window. How I wished he would be coming home, too. I didn't want to think that the knock was his last good-bye. In my heart, I knew he couldn't have survived the harsh camp life in Russia and the hard work they most likely had to do. Several years later, when my mother received the letter from the stranger who had befriended my father in the Russian camp, I discovered that the time of father's death coincided with the time in September when I heard the hard knock on the window.

Arianne and I were ready to leave at a moment's notice. We planned to put on most of the clothes we had. I still had my potato sack. Her home had burned down, and she thought her mother might have traveled to stay with relatives in the western part of Germany; her plan was to join them there.

The barracks around us were gradually becoming empty, and we waited anxiously for our turn. But we were still in the sick barrack. The nurse was the only person who gave us little tidbits of information. One morning she rushed in and told us to pack up and transfer to another barrack. Here were all the really sick people who were unable to walk. It was scary. Arianne and I didn't want to stay behind, but we didn't feel that sick anymore. We were weak, but we kept thinking that we might be able to walk. The nurse had become our daily reporter. One day she burst in with a wonderful message: "You are all going home by train." What great news! Would they really do that? Something had to be done with the very sick; they couldn't just leave them there. All we had to do now was wait.

Finally, our day came and we were handed our bread, and a truck took us to the train station. Arianne and I tried to guess how far they might take us. How glad we were that we didn't have to walk.

The weather was clammy and cold, and I knew that with my footwear I would have had a hard time walking. My coat was very worn from using it as a cover all these months, and my jacket had started to fall apart. This time we didn't mind climbing into cattle cars; we were going in the opposite direction, towards freedom.

Our car must have had the sickest people. One side had a few bunks; Arianne and I settled on the floor. It was slow going. The train stopped so often that we lost our sense of time and could not judge the distance. It rumbled along on the bumpy rails, which were a torture for the very sick.

One young pregnant woman who had been raped by Russian soldiers started her labor. She moaned and cried out, and two of the women tried to walk her back and forth in this cramped place. This was an amazing experience at my age. I didn't know anything about childbirth. It was a blessing that the nurse and a few older women were in this car. It went on for quite a while. Her moaning turned into painful outbursts; I wondered, how long will this take? Can't they do something? It was painful to listen to her.

There was no water, wraps, or towels; the women asked who could spare a piece of clothing. It was dark in the car, too; the only light that came in was through very small openings at each upper corner. Finally, she gave birth. The women around me murmured that it wasn't good the baby had an open back, but it was alive, and it cried. Arianne wrote years later that both had died in a Polish hospital. It made me very sad.

Someone squeezed by me with a bowl containing the bloody placenta to throw it out through a small opening high up under the ceiling, which was difficult to reach. In her struggle to throw it out, she spilled some of it on a young woman who was half-sitting in that corner, delirious and full of sores. It was heart-wrenching to see her. I kept hoping that she wouldn't feel this bloody spill that oozed down her front. She just had a flimsy summer dress on, and nothing on her legs. How cold she must have been. Who was she? Did anyone know her name? Did she have children waiting for her? There was nothing anyone could do for her, and she soon died. This scene has been in-delibly printed on my mind.

Not far from where I sat, another woman was dying. She begged for water, but we didn't have any. The women debated whether she should get some of the milk that was for another baby who was born in the camp. No one knew how long this trip would take, or where we were going. Reluctantly, the women decided to give her a little milk, but she begged for more over and over. We were helpless. How glad any one of us would have been to give her a sip of water or moisten her lips, to fulfill this dying woman's last wish.

How can anyone wish for someone to die? But I wished for this woman to die. It was gruesome; no one could make this last struggle easier for her. I was still dealing with the experiences and emotions of witnessing many deaths in the camp and my own near-death experience. Life had become very precious. It must have been meant for me to live. Soon we would be free and on our way home, reunited with family, but these lives were snuffed out so tragically when a little more time might have saved them.

The train rattled along. At some stops we heard noises outside, and the nurse banged on the door calling out, "Exodus," hoping someone might understand and open the door. Nothing worked. The doors had been tightly locked, and we just had to wait and bear with it. Arianna and I sat close together; we were the youngest, and in awe of the indescribably sad experiences we were witnessing—the women dying and at the same time a baby being born. Each of us had to deal with these emotions in our own way.

In the beginning of this trip, happy chatter was all around us. Women talked about their families, and some especially talked about their children. But when we finally reached our destination and the doors were opened and we were free, there was no jubilation. We helped each other down from the rail car. Arianne and I hugged; our eyes glistened with held-back tears. We both carried our bundle of sparse possessions under our arms—our security blanket. Timidly, we looked around, realizing that we were on our own now, but where?

My eyes searched the train station. There had to be a name somewhere. Then I discovered high up on an old brick building the name Landsberg a.d. Wharte, and now I knew exactly where we were. This wasn't far from home. One of father's brothers used to live here though I had never visited them. They had come to my confirmation party. Home couldn't be more than three or four hours' train ride from here.

We had to make a decision about how to go on from here. Arianne stuck to her plan to travel to find her relatives, hoping her mother and sister would be there. I planned to return home to Köselitz; I couldn't think of any other place to go. I was sure that mother would be there. We asked around to find out what other people were planning to do. Most everyone was not very healthy or strong, and couldn't think of traveling by foot. Arianne joined a small group that had plans to go west. We promised to try to find each other wherever we might end up. A last hug, and then she left with her group.

Small groups of women were still standing around. I had to connect with someone; going off alone was too scary. I looked around and overheard three girls, maybe a little older than I, mention Pyritz. I quickly stepped over to them and asked if I could join them, and of course they didn't mind. We were all in this together, trying to get home. They came from villages not far from Köselitz.

One of the girls pointed at the trains. "I wonder if one of these trains would be going in the direction of Pyritz? " Wouldn't that be wonderful? Our faces lit up, "We might get home in no time at all." This station seemed to be a junction, because several passenger trains were sitting on tracks. "Let's find out," we said. All of the sudden it dawned on me that the people around us spoke a foreign language; then I realized it was Polish. With all our worry about the trains, I hadn't paid much attention to the people. I knew I had seen the name of the station. What had happened here? What were the Poles doing here? How could I have known what happened to our country while we were in the camp?

A woman approached me and kept asking "Niemka? It was Polish for German. I knew what she meant. I showed her my small piece of paper documenting my release from the Russian camp. Even though she couldn't read it, she understood, and must have guessed that I was on my way home. We were probably not the only ones coming through this busy station. She indicated that this was Poland.

I kept wondering, what is she talking about? We are not in Poland. She kept shaking her head saying, "No more Germans here," raising her arm and pointing west, saying "Sa odra." What did she mean by "Sa odra?" We looked at each other; did she mean the Oder River? Have all the Germans gone over the river? I was stunned; that couldn't be true. Doubt crept into my mind. Did my family have to leave too? Köselitz was east of the Oder River, so it would also be in Poland now. The idea of what had happened in such a short time was incredible. I just couldn't conceive of not having a home anymore. Köselitz was the only place I had ever known. How did this happen? Is the Oder River the new border? How could we have known in the camp? We had no communication with the outside world. We decided that boarding a train provided the best hope of reaching our hometowns.

Finally, we found a station official, and indeed there was a train leaving for Pyritz; what a lucky break. We had to wait a little, but soon boarded a train and found enough seats so that we could stay together. It was a slow, miserable trip. All the train's windows were broken, and it had no heat. We were chilled to the bone, but we didn't dare look for another car or other seats. We had no money, and were glad the conductor let us ride for free. One of the girls had many sores on her body; she couldn't sit, so she knelt the whole way.

At one stop during the train ride, I noticed people in freight cars who had livestock with them. The doors were open, and one could see a cow here and there. It gradually dawned on me that these people could only be more Poles coming from somewhere to settle in our homeland. At the time, I didn't know how this came about, but I found out later that these Poles were forced to leave their homes in the Eastern part of Poland due to its annexation to Russia. They had been relocated in Pomerania, where the Germans had been driven out. They were given the German farms and establishments. The Russians had taken all the livestock from the farms. They had forced young boys and girls to drive and take care of the cattle for several weeks until they reached the transport destination. From there, they were shipped to Russia. There was nothing left for the Poles, at least in our area where there had been heavy fighting and destruction. Many villages were ravished by fire, and looked like ghost towns with burned-out houses and barns. The Poles were bringing their own livestock, and had to start with the little they brought with them.

It was late afternoon when we arrived in Pyritz. Daylight was fading quickly, but amazingly, everything so far had worked in our favor. We were glad we did not have to make another connection, and we knew that eventually we would get there. Being finally free started to sink in. It suddenly dawned on me that we might not be able to go further because it was late in the day.

The train station was hardly recognizable. For five years, six days a week, I had traveled through this station, and now I felt like I had never been here before. The station was in ruins. Seeing soldiers was a daunting sight. I walked to what used to be the street, but instead there was no street, just rubble. I didn't venture any farther.

The town had been encircled by the Russians in February, and resisted four weeks of bombardment by tanks and artillery. It was almost leveled. Our beautiful little town, embraced by its ancient wall and its massive towers—sentries of the past, which had withstood many invasions and wars in the Middle Ages—was now only rubble.

chapter nine

SEARCH FOR MY FAMILY

W e were now on the last leg of our homecoming journey. It had been a dreary day, and dusk was settling in early. Luckily, a man looking a little more official came to our rescue—he could have been the stationmaster—and told us that there was a late-night train. Was this a miracle, or were our prayers answered? Surprise and gladness must have shown on our tired faces.

What a relief that we didn't have to spend the night at the station! After a long wait, the train was finally ready, and again we boarded without paying. Thankfully, the windows on this train were all intact. We were now really going home. I remember that in past times there had always been a late-night train, but how long ago was that? Was it really just a year ago?

How well I knew every curve on the line; I had walked these tracks countless times. Hopping from one railroad tie to the next, even sometimes striding over two ties at once. It was the shortest way between Pyritz and Köselitz. For almost five years I had taken the train twice a day to school in Pyritz. What unimaginable changes had taken place in just one year's time! I had been caught up in the Russian invasion, witnessed the destruction all around, and saw people forced into camps and transported to Russia. I had seen many people who died or took their lives. It was more than anyone normally would experience in a lifetime. My carefree school days seemed ages ago.

The train ambled along. I strained my eyes to see if I could make out a familiar landmark, but it was too dark. My anxiety grew; it won't be long I thought. Will I really be united with my family?

The girls were silent. Their thoughts were probably the same as mine. I tried to push back the doubts that crept into my mind. Was the Polish woman correct who earlier today in Landsberg had told me that all Germans had to leave? I just couldn't comprehend it; what happened to all the Germans, and where would they go? We had land and houses; my mother was born in Köselitz. Why couldn't they stay there?

Köselitz was the first stop; the ride didn't take more than fifteen or twenty minutes. Now I had to say good-bye to the girls, since their towns were farther up the line. I was the only one getting off the train. My heart was pounding and my chest felt tight. I was scared. Watching the taillight of the train disappear around the bend felt like the cord that had held and connected me with these girls was cut. I was now on my own. Tears rolled down my face. I was home.

The sky had been gray all day, and it was a dark, starless night with no lights anywhere. I had to take a few minutes to orient myself. Russian tanks had destroyed part of the railroad station. It must have been nearly midnight. I had no way of telling what time it was. Frightened and apprehensive, I walked in the middle of the cobblestone street, watching out for deep ruts. For just an instant, a thought flashed through my mind; hadn't I walked down this street at midnight just a few years ago, coming home from a wonderful summer vacation? It was the only other time that I had ever come home alone on the late-night train.

The village seemed like a ghost town. Soon I stood in front of our house. I noticed a different front door, a sign that it was occupied. Only three steps separated me now from the door. My body was trembling. I knocked several times, and called out "Mother?" but no one came to the door. It was the most devastating moment; it was like swimming in the ocean and not being able to reach the shore. A profound realization came over me: all my hopes of being reunited with my family vanished. They did not wait for me; it had been a wishful dream.

The Polish woman earlier had told us the truth when she said that the Germans had left. But that was in Landsberg, in a different place; I didn't want to believe that everybody had to leave. All these months in the camp, the hope of being reunited with my family had kept me alive. Now I had to bury my dream.

I had never felt more alone than at this moment. I sat down on the step in front of our door, trying to think of what to do next. It was too cold to stay outside. What if I knocked on another door and no one responded? But knocking on doors was my only option; it was getting later and later at night. As I was looking around searching for any signs of light or life, I noticed a faint light at the end of a narrow alleyway across the street. We used to cross through this alley to the other street.

Gingerly, I tiptoed across the street and through the so-familiar alley to the house, and looked into the window. A kerosene lamp sat on the table, and an old man stood bending over the table, turning his vest pockets inside out to collect tobacco remnants for a cigarette. After watching him for a moment, I knocked on the window. He looked up, startled. I knocked again. Grabbing the lamp, he came to the window. I asked him in German to let me in; that I wanted to talk to him. He must have thought that he was seeing a ghost. He hurried out of the room, and after a few minutes several people came to the window. I pleaded with them again to let me in. They finally opened the door. Surely they never expected a girl knocking in the middle of the night.

We communicated with gestures. Cozy warmth was radiating from a big tile stove. I motioned to the bench in front of it; all I wanted was to sit there for the rest of the night. They were sympathetic; one of the women went out of the room and came back with a piece of bread and a cup of warm milk. It didn't taste like the milk I remembered, or perhaps I had forgotten what milk tasted like. It was probably goat milk, which I had never tasted before. It was heavenly. I kept eying the bench with its cuddly-looking blanket. Would they let me sit on it for the night? I could probably stretch out on it, even though it looked a little narrow.

After I had eaten, the women led me to a room where a bed was made up with white linens. I couldn't believe they offered me a nice bed. I would have been happy on the bench at the stove. I wasn't clean, and my clothes were worn and dirty; the bed looked so inviting. It had been a long time since I had slept in a bed. It felt wonderful to stretch out on a soft mattress and cover up with a feather quilt. Tired and exhausted, I fell asleep.

The next morning, the woman woke me and gestured for me to dress. She made me understand that she wanted to take me to the only German person left in the village. Now I became anxious; who could that be? I dressed quickly, and we were on our way.

This was my first walk through Köselitz in daylight. It was worse than I expected. It seemed that nothing had been repaired; the broken-up road had cobblestones lying on the side, and the skeletons of burned-out barns were a grim reminder of the fury of fires and destruction. I walked by piles of rubble where a year ago the school building had stood. It had burned down in the first days of the invasion. Many windows were still boarded up. I could see our house. Not much had changed on the outside; the two large elm trees were still there. I hoped that I might have a chance to get closer to it, or even look around in the farmyard. Unfortunately, we were heading in the opposite direction. The Poles had come during the summer of 1945, and many houses looked occupied.

The woman walked me to an old, dilapidated house, one that probably none of the Poles wanted. I knew the house; a cobbler who once lived in it had shot himself. This history had stuck to the house. Walking by as children, we always reminded each other of what had happened there. It looked like the first blow of a strong wind would topple it over. Uneven stone slabs led to the door. I knocked on the door, wondering who would be the one German woman left behind.

Aunt Hedwig opened the door! How could I have ever imagined that I would stand in front of a relative; she was a cousin of my mother. "Ingrid," she called out, "How did you get here? Where are you coming from? Tell me I'm not seeing things."

She embraced me and pulled me inside. All I could say was "later." I needed a moment to grasp the unexpectedness. It was a miracle. I was relieved and very happy that it wasn't a stranger.

I thanked the Polish woman and tried to tell her that this was someone I knew. Hedwig Stresow welcomed me into the house; it was very small, but it was warm, and I knew I had a place to stay. I was

Aunt Hedwig Stresow.

extremely anxious to find out what had taken place. We talked for hours. So many people, young and old, had died. Staying behind had isolated my aunt, and she had no idea where anyone had gone or what had happened outside the village.

Aunt Hedwig's Account of the Köselitz Exodus

The first expulsion from Köselitz was in February 1945. That was the time I was still with my family. The villagers had settled in surrounding towns, but in early June, gradually a few returned. If they couldn't get into their houses, they stayed with others. Rumors had started to circulate that they might have to leave again since this was now Poland; then, at the end of July, the rumor became reality. They had just one day's notice to pack up and get ready. The order was to assemble at the end of the village, then to walk to the Oder River and cross the new border into Germany.

Mother, Christa, and Werner had ventured back to Köselitz in

June. At the time of the invasion a traveling Romanian missionary lived with Aunt Hedwig and her husband. They had offered him a place to stay while he held Bible studies in their home. Aunt Hedwig's husband was very ill with cancer; they knew he didn't have long to live, which made it impossible for them to join the villagers and leave. The missionary stayed behind with them and several other older people who were unable to travel. Aunt Hedwig's husband died, and she and the missionary buried him. The missionary made a crude casket from boards that he found in the rubble. They did the best they could. The other old folks died one after the other. Aunt Hedwig helped them; they had very little food and no other care at all. She and the missionary buried all of them as properly as possible. He had to push the caskets on a wheelbarrow to the cemetery.

Aunt Hedwig had been in her own house up to the point when the villagers had to leave. Then when the Poles moved into the village, she had to leave, and was ordered to move into this small house. She had taken in a little five-year-old girl who was orphaned when the villagers had to depart. The Russians had taken the orphan's father away, and her mother, who had been savagely raped, had drowned herself, leaving five young children behind. When I heard this tragic story, I couldn't help but wonder why Aunt Hedwig took one of the children; she had never had any children and now, at sixty-eight, she perhaps fulfilled a life-long wish to have a child. But it was neither the right time nor place.

They had very little food. I tried to keep the potatoes out of the water in the tiny basement, and I wondered how long they would last. She baked bread using a wood fire in an unbelievably primitive oven. I was amazed how good plain old rye bread tasted when one had nothing else. I had learned how precious bread was. The fragrance of the freshly baked bread wafted through the little house and made our mouths water, but we were very careful because the bread had to go a long way. Only a short while ago, I had eaten my last piece of bread from the provisions given to us as we left the camp.

Aunt Hedwig made sourdough bread, and showed me how to preserve a bit of dough for the next bread-making. Quite often, the little girl was sent out to beg for milk at various homes in the neighborhood. She usually came back with some, but sometimes she drank it on the way. It was a miserable life for this five-year-old child. I was sad that the five children could not stay together.

Winter was on its way. It was raw and clammy. We kept the tile stove in the living room going; it heated the rest of the very small house. Next to the house was a broken-down shed. The missionary must have piled enough wood into a corner for the winter; at least we didn't have to worry about keeping warm. Of course, we cooked with wood, too.

Another household member was a no-name cat. He was supposed to chase away or preferably eat the hordes of mice that lived right along with us. The cat probably ate as many as he wanted, but that didn't seem to make a dent in their numbers. Once, I watched the cat sleeping by the tile stove when a mouse ran almost over his nose; he didn't even stir. I was glad that the mice didn't frighten me, although I hated that they practically had the run of the house.

At night, Aunt Hedwig and I, our beds next to each other, slept with a switch on our covers, ready to grab it if a mouse came too close. They went everywhere with the most amazing boldness, not afraid of either the cat or us. If I sat at the table to eat, they waited, ready to devour any crumb that might fall on the floor. Several hooks in the ceiling, which had actually become the only safe place for food, held pillowcases with flour and bread. We tried to find places where these marauders were unable to reach. We constantly washed and scrubbed the dishes and the table.

Aunt Hedwig developed a sore thumb. It began to fester and was very painful. She bathed it in warm water; we had nothing else to treat it with. Then she came up with an old home remedy. I had to chew a little piece of bread and then put it on her wound. I had never heard of this; it seemed like magic. Could it really work? It was supposed to draw out the pus. I tried it and it did give her some relief; we repeated it over a few days. I bandaged it the best I could with strips torn off a sheet, and then one day a bone came out. It was so strange that both of us were shocked. After this, the wound began to heal slowly; however, her thumb was forever deformed.

Another straggler knocked on the door one day; it was Dora Abraham. I knew her as a school friend of my sister. Where did she come from? Of course Aunt Hedwig asked her to come in.

No one had any idea that another German was still in the village. Dora had been working in the bakery that was run by the Russians. Apparently, they hadn't let her go when all the Germans were forced out. She had been raped by the soldiers and was free game for all. When she came to us, she was ill and needed help desperately. She had large boils all over her head, which had most likely been caused by the infestation of lice. She was in pain. We let her sleep on the sofa, but something had to be done right away. I was worried that we might all end up with lice. I was happy I had been able to keep myself clean, despite my ordeal in the camps.

Dora had been reported to the Poles, and they wanted to get rid of her. This barbaric news was very upsetting to me. Hadn't they destroyed enough lives? I knew I was the only one there to help her, and I had to do it right away. The most important task was first to get rid of the lice. I cut off all her hair, and then soaked her head. The water had to be brought in from a pump outside. It took days, until gradually the boils opened, and she had some relief and could take care of herself. I don't know if I could have done it if I hadn't experienced so much in the camps. Arianne had had sores in places on her body where she needed help. I was determined Dora's head would be healed. I didn't know anything about venereal diseases until I'd heard about them in the camps. It was a subject no one talked about. Many Russian soldiers were infected, and they in turn infected their rape victims. Soon after Dora's appearance, Inge Propp showed up at the door. She was someone I knew better; she was a little older than I, and had also been in the camp in Posen, though I hadn't met her there. It had taken Inge all these weeks to get home. She was stopped several times and put to work. This could have happened to me, too, if I had decided to walk home. I was thankful as I realized how lucky I was with my return to Köselitz.

Two more people were too much for Aunt Hedwig's sparse food

supply. Even though she had welcomed us all, we knew we couldn't stay with her any longer. We wanted to get out of Poland, but we had to have papers or some kind of permit, since the border had now been established and secured. We had to get across the big river, and the only way was over a bridge. Attempting that in our poor condition and the cold weather was impossible. We had to find a legal way. The Polish mayor of the village was our first contact. We knew he had the authority to give us a permit. But he was an unpleasant person to deal with, and refused our request.

We had to come up with another plan, but what? It was winter, and our clothes and footwear were in poor shape. Going back on the road to try our luck getting across the border was out of the question. We had to wait at least until spring. We were in a terrible bind. I kept thinking, we had made it so far, there had to be a way. Then we thought we might find a Polish family to hire us as maids. We decided to offer to work just for room and board. A place to stay and food was all we needed at the moment.

We always had a maid or two at home, so I knew what would be expected of us. This was our only hope to make it through the winter. We were malnourished, and needed to get a little stronger before tackling our plan. To our great surprise, it wasn't hard at all to find families to accept our deal. They may have taken us out of pity. Probably any mother would have empathy seeing us and hearing our story about searching for our families.

The Poles had been there less than half a year. Most of them had come with one cow and perhaps one horse and a few chickens. They were poor, and really hadn't established themselves. When they had to leave their homeland, they were told that it was only temporary and that they eventually could return. The family I stayed with hadn't even unpacked everything. I felt that they really wanted very much to go back to Poland. The house they had moved into was that of a Köselitz carpenter who also had a small farm.

The family had two boys. The older one was an electrician and the younger one was still in school. Our conversations took a long time; Polish is a difficult language. They didn't know any German because they came from the eastern part of Poland.

I learned the most-used words in the household, but I couldn't make them understand that I wanted to form sentences. So most of the time, I used the word of an object and the rest was conveyed in sign language and gestures. Inge Propp also found a family to work for. We were not far apart, and found plenty of time to share our first experiences. She had her own room. I slept in the same room with the family, the only room besides the large kitchen that was heated. I was glad to have a warm bed to myself, and sleeping with others in the same room was nothing new, although it was often uncomfortable. The family owned one cow, and now that I was the maid, I was sent to do the milking as one of my chores. My initiation was less than successful, and since every drop of milk was precious, the man of the house decided it was better that he continue with the milking.

I was often bored; time went by slowly. I had very little to do and couldn't converse with them easily. I asked the schoolboy to show me what he was learning, but only the math looked familiar to me.

It was getting close to Christmas, and I wondered what was going on in the attached washhouse. It had become, all of a sudden, a very busy place. Something awfully smelly was cooking on the kitchen stove. I hoped I wouldn't have to eat it. What were they up to? The wash kettle was filled with this mushy, smelly substance, and the cover was then tightly sealed. Spiral tubing was connected to a little hole in the cover and fastened on the ceiling. The piping then came down into a large barrel filled with cold water, where it was connected to a spigot at the bottom of the barrel. I learned that this was a homemade vodka still. The tubing had developed leaks, and the room began to fill with steam. All the precious alcohol seemed to go up in steam. But at the end, after sealing the pipe again and again (it was primitive metal tubing for electric wiring), alcohol slowly dripped into a bowl placed underneath the spigot.

I celebrated Christmas 1946 with the Polish family. I was with strangers who were kind enough and took me in. It all seemed bizarre and unreal. It was the Poles' first Christmas away from their homeland, too. Even though we couldn't communicate well, I gathered that they missed the familiar traditions, and perhaps relatives they had left behind.

I spent most of the days with Aunt Hedwig. We reminisced about the wonderful roasted Christmas goose we had just a year ago, and how much had happened in just one year.

Besides the Russian occupation troops, Polish soldiers were also stationed in Köselitz. One cold winter morning, a Polish soldier came to the door and asked for me to come with him; they needed workers. Inge Propp was rounded up, too. We had been very careful not to go outside for fear that the Russian soldiers might find us, but now that we were with families, we felt we had protection. Word had finally bubbled out that we were there.

Grain from the last harvest had been collected and stored in houses next to the railroad station. Now the grain was to be shoveled into sacks, which then were taken to the train for shipment. If the Polish civilians were asked to do this, they would have had to be paid; we worked for free. But there were just the two of us; how much could we do? Polish soldiers had to do most of the work. It was hard work; the grain shovels were large and heavy.

Our families weren't happy with this situation. We only came back to sleep or for the evening meal. One evening, a Polish officer asked us to come to see him. Our thoughts immediately were that perhaps we could obtain papers from him to leave Poland.

Unfortunately, the conversation was about other work. The house was totally dark except for his room. Electricity had not been restored in the whole area. The basement door in the dark hallway had been left open, and not being able to see, I tumbled down the brick steps. It was such an instant shock that I didn't know what had happened. I had taken a step into thin air. I was terribly bruised; my knees and elbows were bleeding. This became the beginning of my own battle with sores. I remembered Dr. Duerholt's words when I had asked him in the camp why I didn't have the awful sores like everyone else. He said that I would probably get them afterwards, but had been hard to believe. The wounds began to fester and spread. I made bandages from a sheet that Aunt Hedwig gave me.

Weeks later, a group of German women of all ages arrived by

train. They came from different towns, had stayed behind for various reasons, and now had been picked up and brought to Köselitz. Not far from the railroad station were several large potato pits. Here potatoes were kept through the winter. The potato pits were opened, and the potatoes had to be picked out and sorted. The German women were brought to do that job.

Before the war, we always had one or two of these pits behind our garden. Most farmers didn't have enough cellar space, and this was a way to preserve potatoes for the spring. The potatoes were placed in shallow dugouts in the ground, often more than twenty feet long, and covered with lots of straw and dirt. We mainly preserved the potatoes to feed the pigs.

Inge and I were ordered to join this group of workers. Our Polish families rebelled at this order. They weren't willing to keep us any longer, feed us, and provide a place to sleep. Later, I was glad we were forced to leave our maid work for a couple reasons. First, for safety reasons, it was always better to be in a group. But in addition, Inge and I had become somewhat isolated by living with these Poles. Perhaps this change in our lives was a step closer to leaving Poland. I knew in my heart that I would find my family if I could only get out.

When Inge and I joined the German women's group, they had already settled in a vacant farmhouse near the potato pit, which was in the vicinity of the railroad station. Once again, I had to sleep on the floor. A layer of straw was spread on the floor, and we all slept in one room. When not working, we spent the rest of the time in the large kitchen. The cooking stove was a welcome source of heat. We made sure that the wood fire in the room where we slept kept burning day and night. The Polish soldiers didn't care how we managed, and they didn't seem to intend to feed us. The work was dirty, and it was cold outside. We had to kneel on the ground to pick up the potatoes, sort the bad from the good ones, and place them in baskets next to us. Our clothes became very soiled, and we had no soap to wash them. Aunt Hedwig gave me a pair of old gloves. I treasured them. I washed and dried them on the stove. We elected one woman to stay in the house, primarily to cook for us.

Every day, each of us brought a few potatoes home for the next meal. The woman who cooked made gravy with flour and water for the potatoes, and that was our meal. One time, she remarked how wonderful it would be to have an herb to flavor the gravy. I knew every household had herbs in the backyard, and also that thyme was a favorite—though not really mine. I was sure if I searched around I would find some. I didn't give up until I found a little dried-up patch of thyme. The leaves were gone, but the little stems were there, and I knew that mother used to pick those in the winter to flavor soups. We had long forgotten to be choosy eaters; we thought that with this added flavor, we had delicious gravy.

Living with these women didn't mean total security, though it gave us some protection from being molested by soldiers. But there was always the unexpected. One night, a Polish soldier demanded to be let in. It was scary, and became even scarier when he read off Inge Propp's and my name to come with him. I threw on my old coat and slipped into my crooked boots. I didn't even lace them. He marched us to the other end of the village. It was a cold moonlit night. The only sounds were our footsteps on the street. We were frightened and didn't dare speak to each other. I remember that he took us to the house where the mayor lived. We had been there when we asked for papers to leave.

The mayor interrogated us; he wanted to know where our fathers were. He kept saying to me that I was in the youth movement and I was the right hand of Adolf Hitler. What an absurd statement! My little knowledge of Polish helped me to understand that much. How could I have been? After I denied it fiercely, he probably realized how silly that was, and told me to go back. I wanted to wait for Inge Propp, but was ordered to go back alone. I was relieved to be let go, but very scared to walk back alone.

However, Inge Propp didn't fare that well. Whatever they had in mind with her was even more puzzling. They kept her there all night. I began to worry when she didn't come back that night. We weren't interrogated together, so I had no idea what she could have said to make them keep her. When she didn't come back the next morning,

I really worried. Another day went by, and then, all of a sudden, she walked in. What a strange story she told. They had transported her the next day on a horse-drawn wagon to a village nearby. She had been dropped off there without any purpose; at least she didn't know why. With the help of a Polish woman, she met a few Germans. Her description of the situation there and the people she met sounded more alluring than our work project. Girls she talked to were well-treated, and lived with families. This sounded so much better than our situation.

We decided to travel there, and talked it over with the group; there wasn't a headcount and the work was loosely run. We knew no one would come looking for us. The work here would come to an end, and then what prospects would we have? We rolled up our belongings. We didn't want to walk on the open road, so we hiked over the fields until we were a little farther away from town. The first contact we made was not very encouraging—a single German woman who lived in a little house. She didn't want to help us. We needed a roof over our heads, so we hired ourselves out as maids again. It wasn't easy to find a family so quickly, but I think sympathy for our plight always won out. It didn't work out for both of us, and lasted only a few days. The girls we met weren't as willing to help us as Inge had thought. They had to look out for themselves. I realized this had been a bad idea, so we hiked back to Köselitz. The work group was still there, and we joined them again. Our little excursion went unnoticed, and it gave us courage and hope that we would find a way out. I was always thinking about a plan.

The sun was climbing a little higher each day, and the days stretched a bit longer. The frost had gradually given way to warmer temperatures. Inge Propp found out that several Germans in Naulin had to stay behind to operate a still which was part of a farming estate. She also used to have relatives in that village, just as I did. Our hopes were slim, but perhaps someone she knew was still there. I didn't expect Aunt Adelheid and Uncle Hans to be there.

I think it was March by now. I went to Aunt Hedwig, who I visited often, and talked with her about our plan. I felt a special gratitude to Aunt Hedwig. She was my little oasis, where I had initially found shelter that first moment of my arrival, and now the time had come to say good-bye.

She gave me a piece of material so I could sew a little primitive knapsack. She also handed me a one-hundred mark note. "Who knows," she said, "It might still be in circulation on the other side." Calling it the "other side" always meant Germany across the Oder River. She also gave me her husband's overcoat. With a heavy heart, I finally threw away the coat that had been my companion since the camps, keeping me warm and also serving as my pillow when I didn't need to wear it.

While we were staying with the work group, a Russian soldier had broken into the house and raped Aunt Hedwig; apparently he had been looking for us. Being singled out and raped was always my biggest fear. Aunt Hedwig later found out that he infected her with a venereal disease.

I still had with me the little things that I made in the camp. Mother's 43rd birthday had been in August; I had sewed and embroidered a little heart for her. I celebrated all my family's birthdays in the camp, including my own seventeenth, with lots of hope and prayers.

Our plan to walk to Naulin gradually matured. Perhaps this attempt would bring us closer to our goal of getting out of Poland. The day came when I said good-bye to Aunt Hedwig. We cried and hugged. What would I have done without her? She never complained, and put her fate into God's hands. I felt that I probably would never see her again.

I knew the road to Naulin by heart from all the visits to our relatives. The road was unpaved and was, at this time of year, very muddy. The plowed fields on either side didn't look much better, but the large chunks of earth weren't quite as soft. We chose to walk on the field. Our footwear was pitiful. I still had my worn and crooked boots. Inge had a hard time walking in the muddy earth; it was still cold and raw. She had no socks or stockings on and wore very primitive wooden sandals. We planned to go to the house where her relatives used to live. Luckily, we bumped into a German on the way, who took us to the house where most of the Germans now lived. The men worked in the alcohol still, and the women performed farm labor. Their work at that time was spreading manure in the fields. We learned from them that we could probably stay, but would have to sign up and work. This didn't appeal to us. It could be arranged very easily, they thought, but they were afraid to hide us. These people received a little pay for their hard work.

By this time I was in poor shape with the sores from my stairway fall. They had spread all over my legs and arms. I had bandaged them as best I could, but I desperately needed to see a doctor. The people in the house had no idea where I could go or where there was a doctor. I was afraid to talk much about it, let alone show them to anyone. I had used up all the strips of sheet Aunt Hedwig gave me. All I could think of were the women in the camp who had died from them. I was suffering, and very scared. My fear fueled my determination to get out of Poland as soon as possible.

It seemed to me the people weren't happy with their situation, but they didn't do anything about it, either. I stuck to my plan to find a way to get out. Fortunately, these people gave us a little more information. Naulin was still a train stop, and the train went directly to Stettin, the big city right on the new border. We planned to take the train, although it was a big venture. Perhaps somehow we might get across the border there. I thought Stettin was the only possibility, since all the bridges had been destroyed along the river during the war. We had no way of knowing the location of any temporary bridges. Perhaps we could even get out legally in Stettin.

The people gave us enough money to pay for our tickets. We mustered all our confidence and boarded the train, planning not to talk if anyone else would be in the compartment with us. Our attire was less than attractive; I could almost hide in my big overcoat. Inge still had only her wooden sandals.

The trip took longer than we thought, and it was early evening when we arrived. Stettin was the last station, and everyone had to depart the train. Police and soldiers were everywhere, with lots of commotion. The minute we stepped off the train, a soldier stopped us and asked us if we were Germans. We couldn't deny it; it didn't look good. We had to follow him; my heart sank. Please God, not again to a camp, was my prayer. We reached a place where quite a large group of Germans were assembled. I felt a glimmer of hope. Little did we know at this point that it was the best thing that could have happened to us.

People had come from different regions, and all were trying to get across the border. Here, being in a group meant a little more security. People were hopeful that we would be sent across the border. This was wonderful news. One family had come with horses and a wagon. This was another step closer to our goal. I was glad that we had undertaken this venture. All I thought about was getting away as soon as possible. I needed medical help desperately; there was no privacy, and no place where I could look at my arms and legs.

It was dark by the time we were led to a large warehouse-type building, which was a holding place with many more people already waiting. Inge and I were the only ones who had practically nothing to carry. Most people had come with their belongings in sacks and suitcases. They hadn't had occupation troops ransacking their homes, and now here they were with their silver and their best tableware and linens. Everyone had to stay in this building, and we sat on the cement floor. I can't remember if we had sandwiches with us or if food was brought in.

After a day or two, officials arrived with the good news that we would be shipped to Germany. I was overjoyed; I knew help was on the way. I didn't know how and where I would find my family, but I knew that once I was in Germany, I would find a way.

An announcement instructed us all to walk to the railroad station. Having no transportation was devastating for the people who had much more than they could carry. People started to rearrange and rethink what they wanted to keep. Many people were giving away some of their precious items, such as silver and linens. Inge and I were on the receiving end, but we had no bags or containers. A woman offered me stainless steel tableware, and I took a single set. I can't remember if I took anything else. I felt sad for the people who had carried these things to the very last place on their journey. Now they had to leave most of it behind. They begged others to take things.

The railroad station was quite a distance away, and the departure was in the evening. People were determined to carry more than they really could. They shifted their burdens from their hands to their shoulders. Muffled curses were heard here and there. The pace was very slow. Polish ruffians were waiting along the way. They jumped into the lines and grabbed bundles and bags, whatever they could get their hands on, and ran off. The guards didn't try to help people. Despite the screaming and shouting, the guards looked the other way. I just had my little knapsack, and didn't have to worry. Despite our slow pace, we eventually made it to the train station. Now many people had a lot less to carry. This time we didn't ride in cattle cars, though from the outside the train looked like we would. The cars had been modified by the Germany military for troop transports, and had bunks inside. I climbed eagerly into the third tier of the bunks. We had no idea where we were going, but one thing we were sure of: we were being shipped out of what was now Poland.

I knew by now the Oder River was the new border between Poland and Germany. I hadn't heard that Germany was divided into an East and West. The river had always been the division of the Province into Vorpommern and Hinterpommern—one could say, the eastern and the western part of Pomerania. Now the eastern section had become Poland, and the western part remained Germany.

Finally the train left with at least two very happy persons aboard. From now on, things could only get better for us. Every time the train stopped at a larger station, Red Cross ladies walked up and down the platform offering coffee or tea. Food must not have been my priority, because I can't remember what or where we ate.

The train rattled along all night, and made many long stops. Once in a while, the person near the window called out the name of a train station. I was content; freedom and help were at the end of the train ride. Of that I was sure, wherever that would be.

A New Chapter in My Life

At long last we arrived in the town of Bad Segeberg in the Province of Schleswig Holstein, in the most northern part of Germany.

This was the English-occupied zone. Here, a large influx camp had been set up, some of it under tents.

When we arrived, we were registered and given a medical check-up. I could finally remove the bandages and look at myself. I was shocked; my sores had spread all over my arms and legs. The bandages I had put on should have been changed days ago; I could not have gone on much longer. At last, here was help. The doctor's encouraging words helped me to let go of my worries and fears. The doctor reassured me that I would be all right after it all healed. To my amazement, as bad as it was, it healed in a short time. They took X-rays of my lungs and confirmed what I told them about the pleurisy in the camp.

A school gym had been turned into a temporary hospital. I was cleansed and treated with a salve from top to toe. I had a bed with clean white sheets, and best of all, someone was taking care of me. The meal was brought to my bedside. What luxury! I thought it was the most wonderful food, and savored every morsel of it.

Words couldn't describe my feelings when I was discharged from the hospital. My legs and arms were healed, though I had scars all over. But that didn't bother me, because my body was whole again, and I was ready to face the next challenge. In the last few days of my stay there, I had already started to look for my mother and siblings. Anyone who had gone through this camp was registered. Large books in the office area were available for anyone to check. I spent many hours looking through the files.

Inge Propp had disappeared while I was in the hospital. The camp organization was placing people all over the state. I was a single, homeless youngster, a schoolgirl, and they had to find a place for me.

When my turn came to leave the camp, I was handed a slip of paper with the name of the town of Rade. Someone had assigned me to this town. I had no idea where it was or how to get there. Information in the camp was sparse. Once again, I rolled up my belongings, and my first thought was to go to the railroad station and take the train. I had meanwhile found out that the hundred-mark note I had from Aunt Hedwig was still good. I felt very lucky; I had real money.

The information I received at the station was not very helpful. The man at the ticket counter examined my slip, and told me that this was a small town without a railroad station. He didn't exactly know the directions, but he thought I could walk there. I was disappointed.

I was physically weak, and my footwear was beyond description. I put on the overcoat from Aunt Hedwig's husband so I didn't have to carry it. I found someone to give me better directions to be sure I was taking the right road.

It was a country road much like the roads at home, with cobblestones and a narrow walking path on one side. I looked like a vagabond with my big overcoat, the little white knapsack, and the crooked shoes. But I was as free as a bird, my sores had healed, and whatever was ahead of me could only be better than what was behind me.

Determination is a wonderful mindset. I knew I would make it. I don't know exactly how far it was or how long I walked, but I arrived there. My instructions were to contact the "Bürgermeister," the village mayor. It was his responsibility to find a room for me. I hadn't quite realized that I was now on my own. I had always thought of myself as a student. What will I do when I get a room? Can I go to school somewhere? How will I support myself? Those questions hadn't even entered my mind. These thoughts kept me busy as I walked to Rade. I was glad that I had the money from Aunt Hedwig; it felt good to have this safety net.

The countryside of this part of northern Germany, especially this province, had not been touched by war, except the large industrial cities of Hamburg and Bremen. It was farming country with large farms. Homeowners and farmers who had extra rooms had to take in refugees.

It turned out that Rade was a small farming village. The mayor was also a farmer, and lived in a stately home. My appearance must have been shocking when I knocked on their door. The woman of the house listened to my story and was quite sympathetic. With a cheerful voice, she told me not to worry; to come right in and they would help me. I was astonished at how easy this had turned out to be. I gave a brief run-down of my stay in the Bad Segeberg influx camp. She mentioned that I would probably have to stay with them for the first night until they found a proper place for me. I said that was fine with me, and then she asked, "Would you like to take a nice hot bath?" I was embarrassed; I knew anyone who looked at me probably didn't want to get near me. In no time at all, a wooden tub was readied in the washhouse, and I was ecstatic as I wallowed in the nice warm water. I felt like a new person. I will always think of this day as the dawning of a new chapter in my life.

The day had started with apprehension and uncertainty, and a long tiresome walk. Then this family embraced me with sympathy and good will. They had not suffered in the war, just like we hadn't until the very end when the Russians came. Their life had been normal all those war years; not much had changed. Even now after the war, when many people experienced hard times, their daily life was undisturbed and comfortable.

The Mayor's wife had two young girls working as apprentices to be trained in running a household. This was still customary in the north where most of the large farms were located. Daughters from small farmers often apprenticed in these households to learn cooking and the finer art of entertaining. Oftentimes, it was an aristocratic household.

That night I stayed with them. I was a bundle of rags compared to the normal lifestyle I saw here. I realized that my life had been changed forever. Right now I was a homeless teenager, a student, and had no skills where could I fit in. What could I do? I couldn't depend on the kindness of others very long.

The evening meal was the first big home-cooked meal after a long, long time. I thought of the last meal when we were still living peacefully at home. The dining area was off the kitchen, and the large table caught my attention. The top had been scoured and buffed, and had a wonderful smooth and silky surface. I guessed that this was probably one of the girls' chores.

The family and all their help sat around the table and shared the same meal; I was welcomed in their midst. I still remember the dessert; it was a steamed pudding made with the first milk from a cow that had just calved. I always thought that this milk, which was very rich, couldn't be used for human consumption; at home it was given to the calf. Here, in this part of the country, it was used for this special pudding.

The next day I was introduced to the Wales family. Mr. Wales was an architect who worked in the city and only came home on weekends. Their two young sons were about eight and ten years old. The family had been bombed out in Hamburg, and had found refuge here in the countryside. They lived in a charming cottage with a thatched roof that reminded me of fairy-tale pictures. It had big old oak trees in front and a vegetable garden in the back. Mrs. Wales confided that she wasn't much of a gardener; she had lived in the city all her life and knew nothing about gardening until she came here. The house was part of the farm next door; the "retirement home" for the elder farmer when he would hand over the estate to his heir.

The Wales had been lucky to have this lovely little house all to themselves, and now they were asked to give up the small room next to their bedroom for me. This was a very peculiar situation. In order to get to my room I had to go through their bedroom. I hated this arrangement, and it became stressful, especially on weekends when Mr. Wales was home. Times were tough finding housing for all the refugees; not only did they need a roof over their heads, they needed food and clothing. Most of them had lost everything.

Mr. Wales had not been in the Nazi Party, and this had given him the opportunity for a top position in the new provincial government. Rebuilding was very necessary, since people were ready to start anew. He was in charge of issuing building permits for all sorts of constructions. New entrepreneurs lined up at his office with their plans to build. Businesses which had lost much in the air raids wanted to get back on their feet. He had an enviable position. Bribing helped to speed up the requests or let them be granted. It always seemed to be food, which wasn't so easy to reject. Food was scarce; nothing could be bought without ration cards. A chauffeur brought him home for the weekend, then the unpacking began. He had things I could only dream of, like butter, white bread, all kinds of sausages, and live fish in a tub of water.

Because I was malnourished, I was given a special ration of milk, just a quarter liter of milk, a cupful, which I picked up every morning. I usually had it with my breakfast. Sometimes Mrs. Wales wanted it because even though they had two young boys, they were not eligible to receive milk rations. It was a strange situation. We had decided that I would buy my bread and jelly and eat my breakfast in my room. There was no way for me to start cooking for myself in her kitchen. She took my ration card, and I ate the main meal with them, for which I further compensated by helping to clean the house.

They didn't really like to share all the food the husband brought home; but there I was, and I had to eat. I always felt at the meals that I should be thankful to eat with them. My subservient status bothered me, but I knew I had to compensate for the food. I actually worked for room and board.

The most important task on my mind was to start searching for my family. I remembered father had had a friend from WWI; they visited each other once in a while. He lived on the German side of the Oder River. This was now East Germany, and the Russian occupied zone. I thought mother might have gone there or traveled through and left word of her whereabouts with him. Actually, I only knew his name and the name of the village. I wrote a letter querying him about my family, and I hoped the postal service would somehow deliver my letter to him. I settled into a daily routine and did my chores. Sometimes I visited the refugee family from East Prussia who was placed in the main house; we shared the same fate.

Every day started out with hope of getting a letter. And then one day, I finally had a letter in my hand. It must have come three or four weeks after I had written to my father's friend. It was in mother's familiar handwriting! My hands were shaking. I pressed the letter to my heart and couldn't open it fast enough. Then I read it again and again. Mrs. Wales put her arm around my shoulders as happy tears ran down my face. The feeling of not being alone anymore, and to know that my family was alive and well was an indescribable joy. The Wales family shared my excitement.

We took a map out and looked up the town of Tangerhütte. My mother had been resettled near this town. The little village of Malphul was not on the map. It was most disappointing that they were in the Russian-occupied state. I still couldn't think of that part of Germany as a separate country. Many negative things had been circulating; much centered on scarcity of food. The Russian occupation troops drained the economy. Now that I had found my family I wanted more than anything to be with them. I started painting a more positive picture in my mind, even though I heard about the disadvantages. I thought that together we could have a new start.

Planning to Join My Family

Since the border between East and West Germany had already been established, East Germany was now a separate country. I still had trouble comprehending all the changes: first losing my homeland, then discovering a new border between Poland and Germany, and now finding out that Germany was divided. Too much had happened in one year.

I now required an entry permit, which my mother had to obtain from the authority in her town. All that separated us now was one more trip. The waiting was dreadful. It was nearly summer, and I knew that eventually I would be leaving. But it took so long.

My life in Rade didn't change. A few times on Sundays, the apprentice girls from the Buergermeister's farm stopped by and invited me to go for a stroll with them. It was their day off, and there was really not much else to do. I enjoyed coming to know the local surroundings. Rade was a charming little village comprised of several large farms with stately farmhouses. Some still had thatched roofs with large prominent chimneys.

On one of the early warm summer days, the farmer from the estate asked me to come along to the moor. He needed a few extra hands to cut peat. I was surprised to find out that not far from the village was a large peat bog. Different farmers owned sections of it where they cut peat. I welcomed this change of my daily routine; this was exciting. Now I had a chance to see a real moor. I had learned about moors in school, and stories and poems had added a supernatural element to them. I wondered if the ground was really soft and spongy with little pools of dark murky water. Perhaps I could find that little bug-eating plant I had learned about. Poems and stories described mysterious sights and happenings in the moors, like gray mist rising from the damp ground that moved like floating veils, enveloping tree stumps, looking like phantoms stalking lost souls.

We went on this outing with a horse and wagon. The special spades with their knife-sharp edges gleamed in the sun; the men held them carefully. We arrived at the designated place following narrow paths that weren't really roads, but solid enough for horses and wagons. Brick-like slabs were sliced from the ground. The men in their rubber boots soon were standing in holes which filled quickly with water. We picked up the wet slabs, and put them on a wooden pallet next to us. This was then pulled by the horse to a drying place, where we stacked them, overlapping, to dry. The slabs were a thick mesh of decaying roots, moss, and grass-like material that had aged and rotted in these bogs for a long time. I loved the musty earthy smell. The dried slabs were used as fuel for cooking and winter stoves. It was a nice change of pace in my everyday routine. I had cut my hand once on a spade while I grabbed a slab. Worried about what to do, the men said, "This turf has a great healing effect; don't bother with anything." I wasn't sure I should trust this philosophy, but I kept working with blood running over my hand. The next day it was practically healed; the men's belief was the truth.

The permit took many weeks and tested my patience. However, my mother and I wrote letters back and forth, and I learned about their everyday life. Meanwhile, June and July passed while I waited. It was hard; most of the time I spent around the house.

The town of Rade was near the Kaiser Wilhelm Canal that honored the German Kaiser, during whose reign in the late nineteen hundreds it was built. It connects the North Sea with the Baltic Sea. This was a very important and busy shipping channel. People talked about things they found on the shores. What was most enticing to the boys were the crates of oranges people had found. Oranges—who could remember the taste of oranges? The boys were excited; they had to check this out. They flung their school bags into the corner, and were ready to go. Mrs. Wales allowed them to go; she didn't want to spoil their excitement. I went to keep an eye on them.

I had learned all about the Canal in school, and never thought that one day I would walk along its bank. I had pictured it being much wider. It was so narrow that two large ships couldn't pass each other. We happened to stand at an interesting spot, across from a cove. A ship needed to move into the cove to allow the ship going in the opposite direction to pass. I thought that was pretty unique. We scoured the bank back and forth. Coarse reeds hampered our search, and we were careful not to cut our hands, but no oranges or other interesting items turned up.

Men were fishing from the shore, and soon the idea of looking for crates of oranges was tossed aside; the boys wanted to fish. On another day back at home, they had made simple rods with some old fishing line they had found in a shed on the farm. We heard it was especially good eel fishing in the evenings. There were earthworms galore in the garden behind the house, and after collecting a container-full, off we went. To our delight, we reeled in several eels—not very big ones, but they were like trophies for us, and we took them all home. The boys loved it so much we went often. They even anchored the poles on the shore overnight.

Then we hit upon the idea to smoke the eels. Europeans like smoked eels. In these times when food was scarce, no one could buy smoked eels. You had to do it yourself. The boys where so excited they couldn't wait to start. I had no idea how it was done. But they explained how they saw people do it right outside their homes. All I could think of was our smoke chamber in the attic in Köselitz, but there wasn't anything like that in this house. The boys knew where they could get a barrel from a neighbor's yard. They promised him a taste of our catch.

We rigged up the barrel outside the house with a layer of sawdust on the bottom. The eels were strung on a metal wire over the barrel, and the sawdust ignited. The trick of smoking was not to have any flames. Soon, grey smoke poured out of the barrel and quickly spread around, not very pleasant for the people who were near. Our eyes filled with tears as we peered into the barrel, trying to see how the smoking was coming along. We knew we had to give it time, but how much? The skinny little eels were still hanging there, just the way we had put them in. Hours went by. We kept checking, but they still didn't have the glistening shine the way they had in the stores. Our enthusiasm weakened, and we pondered what might have gone wrong. Adding more sawdust would cause more smoke; it was already bad enough for the neighborhood. Mrs. Wales wasn't very happy seeing the smoke wafting into the house. Finally, we came to the conclusion that the barrel was much too large for our small catch—all the heat was literally going up in smoke. Sadly, there wouldn't be smoked eels for dinner. All that smoke had made the eels pretty sooty, and under closer inspection, we saw that our wonderful idea wasn't working out. We covered the hot sawdust with dirt, and returned the barrel. Smoking eels wasn't as easy as we thought.

chapter ten

THE FAMILY'S RESETTLEMENT
IN TANGERHÜTTE

After I was taken from Marienwerder in March and detained in the camps, mother, Christa, and Werner remained in their situation. Christa became well again after nearly dying from typhus. After the war ended, the Russian occupation settled down. At some point in June, little by little, people began walking back to Köselitz. Mother, Christa, and Werner packed up and left Marienwerder, hoping that they could move back into our house. With their bundles under their arms and much anticipation, they started the long walk; they were almost happy. Mother said in a quite confident tone, "We are going home."

On the walk, they talked about what they might do first, and wondered if there was anything left in the house. When approaching from the distance, they could see activity around the house. Their hopes were soon shattered when they found that Polish families had begun to move into the village. Our house was occupied by Russian soldiers. Mother, Christa, and Werner moved in with Agnes Thöns, a distant relative of mother. She was alone after her husband and son were taken by the Russians and her daughter died of typhus. When Mother, Christa, and Werner arrived, the unforeseen lack of food was frightening. Nothing edible was growing. They dug up potatoes outside in a pit from the last harvest. The barn still had straw with grain on the seed heads. Again, they threshed it with sticks and then ground it in the coffee grinder the way they had done it in Marienwerder. Werner hung around the soldiers' butchering place and grabbed what they threw away. That became dangerous because sometimes they shot at him. He had to sneak to the backyard when nobody was around before the innards were buried. Mother and Agnes made lard from the fatty parts. They all ate a lot of fried potatoes. The soldiers had been very thorough in taking all the food that had been stored and saved in basements and pantries. Worry about their future was very acute. Christa didn't dare go outside in the street for fear of being seen by soldiers; rapings were still one of the most-feared incidents. In Marienwerder, they had the community of friends and neighbors sharing resources. Here, where they were "home," was a town entirely emptied of the connections to family, community, comfort, and safety. All the livestock had been driven away in the winter, except what the soldiers were now butchering. The chickens had been the soldiers' first shooting targets, eaten long ago. The same with the pigs; not even a dog remained. They felt that if they could only get back into our house, they would at least feel at home. Consoling themselves that it was becoming warmer with spring, they fought not to lose hope, and believed there had to be a way to start again.

Exodus from Köselitz

By the middle of June, many more people had gradually come back. But at the same time, some people noticed small groups of Germans walking on the road, not through Köselitz, but on the main road a little from town. It should have been a forewarning, but they didn't know what it was all about. They soon found out when Polish officials came around and announced that all Germans had to leave this part of the country. This was Poland now, and they were given twenty-four hours' notice. Surrounding towns suffered the same fate.

The shock was so intense it almost paralyzed their minds. Leaving the village permanently was unthinkable; where would they go? There was no time to waste; every minute counted. Werner quickly looked around; he wanted to make a pull-cart to take all they had with them. He had no tools. Searching in the barn, he found a crate, and mounted it on a set of two wheels he took off a farm machine. Somehow he fixed a handle on it so it could be pulled. The next morning, a heavy-hearted group made the painful walk to the end of the village where they had to assemble. As they walked by, they took a last look at our house. How was this possible? It was beyond their imagination. In Marienwerder, there had been hope, since no matter how long they had to remain there, the house and farm was something to hang onto. Mother was already grieving about the loss of father and my disappearance and potential death; how much more could she bear?

No one knew what was going to happen. They were told that they had to walk to the Oder River, which was the new border. Even after hearing about the border change, many of the townspeople would have probably stayed in Köselitz; most of them had properties there. To be forced out of our homeland was an unbelievable event. Who would have ever thought of that? Once across the river in Germany, they were told they were free to go wherever they pleased.

Looking back into history, neighboring countries had off and on claimed border provinces, but never forced the people out and replaced them with their nationals. It was bad enough to leave our hometown and stay in Marienwerder, but it wasn't far, and we knew it was only temporary. Would this be forever? How could they do this to us? Our land was here. It was ours. It had been ours for generations. We belonged there. There were no explanations, only despair and grief.

Long columns of people were slowly moving West, pushing carts and carrying sacks on their backs. Most were women and children, and a few older people who didn't want to stay behind. At the last rest stop before crossing the Oder River, Poles vandalized the group and stripped many of the few belongings they had saved. All these months Christa had been able to hold on to her watch, and now she buried it under a big tree. She wouldn't let them have it, too. She claimed to remember the spot forever.

At the Oder crossing, groups from other areas had also arrived, and people mingled, searching for friends and relatives. Here, in all this confusion, Mother bumped into her sister Adelheid and her husband Hans. To meet at this crucial moment, after all the tragedies and unbelievable events that they had experienced, was a miracle. Over and over again the sisters hugged. An endless stream of tears rolled down their cheeks. They believed that God had worked in mysterious ways. How glad they were to have found each other! It was the first time the two sisters had seen each other after that fateful day in January when they came to our house with the news that the Russians had already been in Naulin for three days.

An invisible force had thrown Mother a lifeline. A weight fell off her shoulders. Decision-making was now shared. How she welcomed that! For Mother, leaving the only home she had ever known was an unbearable stroke of fate. It broke her heart and spirit. Never before had she have to worry about providing for the family, and now she had nothing, not even a roof over her head. She remembered father's words when he said, just before the Russians came, "They can take everything from us, but they can't take our land." He probably never found out while he was still alive in a Russian labor camp that they had indeed taken our land, and not only that, but forced us to give up our homeland too.

Even though mother was only forty-three years old, the terrible experiences, the shock of having her husband pulled from her side without a good-bye, and my disappearance left an indelible imprint of sadness and grief. She withdrew, and was never the same again. Having had a good life and losing it all, almost one could say in a day, when they were forced out, was more than she could bear.

Martha Buchholz.

Mother now needed her children to become her support, not so much physically as emotionally. My heart aches when I think of the psychological damage the war caused. There was no place to turn to, only the struggle to stay alive. To overcome this tragedy, one had to be strong. Survival was the imminent test, and my gentle and loving mother had a very difficult time. She was looking for a place where her soul could find peace, understanding, and compassion. For many weeks, they walked through the land and were rejected by people who couldn't relate to their terrible fate. That was hard for her to accept.

Aunt Adelheid's and Uncle Hans' hearts were heavy too. The Russians had taken their young son Sigismund, only fourteen years old, and they didn't know what had happened to him. Ultimately, Sigismund was held captive in a Russian camp for three years before being released. Their other son, Hans Dietrich, just seventeen, was drafted in the last year of the war and they had not heard from him. They never did. Their two older daughters, Elisabeth and Brigitta, were married and had moved before the end of the war to the western part of Germany, to a safer place, while their husbands were still in the service.

The families walked together and crossed the Oder River on a makeshift bridge. The area west of the river was still a part of Pomerania, Vorpommern. It was now occupied by Russian forces. Here they were free to go where they wanted, but where should they go? Uncle Hans remembered a distant relative on the west side of the river, and that became their goal. Fortunately, this little section were these relatives lived was like a hidden pocket practically undisturbed from the onslaught of the Russians forces. The families were welcomed into the home, and shared food and shelter with these relatives. Now they could rest up, and sit down and make plans. Uncle Hans was sure if they headed to Berlin, they would find help there. He thought that must still be the capital, and surely there must be an organization which would find towns and places for all the homeless people.

Again, they packed their few belongings into the pull-cart. It was amazing that Werner's pull-cart had held together for so long, a testament to his handiwork, and was ready to go further. They thankfully accepted provisions from their hosts, and started walking. They trudged from village to village with little to eat and no place to sleep. Luckily, it was July by now, and warm enough to sleep outdoors in the fields. If they came to a field with vegetables, they helped themselves. They picked peas in the fields that were just maturing, and mushrooms along the way. At times, they begged food from villagers; it was the most degrading and hardest thing for them to do. They came through villages that hadn't been touched by the war, and often were met with harsh words. They sometimes were treated like gypsies; looking the part with their cooking pot tied on top of the cart. People locked the doors when they approached, and wouldn't even give them water. They were begging in order to stay alive.

Of course, they knew Berlin had been badly bombed, but seeing the devastation with their own eyes was overwhelming. There was no place to stay. They eventually connected with authorities who were trying to help the refugees who poured through day after day, directing them to resettlement towns farther west. Now they were told that the Elbe River was the zonal border between the Russian and the American occupations. Uncle Hans kept saying, "Let us walk until we come to the American Zone, and let's get away from the Russians." Fortunately, the destination that had been given to them was in the American Zone; this was encouraging. It boosted their spirits, and after many more days they finally reached the Elbe River and found a man who ferried them over by boat. The bridges had all been destroyed.

Tangerhütte and Briest

Dirty, hungry, and exhausted, they arrived in Tangerhütte, their destination. A little town not far from the Elbe River, Tangerhütte was very rural, with a cobblestone main street. It was the central place in the area with a town office and police department servicing the surrounding villages.

Mother, Christa, and Werner were sent to Malphul, a tiny farming village a few kilometers outside of Tangerhütte. Christa was placed with a farming family, and Werner had to live with another family since he was still going to school. It was sad that the family was split up; another setback for mother's fragile emotions. Her job was running the household for an elderly farming couple; the woman was ill. Mother had only one room. They practically worked only for room and board.

Uncle Hans and Aunt Adelheid were directed to the very small village of Briest, which was on the opposite side of Tangerhütte. In Briest was the von Bismarck estate. Most of the local families there had ties to the estate, either working in the fields or the forest. The estate consisted largely of woodlands, a sawmill, and a carpentry shop.

The von Bismarck family had to open up the manor and give rooms to arriving refugees. Aunt Adelheid and Uncle Hans, along with other homeless people, had been assigned to the manor.

This historic old manor with its half-timbered walls and artfully masoned brick squares in different patterns was an example of how much went into the construction of beautiful details a few hundred years ago. A niche above the main entrance held their coat of arms. It sat in a large park with huge oak trees probably as old as the manor itself. Groups of ornamental trees skirted a small pond. The scene gave a hint of past idyllic times.

Some of the villagers had their own little houses; others lived in housing provided by the von Bismarcks. A tiny chapel, a place of worship, was built in later years to commemorate a member of the von Bismarck family.

This was their place to start anew. Glad to have escaped from the Russians, they wanted to start farming again. Uncle Hans wanted to have something of his own, even if it was just a few acres of land.

The von Bismarck manor, the "Schloss", Briest, where Martha Buchholz resettled in 1946.

He wanted to be his own boss. How could the people running the towns understand that many of the refugees had suffered indescribable losses and wanted to start again?

After several months of American occupation, the Allied Powers finalized the post-war boundaries of Germany. Unfortunately, the Russian territory was enlarged and new borders established. Tangerhütte, Briest, and Malphul suddenly became Russian-occupied land. The Americans had left without fanfare, and the Russians moved in. It was a surprise and a huge concern to many.

The von Bismarck family packed up and left. Frau von Bismarck's husband was killed in the war, and she had two little boys. Her home was not her own anymore, and she knew nothing good would happen to her. She moved farther to the west to be with relatives. She took whatever fit on two horse-drawn wagons and left everything else behind; these goods were there for the taking by the refugees and everyone else. It was a tragedy, since much old, priceless furniture, china, and crystal heirloom treasures were lost from the family.

There were broad changes when the new East German government passed new laws. Land reform and communal farms were established. Many farmers were stripped of their ownership and had to work for wages. Before this happened, Uncle Hans was given a few acres of land and a horse and wagon. He didn't want to give this up, and tried to hold on to it. Of course, he didn't know the future and the consequences of the Russian occupation.

In the first few years, the new border wasn't fortified, and it was still possible for people from East Germany to flee to the West; many did. East Germany was losing its workforce, and to halt this, tall fences were erected and a "no-man's-land" was developed all along the border, making it impossible to cross, though many tried, and some lost their lives.

Mother was glad to have her sister, Adelheid, nearby. Lydia, her younger sister, and her family had stayed in the northern part where they fled. Uncle Ewald had returned from the war. They felt it was time to make a change. They decided to move to Briest and join mother and Aunt Adelheid. Now the three sisters were together and they could support each other. Two had their husbands, and Ewald's elderly mother was also with them.

After several years in Briest, Uncle Hans and Aunt Adelheid secretly planned to move to West Germany to join their married daughters. They had diligently saved every West German penny the daughters had sent them. It was illegal to have West German money; the government wanted people to exchange it into East German currency. The West German Mark had good value, while the East German Mark was hardly accepted outside the country.

*Ingrid, first photo after
reuniting with family, 1946.*

Someone found out and denounced them. Police came and searched the apartment, found the money, and Uncle Hans went to jail. What a shock! Aunt Adelheid, too afraid to stay, fled to Berlin while he was still in jail. From there, she was able to fly to West Germany; it was still possible at that time. She moved in with her daughter Elisabeth. The arrangement was that Uncle Hans after his release would go straight to Berlin and fly out, too. During his incarceration, mother and Aunt Lydia took over and visited him in jail, taking him food. Luckily, Uncle Hans was able to travel to Berlin after his release, and managed to fly out to West Germany, too. Soon after that, travel for East Germans to West Berlin was terminated, and this option to leave East Germany via Berlin was no longer possible.

chapter eleven

OUR FAMILY REUNITED

One of the first things I had learned at my arrival in the Spring of 1946 at the influx camp in Bad Segeberg, Schleswig Holstein, was that the allies had divided Germany into East and West. The East was occupied by the Russians and the West by the Americans, British, and French. Worst of all, Germany became two different countries. It made me sad to find out that my family had ended up in East Germany.

People no longer were allowed to move back and forth across this new border without identifications and permits. Though the border was not sealed until several years later, the border patrols were on both sides. It was still possible to sneak across. People who lived right at the border helped others with traveling across. All I could think of was to be reunited with my family as soon as possible. I never thought twice that I wouldn't go to East Germany. I missed them very much, and all I wanted was to share their life. I was seventeen, and had no place to go, and was too young to strike out on my own. My stay with the Wales family was of course only temporary. I didn't know at that time how fortunate I was to be in West Germany, and of course I couldn't know that once in East Germany, leaving there was impossible for a young person.

Legal crossing points were established to enter the new East German state. I had to obtain a permit from the East German city hall where mother lived. There were no doubts in my mind that I wouldn't be permitted to travel there, but I had no idea that it took forever to get a permit. Exchanging letters made the waiting a little easier. Mother had described her situation and her job of running a household for an elderly farming couple. She sounded depressed, though she never mentioned anything directly in her letters. But I could read between the lines how she felt. I thought that once I arrived there, I might help to change her predicament. I was happy to be alive and to have found them, and this was the last hurdle to overcome.

June and July went by, and I did my usual chores; the days seemed endless. The boys had school vacation, and we often went to the Canal, watching ships and barges float by. We stood at the shore and waved, but no one threw us crates of oranges. Once in a while we tried our luck with fishing eels, but that novelty had worn off a bit.

The food situation, even a year after the end of the war, was still terrible in both German states. With the assistance of the American Marshall Plan, West Germany had help. Bombed cities everywhere were still in shambles. Women volunteered to clean up the rubble. They called them "Truemmer Frauen," rubble women. Many men were still in Russian POW camps.

Finally, in August, mother sent the long-awaited permit. It was just a small piece of paper, and I had had to wait so many weeks for it. Mrs. Wales and I studied a map to pinpoint the nearest border crossing, and I had already done my homework charting my trip. My excitement was contagious; the whole family celebrated with me. I ran to the neighbors who were also refugees, and told them the good news.

My faithful companion, the little white knapsack, and I thought we could do it again—one more time. All I really needed now was to get on the train and get there. I had enough of Aunt Hedwig's money left to buy my train tickets. Mrs. Wales had taken me to a dressmaker, who made over one of her dresses for me. I still didn't have much to wear, and what I had fit into my little knapsack. I rolled up the winter coat from Aunt Hedwig, and I was ready to go.

With the help of a neighbor, I traveled to the railroad station in Bad Segeberg, and from there I boarded a train south to Hamburg where I caught a glimpse of the city's destruction. It was an awesome sight; it seemed not a single wall was standing. That's where the Wales had lived. Now I could better imagine the time when Mrs. Wales talked about the air raids and practically living in bomb shelters. Here in

Hamburg, I changed trains, and from this point I rode to the last town at the border crossing.

The end station was bustling; every person on this train disembarked. Piles of luggage, boxes, and knapsacks filled the platform. And there was I with my little white knapsack and my bundle under my arm, unhampered by anything. I followed the stream of people who were all heading in a certain direction, thinking it had to be the way to the border. It meant walking again; my footwear was still a big problem. Someone had passed along some old shoes which were much too big; I had had to make special insoles so they would fit better.

It was mind-boggling to see so many people wanting to cross over to the other side when it was already known that they wouldn't fare as well as here in the West. Family ties are strong, and many probably wanted to rescue what was left of their properties, or just be together with family, and it was too early to know what the future would bring.

As I came closer to the border, I could already see the long line; it seemed endless. The checkpoint wasn't even in sight. It was a slow process, and the line hardly moved. People were on foot, others had horses and wagons, and some had farm machinery. It seemed like another exodus. I knew then that it would take days before I had my turn. Realizing this made me very nervous. What will happen at night? What will everyone do?

Perhaps they will all stay where they are so they don't lose their places. I didn't know what to do, and asked the people standing next to me. They talked about looking for a place to sleep after the checkpoint closed. Thinking they must have something in mind, I followed them. There was a barn nearby, and that's where they were heading. I quickly went in, too, so at least I would have a roof over my head. Straw was all over the floor; many people must have slept there before from the look of all the remnants of discarded food wrappings and bottles. This was no time to be choosy. I found a little corner and tried to sleep. More people came in during the night; their whispering and stumbling around was annoying and interrupted everyone's sleep.

The next day, I stood in line until the border closed in the evening. That night I slept outside on a mound of straw. Finally, I had edged up close enough to expect to get across, but as fate had it, they closed the crossing barrier right in front of me. I was crushed. I had such high hopes. Now I worried about my place in the line the next morning; I couldn't lose it. Officers were still standing around, and I quickly asked one what to do to get my place back the next day. The officer suggested, "Go to the front of the line the next morning and let someone know." I hardly slept that night. I worried whether anyone would listen to me, but despite people's unpleasant remarks for just walking up front, I was in the first group the next morning to go across. It was hard to believe that I was now in another country, even though it was another German country. Looking around, everything seemed the same—the land, the people, and the language. How was it possible that our country could just be divided like that? It didn't make any sense.

I followed a group of people who were looking for the train station. Only hours now separated me from mother. She had written me all the information. I needed to get off in Tangerhütte; the little town I had never heard of before. From there I had to walk one or two miles to the village of Malphul where she lived. I arrived towards late afternoon on a bright sunny day. I had asked someone for directions, and before I knew it I was on my way to Malphul. Soon I saw the church steeple, and my pace increased. My heart began to pound; it was hard holding the tears back.

From our letters, I knew mother lived with an elderly couple, and it didn't take me long to find the house. I was coming "home." Home was where mother was. I had longed and prayed for this moment, to feel her arms around me. My long and hard journey had come to an end.

I arrived unannounced. Mother was right there when I entered the house, and she let out a little shriek, calling my name perhaps to make sure it was I she was seeing. This moment is etched in my heart. Nothing mattered—not the loss of my home or the experiences in the camps, nor having been so close to death. Feeling mother's arms around me was all I wanted. We let the tears flow. Everything else was irrelevant; only the present existed. After hugging and kissing, we sat and just held hands. She whispered, "I don't want to let go of you." We had plenty of time now to tell our stories.

I didn't know where I would fit in. I was appalled at the situation mother was in. Something had to be done. She didn't have the strength to change her situation, not at that time. Her will was broken, and she wasn't the same person anymore.

On one of my visits to Aunt Adelheid in nearby Briest, I worked out a plan with her. If possible, mother and I would move into the von Bismarck manor, too. Werner and Christa stayed in Malphul for the time being with the farm families they had initially been placed with. It was not an easy decision for mother, but she finally agreed. She did this just in time to acquire a little piece of land, about one acre and a small section of a vegetable garden on the outskirts of the village. She was delighted. This little garden had a plum tree, and the plums would be all hers. Food was a major priority, and having a garden was a great advantage. Whenever we had time, we roamed through the woods to pick wild mushrooms, and soon learned which mushrooms were safe to eat. I enjoyed that very much and often went alone, one time meeting up with a big wild boar. If we had too many mushrooms, we dried them.

The refugees had no resources; life was an everyday struggle. Everything was rationed just like it was in West Germany. A ration card was very important. In addition, everyone was asked to work. What I really wanted was to go back to school. I learned that I could enroll at a city University, but perhaps did not have enough school years. With all the uncertainties and dramatic changes, it was too soon to make a decision. The new East German politics, still in their infancy, began with new rules and regulations. And then I found out I had to join the Communist Party to study for free. It frightened me to think that I might have to march around waving a red flag with the hammer and sickle.

Near Briest, where mother, Werner, and I now lived, was a huge Russian garrison. The woods around Briest were off-limits to the German civilians; it always gave me an uneasy feeling. Even though the Russian soldiers were not allowed outside their camp, one would still see them now and then. It wasn't so much that I was afraid to be there; I just didn't see any future for myself there.

Meanwhile, I had registered in the town hall. I had to have a ration card, and they also wanted to know if I worked. We had no money, so we all needed to work. I had studied at one of the best schools around, and the only opportunities were working in the fields. I didn't want to do that. I was frustrated, and life looked very bleak. There had to be a way out of this depressing situation; it was constantly on my mind. I talked with mother, but what could she do? She was helpless. She had to go out and work, and I had to look for work also. Everyone's life had totally turned around. This stage was challenging and frightening. The future looked scary. We could no longer think of who we were and what we once had; that was the past. We had to think of building a new life.

I heard of a job at a sawmill. The mill was quite a walk, but I joined several other people and started working there. A young girl and I stacked freshly cut boards into large piles for drying. The work wasn't all that stressful, but the long walk home was exhausting after working all day.

Werner, who as a little boy wanted nothing else but to be a farmer, needed to look for something else now. He had finished school, and mother thought learning a trade was the best way to go. There weren't many choices to pick from; Tangerhütte was such a small rural town. But mother found a cabinetmaker who still owned a business and worked by himself. This man was willing to take Werner on as an apprentice. It was a big relief for mother, who had worried about Werner's future. He would even receive a little pay.

I had a wonderful surprise one day when I received a letter from my Pyritz school friend Eva. It was amazing that she found my address, since I had only been there a short time. A remarkable network had developed. People were looking for friends and relatives and astoundingly had much success. Of all places, she and her parents were in Berlin, and she invited me to come and visit. I accepted the invitation. Of course, this was the worst time ever to see our capital city. I wished I had seen the city in peacetime as our vibrant capital.

Eva had already connected with another schoolmate, and the three of us had a great time wandering around the city, practically climbing over the rubble. None of us had ever been in Berlin. The girls pointed out places where interesting sites used to be. We could only speculate about how beautiful they must have been. For us, it was a celebration of being alive and of friendship. We all had so much behind us.

We climbed the many steps to visit *San Souci*, the palace of King Frederick II, the Prussian King who reigned in the eighteenth century (1744-1797). Vegetables had been planted on the terraces where lawns and beautiful flowerbeds used to be. The palace was damaged and closed. I was astounded that it wasn't totally demolished like most of the buildings around.

At this time, in 1946, Berlin had four sectors, but no physical boundaries. One was able to go anywhere. Eva's parents lived in the basement of a bombed-out house. Everything was done in one room. Coal was piled in one corner for heating and cooking, and potatoes in the other. Everything was makeshift.

I had spent about eight weeks or so in East Germany when my cousin Brigitta asked me if I wanted to come to Bamberg, in Bavaria. My heart leapt; that was in the American zone. I immediately felt that this was my chance, but was I ready to leave my mother again so soon? We sat down together and looked at the pros and cons. I was not happy with my life. I wanted more, such as finishing school, and there was no chance in Tangerhütte. It wasn't easy to persuade mother to see the nonexistent opportunities. Accepting Brigitta's offer was my opportunity. The decision of leaving East Germany won out, and I soon started planning.

My eighteenth birthday was approaching, and I invited Eva to come to Briest. We made the most of this visit. The living situation with us wasn't much different than hers. She stayed overnight and we had no extra bed; we slept together again like we did in her basement apartment in Berlin. It was wonderful to connect with her again. This visit fastened our friendship, and we promised to write. I was getting ready for my move to Bamberg, and that was very exciting.

Brigitta's offer was to help with her two little boys. I could also go to school and live with them. Unfortunately, their house had been bombed and burned down. They were at a point where they had no income. Her husband Georg's punishment for being in the Nazi Party was a two-year period of temporary dismissal from his former marketing job at a big tobacco company. He and another person, also a salesman, worked at the site of his burned-down house, removing the rubble and cleaning bricks for reuse. Building material was hard to come by. Brigitta was looking to find a job.

chapter twelve

THE MOVE TO WEST GERMANY

Therewas another teenager in Briest who had fled with a family from East Prussia. She found out that her sister, the only survivor of her family, was on a peninsula along the North Sea in the northern part of West Germany. She was a tall sixteen-year-old, and was staying with a family looking after their children. Now that she had located her sister, she wanted to see her and asked me if she could join me on my trip, not having the courage to venture across the border on her own. Our plan was to slip illegally across the border. I was glad to have company. I knew it wasn't just a "walk across the border." We planned this undertaking as well as we could: asking around if someone knew the area, where the closest distance was to the border, and trying to find someone who had done it previously. Even though we lived in a very small village, there was a lot of talk about people getting across the border in many places.

It was 1946, and people were still trying to reunite with family by sneaking across the new border. We picked the closest distance to the border, since we traveled by train, and one never knew how often they would run, especially in the direction of the border. I had studied the map to find a town that was very close to the border and had a railroad station. I really didn't know exactly where the border was located; new maps of course were not developed, and one had to find out from people who were more familiar with the area. Getting to the closest point on the border was important; we had to make it in a day, and needed daylight for our walk across the border. I didn't know if I should pray for a sunny or a rainy day—which would make it easier for us?

My handmade knapsack, which I had made from an old piece

of material that Aunt Hedwig had given me, was washed and repaired again and packed with my few belongings. The decision was to leave on the eighth of October, two days after my eighteenth birthday. A lovely sunny fall day greeted us in the morning. I took it as a good omen; we actually needed good weather. It was a sad moment to say good-bye and leave again; it seemed I had just arrived there. I had wrestled with my conscience for some time; should I really leave? Mother wanted the best for me, and didn't think she should hold me back. We had talked enough about this and weighed the advantages and disadvantages. I could only see the positive side, such as finishing my education, and of course, the excitement of living in a city. The only risk was getting there, but it wasn't a trip into the unknown this time. I could come back any time, and this was reassuring for both of us.

We had taken the earliest train to get to the border as fast as possible. The train ride took longer than we thought. It made many stops, and the schedules weren't always adhered to. We didn't talk much; most of the time we stared through the window as we passed little villages here and there where people in the fields were harvesting potatoes and beets. The train rattled along on rails that hadn't received much attention. The locomotive was fired with brown coal, puffing dark smoke into the air, emanating a pungent smell.

Our minds were occupied with what lay ahead of us. I didn't want to think of being caught, and wished it would be over. Not many people disembarked at the end-station. It was the middle of the afternoon, and we were glad that there was still plenty of daylight. We left the platform quickly so as not to be noticed. But we had to find out which direction the border was; we needed to ask someone. Most people seemed to live in this town. I looked around and approached a man who had been walking ahead of us. He was willing to give us directions. I asked him if he could tell us where there was a safe place to cross and how far it was. I gathered from what he said that it wasn't that close. It took all our courage to go ahead; we were frightened.

We knew soldiers patrolled the border on both sides—on one side, the Russians, and on the other, the British. Fences and watchtowers had not been erected in 1946. The man also told us we should come to overhead power lines, which denoted the border in that area. Now we had the direction and also what to look for. He suggested the best way was going through the forest. These woods were swept clean of firewood; also a sign of hard times. There were hardly any bushes or undergrowth, no place to hide if we needed to. We stepped lightly to make as little noise as possible, but it was fall and the dry leaves rustled with every step we took. We only whispered if we had to; most of the time we just used our hands and gestured.

We had walked for a while when suddenly we saw two men ahead of us. This felt like a lifeline. We hurried to catch up with them, and hoped that they knew the way and we could tag along with them. But they didn't want to have anything to do with us, telling us that four were too risky in a group. We stayed a short distance behind them, but kept them in our sight. It was a relief to know we were not the only ones in these woods. How far could the border be? There was no way that we could judge how far we had walked, especially since we didn't have a watch with us.

Suddenly we saw two Russian soldiers step out from behind trees and stop the men. Instinctively I whispered to my companion, "Hide quickly," but where could we hide? The trees didn't give us much cover. I crouched on the ground, and then suddenly, a soldier stood behind me pointing a gun. I hadn't heard him. He must have watched us all along. I looked at the gun and thought he wouldn't shoot us. It wasn't the first time that I had faced a Russian gun. He was a young man, but seemed all business dressed in a camouflage uniform. If it hadn't been so serious, I could have looked at it as a "Hide and Seek" game. He walked us to the other soldiers, who were busy with the men, searching their knapsacks and pockets, and then ours, too. They took our identification slips, which were not more than a piece of paper with our names.

The two men were led away; we never saw them again. We were walked to their barrack, which was a little wooden cabin with primitive beds, a table, and a few chairs. We couldn't communicate with them, but when I saw this, I knew what they had in mind. We started to cry and became really hysterical, telling them we were only fourteen years old by holding up our hands and showing them with our fingers. We told them our mothers were on the other side, and that's where we want to go. I hoped we could evoke sympathy; we were frightened and we knew we were at their mercy. By now the sun had set, and it was getting dark. We kept begging them over and over again that we wanted to find our mothers. It seemed that they couldn't agree on what to do with us; they talked amongst themselves, and it sounded like arguing. I kept praying "Dear Lord, don't let them rape us." This went on for some time as they kept glancing at us. I knew they were talking about us; there must have been four or five of them. We started sobbing again and wailed, "Mother, mother." At least they understood what that meant.

Finally, one came to us and motioned to follow him. What did that mean? Apparently, one of them had decided that we should get out of the barrack, and, I was hoping, out of their sights, too. I knew at this point there was no chance that we would find our way in the dark. Getting away from the soldiers was all we wanted at that moment. He walked us behind the barrack, and pointed with a flashlight to a dugout in the ground with a post in each corner to hold up a makeshift roof. I didn't care what it was, as long as we were safe there. The dirt floor was covered with water. There were no walls, but luckily there was a bench. We managed to get to the bench, pulled up our feet, and spent the night crouching there. It was a long night, and we agonized over what would happen the next day. Would they let us go or lead us back to the town?

An older soldier came the next morning, and motioned for us to come out and follow him. We were now walking under the power lines; this had to be the border. I remembered my inquiries in the village. I whispered to my companion to slow down—the soldier wasn't turning around to watch us. Maybe we could just run across the strip of grass under the power lines to the other side, into the woods. But before our little plan matured, he stopped and waited for us to catch up. He handed us our identification slips and pointed to the other side, gesturing for us to hurry across. No British border guards were there at the moment, and we managed to understand his hand signals. What a surprise! I wished I could have shouted, "Hurray;" he was a sympathetic soul to let us go.

We didn't waste any time, and dashed across into the forest to get away from the border as fast as we could. We wanted to put some distance between us and the British border patrol.

We were now in the British occupied zone. Of course, we didn't want to be caught by the British, either; we avoided open areas, and really just followed our noses. There were no roads, but we saw tracks where vehicles had driven over the forest floor. We were praying that we were heading in the right direction. It was early morning, and I was glad to have the day ahead of us. We walked at a good pace, following the tracks on the ground, and always listening for unusual sounds. The woods were very quiet; the only noises were our footsteps in the rustling leaves. It occurred to me that if we met a British border patrol, I could actually talk to him with my school-learned English.

Gradually, we became aware of faint noises. I whispered to my companion, "Do you hear the noise, too? It sounds like car noises." What welcome sounds! There had to be a road ahead of us. We tried to judge the time, since it was impossible to judge how far we had traveled. Gradually, we came to the edge of the forest and saw the road. I was relieved to be out of the woods, and hoped the biggest hurdle was behind us. We took a moment to figure out which direction to walk, and then just took a chance. We didn't dare walk on the road, but walked alongside, in the grassy part near the adjoining fields. No one stopped us, and eventually we neared a town. I was anxious to find out if it was the town of Helmstedt, the town we had planned to go to. Finally, we saw a road sign, and anxiously walked a little faster to read the name on it. We were on the right road heading into Helmstedt; we had made it! I felt like embracing the post and dancing around. I wished I had a way to let mother know that I was safe, but there was no communication except writing. I knew she had worried about the trip and our safety, and all the things that could go wrong.

The railroad station was our next aim. Once we arrived in town, we started asking for directions. Having made it so far, my bundled-up worries dissipated; all I needed now was the train to Bamberg. We parted ways at the train station. My companion had to travel to the peninsula of Sylt at the North Sea. With happy smiles, we wished each other good luck. I knew I would never see her again.

I had to get from the British Zone into the American Zone. Little did I know that these zones had borders, too, even though it was all West Germany; they were invisible ones. At certain railroad stations between the British and the American Zone were checkpoints. I had no permit of any kind, and was wondering what would happen to me. My only identification was the paper slip from East Germany. I began to worry. My only hope was the guards' acceptance of my plea of reuniting my mother.

Loud announcements ordered everyone off the train, and guards went from person to person to check papers. Next to me was a family with children, and as the guard turned around to talk to another person, I stood quite near the family who he had just checked. He must have thought I belonged to them and moved on; I was safe. After everyone was checked, we were allowed to board the train again. The struggle to find a seat or even a standing place was tough. It was everyone for himself, and this time I only had a standing place.

chapter thirteen

BAMBERG YEARS

S tepping off the train in Bamberg was like entering another world. The late afternoon sun bathed the surroundings in a warm orange glow. My eyes squinted as I took in the scene in front of me. The railroad station appeared perfectly unharmed from air raids. The train had passed through many stations with makeshift platforms, damaged roofs, or wrecked buildings, but here it seemed war had passed by without causing any harm.

People were streaming to the exit, and I just let myself flow with them. Everything appeared so large—or did I just imagine it because nothing was damaged? A grateful feeling welled up in me. It seemed luck had been with me. I felt like embracing the world and spreading my arms to skip across the square in front of the station. This was the end of my journey. I had to let it sink in first.

For the first time in my life, I would live in a big city. I had only visited Stettin and Stargard, two larger cities in Pomerania, and that was just for shopping once in a while. This was a new life. I had visions of going back to school, an opportunity that was now available. Moving here to this much-desired part of Germany—the West—in the American-occupied zone was a dream come true.

The City

The city had been bombed, but hadn't suffered greatly; everything looked nearly intact. The biggest damage was done by the retreating German Army, which had detonated the bridges over the Regnitz River. But temporary bridges were already in place. Two branches of the river wound their way through the city. For a time, the missing bridges must have slowed down the life of the city for working people and school children.

Bamberg is in Frankonia, the northern region of Bavaria, and as an old historic city is often called "Little Rome" because it is also surrounded by seven hills. The massive cathedral, the "Dom," dates back to the seventh century, destroyed by fire once and rebuilt around 1100. Centuries ago, a Bavarian Emperor had ruled here, and ever since the building of the Dom, Archbishops have resided here. The old and new residences are on every sightseer's list. It is mainly a Catholic city, with many old and beautiful churches, monasteries, and cloisters tucked away in the old part of the city.

Statue of the "Bamberger Reiter," symbol of the city.

Quite a number of beer breweries dotted the city and the surrounding towns. The Bavarians like their beer, especially in the summertime. People flock to the beer gardens after work or on the weekends, and many have their favorite places. Pubs along the country roads set up tables and chairs outside for the Sunday strollers.

Arriving at Brigitta's

The struggle at the border had been just a day ago, but it seemed far back in time. How thankful we were that the Russian soldiers let us go. My legs were sore and tired from standing up most of the time on the trains, but this would soon all be forgotten. In a very short time I would be with my cousin Brigitta, and a new phase in my life would begin.

I headed for the street across from the railroad square and old Patrician houses with ornate red sandstone facades, darkened by age, that lined the sidewalk. These were reminders of wealth and culture from bygone times. I noticed people were nicely dressed. With the address handy in my pocket, I asked a woman for directions to Siechenstrasse. "Turn right at the next intersection, you will be on Koenigs Strasse. Keep on going, and on the other end is Siechenstrasse, you will see the street sign. It's not far," she answered.

I was glad that I was on the right track. When I turned the corner into Koenigs Strasse, I noticed shops on either side. I slowed down a little bit, and instinctively read their names, such as housewares, electrician, and optician. Not much was displayed in their windows; times were tough here, too.

Farther down, facing the street, was a large pub sign, "Der Goldene Löwe," The Golden Lion. Looking down a side street, I glimpsed the Regnitz River. "What fun I will have exploring the city," went through my mind. Checking the house numbers, I found I was almost there. My heart started to beat faster; in a few minutes I would be face to face with Brigitta and her family.

There it was, Siechenstrasse 20, a little white-and-blue house number next to a large door, which had a smaller door framed within it. I entered through the smaller door, which led under part of the house and into a small courtyard. The surroundings were not very pretty; garbage barrels leaned along the walls. There was a small shed, and on the opposite side a brick structure, likely the washhouse. Brigitta had described the location and their living arrangement, and this had to be it. The apartment was on the second floor. I entered a large semi-dark workroom, and on my right was the stairway going up. Even though Brigitta and I had corresponded, my arrival was a surprise. I hadn't set a date, since my plan was to cross the border illegally. I hadn't been sure if I would muster enough courage to go through with my plan. The final decision came only when I met the young girl who wanted to join me.

And now here I was, just showing up at the door. The stairs were rather dark, but on the landing was a window and three doors; two had names on them, and one was a toilet. I knocked on the door that had my cousin's name on it. It was a poignant moment; we laughed, cried, hugged, and talked all at the same time.

Brigitta, her husband George, and their two little boys, Rainer and Wulf Dieter, had moved into this small apartment after their house burned down. Their little boys were two and three years old. The apartment had three small rooms, of which one was also the kitchen. The house belonged to George's relative Anna Keller, who was a pastry chef. All this property belonged to her, including the bakery store out front. The bakery kitchen was attached in the back of the house, and Brigitta and her family lived in the rooms above it.

Across the landing from their apartment was another room, occupied by an elderly couple from a big city. They were one of the thousands whose house had been bombed and now had to live in one room. The toilet that was on the landing was the only one for all of us. From there, a narrow stairway led up to two little rooms, and I settled in one of them.

I was happy to have my own little room. The window looked onto a garden where someone had grown vegetables. Stalks of Brussels sprouts were still in the ground waiting to be harvested; their fruit had been nurtured and grown all summer, and the cycle was coming to an end. A row of leeks and cabbages was also still in the ground.

These rooms and the apartment had been used for storage, and also housed the bakery apprentices. Now that everything was rationed and pastries were a luxury, most of the pastry bakeries had closed or changed, making only bread. Anna Keller's bakery was shut down. In 1946, people were grateful to be able to buy bread. The ration coupons allowed only so much; bread was very precious, and more important

Ingrid, 1947.

than anything else. It would have been wonderful to have the aroma of freshly baked cakes and delicacies drift into my little room, but I could only dream of it.

Brigitta had married George Wagner in 1941. George was a widower; his first wife had died. His school-aged son lived with Anna Keller, his former sister-in-law, while George managed a tobacco company in Kiev in the Ukraine during the last years of the war. George and Briggitta had met there. She had taken a secretarial job in Kiev in his company, and became his secretary. We were all surprised when she accepted a job that far away from home, but at that time, the German Army was still advancing in Russia, and no one worried much about it.

The Ukraine was a rich agricultural land, and Germany quickly took over local companies and assigned German managers to run the productions. George, who was a salesman for a large German tobacco company, was offered the position running the company in Kiev. His home was in Bamberg in Bavaria on the fashionable "Lange Strasse." That street had been renamed "Adolf Hitler Strasse," but, of course, had received its former name again. It was obvious when the German Army retreated that Brigitta and George could no longer stay in the Ukraine. Brigitta went to live with her parents in Naulin, where her children, Rainer and Wulf Dieter, were born in 1943 and 1944.

When the Russian Army pushed west, George urged Brigitta to move to Bamberg, where he had his home waiting for her. He didn't think it was safe to stay in Naulin, the little farming village next to Köselitz in the eastern region. He realized that Pomerania, the eastern-most province, would be hit first by the advancing Red Army.

Once in Bamberg, Brigitta decided to find a place in the country where she didn't have to get up at night during the air raid alarms with her two little children; they were also safer there. Unfortunately, one night phosphorus bombs were dropped, and one fell through the roof of their Bamberg house, but since no one lived in the third-floor apartment, which was theirs, and the second-floor apartment had also been vacated, the bomb smoldered for a while until a real fire broke out. The house could not be saved; it burned almost to the ground. It also did much damage to the attached neighboring stores. That's when Anna Keller, George's former sister-in-law, offered them the apartment over the bakery kitchen in the back of her house and store.

Beginning a New Life Wasn't Easy

The first and most important step for me was to register so I could obtain a food ration card. The guidelines were quite strict. Even though I had a place to stay, I had to register at a certain shelter every day and prove I was a refugee. Only with proper registration and citizenship in Bamberg could I receive a ration card, which I had to have, since food was also very scarce in West Germany. There was no way to obtain food without the card.

The thorough German bureaucracy was working hard to help the many refugees who had come from all directions. They were housed in temporary shelters during the process to find them permanent housing. It was a blessing that the city hadn't been badly bombed. Many refugees still lived in schools, and it became necessary to move the people so schools could reopen.

The process was very slow. My place to register was a school. It was the fall of 1946, and since the school was needed, the refugees were moved to a shelter in Fürth near Nürnberg. I was confounded when I heard this, since Fürth was quite a distance away. I was hoping until the last minute for my registration to come through, but to my distress, I had no choice but to move with the other refugees. My situation was dire; I had no money and hardly anything to wear. I stayed during the week in the shelter, and on weekends took the train to Bamberg. Brigitta gave me enough money to buy my train ticket, but that was all.

The shelter was primitive; large rooms with bunk beds provided families and people of all ages, even returning POW's, a roof over their heads. A soup kitchen fed us all. I was glad it was only temporary. The bad memories of camp life were still with me. It was not even a year ago that I had left the Russian camp in Posen, but I felt now that I was so much better off than all the rest of the people. I had a place to return to. When I ate the soup that we received, I thought of the watery soup in the camp, often with frozen potatoes that were all black, and with the teeth from the cooked cows' heads.

There was nothing to do but wait. In the daytime I joined some single girls, and we walked around in the city. I couldn't even do that very often, since my shoes were in such poor shape. It seemed that it took forever, but finally I received my identification papers and returned to Bamberg. Now I was a proper resident, and could pick up a food ration card. Despite all these inconveniences, I had faith in my future, and was confident that my life could only get better. I was glad that I had taken the risk to come here.

Clothing and shoes were still a big problem for me. Brigitta tried to help me. We heard that a church near us was distributing donated clothing from America. This sounded exciting. I rushed there with high hopes, but everything was picked over. I needed shoes desperately, but what could I do with a pair of high-heeled dancing shoes? I practically had to beg on my knees at the agency in city hall which issued vouchers for clothing. When at last I received a voucher for shoes, another struggle began in order to find shoes. I must have visited every shoe store in the city. I wouldn't have cared what they looked like; all I wanted was a pair of shoes. Finally, I found a pair of black Oxfords. It was exciting. They looked like they would get me through thick and thin, and were sturdy, with laces on top. Then, one day I was caught in the rain, and suddenly my feet felt wet. I looked down and saw my shoes falling apart; what looked like leather was just pressed paper. I was devastated.

All these shortages made people quite resourceful. There was no end to the ingenuity of the cobblers. Everyone had to make the most of their footwear, and they patched and soled shoes over and over again. Brigitta had a pair of sandals which didn't fit either of us. I thought there had to be a way the cobbler could make them over for me. Off I went to the neighborhood cobbler, and took along a narrow blue and white leather belt for straps, which Brigitta had provided. I really had to twist his arm, until he reluctantly agreed to work on them. He shortened the sandals in the front, and used the belts for straps across the foot, alternating white and blue. He also lowered the heels a little. When all was done, I had an attractive pair of sandals which lasted me for a long time.

Besides footwear and clothes, I desperately needed a dentist. My teeth had suffered from not being able to brush them during the camp time, plus they were weakened from malnutrition. No dentist in all of Bamberg was accepting new patients. Not even Brigitta's or George's dentist would take me. The situation was frightening; how much longer could I wait? I detected a cavity in my front tooth. Here, Brigitta came to my rescue when she came home one day all excited with the good news that she had discovered a new dentist's office that was taking new patients. This seemed like a gift from heaven, and I immediately went and made an appointment.

I was taken aback, though, when I noticed that the office didn't look like a dentist's office. It seemed to be in the living room of a regular house. The patient's chair was situated in the middle of the room, but I didn't care—I was desperate, and glad to be there. The dentist was a younger man, and had an accent, but that didn't bother me either, since so many foreigners were around. I admired him to set up an office like that. He seemed to have all the necessary equipment, too. He told me my cavities needed to be filled; he started to work right away. I had to come back several times; he didn't have Novocain, and the drilling was very painful. That reminded me of the painful drilling at the dentist at home in Pyritz, where we never received Novocain. But now I had no choice, and the extraction of the nerve from my tooth was so painful I almost fainted.

His waiting room was always full; nuns from the neighboring cloister also came. One time, another man was there to work on my teeth, but he didn't look like a professional at all. He wore riding boots and looked as if he were on a hunting spree. I heard laughter and merriment from the next room; it sounded like they were partying and having a good time, including my dentist.

When I discussed this with Brigitta, we both wondered about the situation, but since I had no choice, I went back. Then one day the bubble burst. The headline in the newspaper reported that this "dentist" was a charlatan; he had had everyone fooled. Perhaps he had been a dental student; the truth never came out. He was arrested for malpractice, and also for being involved in the black market.

These were meager times, with no income. Now that I was there, Brigitta looked for possibilities and ideas to help with the expenses. They wanted to rebuild their burned house, but at the moment it was impossible. In addition, building material was impossible to procure.

Cousin Brigitta's Business Venture

At one point, George's brother, Joseph, came from Munich to visit. He was a hat salesman, and kept himself above water even though there were no hats to sell. He had many business acquaintances, and was ready to help. The three of them sat down and brainstormed.

They wanted to find something Brigitta could do to earn money and help support the family; George was performing the two years of physical labor. I could almost hear the wheels turning in their heads; they groaned when they rejected an idea. Of course, Joseph, who was more familiar with the men's accessory business, was leaning in that direction, and came up with the suggestion of making and repairing neckties. At first, this seemed a frivolous idea, but as they looked at this a little closer, the idea grew on them. There weren't any neckties in the stores, but men still wore them.

Little by little, they decided to look into it. Brigitta knew how to sew, the first prerequisite for the undertaking. Joseph knew a woman who had a necktie business in Munich, and arranged a weekend for Brigitta to visit and learn the method. Her excitement was contagious; all we thought and talked about was ties. Was it possible to learn all that in one weekend? How could this become a source of income for the family? It still sounded unrealistic.

She came back enthusiastically, ready to practice what she had learned. George, with his connections, was able to obtain a business license for her. Indeed, even for a little undertaking like this, a license was needed. They put together an advertisement in the paper, and nailed a small plaque next to the outside door—a very small plaque. I wondered if anyone would look up and read it.

Neckties were now on my mind, too; wherever I went I looked at men's neck ties and noticed how dreadful they looked. I wished I could be a little invisible elf tugging at their coat tails and whispering into their ears, "Have your awful tie repaired; I know just the place."

We waited anxiously for someone to show up. Would they find us? There was the dreary courtyard to be crossed and the semi-dark staircase to the apartment. We didn't have a telephone either. But then one day, there was a knock on the door, and the first customer was there—he did find us. We were elated, and it raised our hopes.

Gradually people came; they brought mostly old stained ties for repair. Many of them were so bad that we had to take them apart and wash them first. Saving a poor threadbare tie was a real challenge. The worn-out section had to be cut out, making the tie shorter, but after the repair was done, and the tie nicely pressed, it looked almost like new. We admired the nice outcome. All this was done in the live-in kitchen.

At first, the income from it was so trivial it wouldn't have fed a bird. But Brigitta didn't give up hope. Little by little, word got around; advertising helped, too. As long as there weren't any neckties in the stores, customers kept coming. New ones were made from all sorts of material like flowery prints, hilarious colors, and, oftentimes, a scrap from an apron or a skirt.

It took George and his colleague friend a long time to clean up the rubble of the house on Lange Strasse. Eventually, we could travel through to the back where a little garden was nestled between the walls. The old magnolia tree had survived; its gnarled trunk was a testament to its age, and it delighted us with exquisite blossoms in the spring, lending the garden an exotic look. The garden was a little oasis amidst stacked-up boards and bricks.

In one corner was a small storage building. A hardware store had been on the first floor before the house burned down; its storage room was now accessible. Brigitta set up the sewing business there. Surprisingly, the tie business grew after the move to Lange Strasse until she even hired a young girl to help her. She continued even after the monetary reform in June 1948.

Soon she could buy new material and make ties by the dozen. She even ventured to hire a salesman. This worked for awhile, but because of the new currency, clothing companies started mass-producing these items. The economy improved all around, and it became harder for a small specialty business to make money. Department stores started to blossom, and competing with them was hard.

Bamberg Life in the Early Years

During this time, I met Inge Dietz, who worked as a nanny for a family in Anna Keller's house as part of her school internship. We were about the same age, and became good friends. Her family were refugees from the Sudetenland, which was now part of the Czech Republic; the German people had to leave there, too. Her father had already built a little wooden house for them on the outskirts of the city. I often visited with them; she had a wonderful mother, and I was always welcomed there. Because of our work schedules, Inge and I met only on Sundays. Sometimes we met in the city, and sometimes I went to her home. Even though the Dietzs were a large family and had many mouths to feed, and despite all the shortages, her mother always made wonderful sheet cakes topped with streusels on Sundays. Sometimes the cakes included blueberries she had picked.

Now a young adult, I wanted to do fun things. My teen years had slipped by. The last years of the war had been bleak, especially for us because we were living in a small village. There had been no amusements of any kind. My school was in the little city, and a good part of the day was taken up by school and commuting. Boys sixteen and older were drafted and one could only dream of how nice it would be to have a boyfriend.

Separation from my family in those formative years, especially the time in the camps, had added an early maturity to my life. I couldn't make up what I had missed, but now I wanted to enjoy what was in my reach. Human nature is extraordinary and resilient; it adapts or arranges itself, stores sad experiences in the far corners of the mind, and continues on with life. Learning to survive had added another dimension to my senses.

In Bamberg, ballrooms began to open for dancing. Of course, Inge and I wanted to go dancing and meet boys. Brigitta and I decided I should first take a ballroom dance course; this was a wonderful start. I met young people my age, and discovered how much I loved dancing. After that, I was confident and ready to waltz away. Lots of American songs were popular, and small bands played them with great gusto. People wanted to dance again; there was no dancing during the war years and no men to dance with. People wanted to make up for the years they had missed.

I still didn't have much to wear. I had one pair of shoes, and my only dress was one I had made over with little butterfly sleeves. Inge and I began to date young men; it was very exciting. We had met two men who were locals and friends, and the four of us went out together. We mostly met Sunday afternoons, and since nobody had a car in those days, we had to go for walks, limiting our excursions to nearby villages. From these walks, we learned much about the city and the neighboring towns we visited.

One of my favorite outings was the Altenburg, an ancient castle on one of the seven hills. The Altenburg dates back to the eleventh century in the Middle Ages. Emperor Heinrich ruled from here. The story went that his Empress Kunigunda came down the hill with baskets of food to feed the poor. Several streets and a bridge were named after them. Their weathered statues, with their once-gilded crowns, were on many church facades. In the twelfth century, the Catholic Church elevated them to holiness.

After a long uphill walk, we looked forward to a rest in the charming café, where we enjoyed coffee and pastries. On a nice summer day, we would sit outside on the terrace and savor the grand panoramic view of the city with the many church steeples, the mighty cathedral, and a sea of red roofs reflecting the sunshine. At moments like this, I couldn't help but think of the dire conditions my family was in at Briest, and how I wished I could share the beauty with mother. If she were only allowed to travel. I felt guilty for my contentedness. I was homesick for my family.

East Germany's Dilemma

The situation in East Germany was appalling. Russia had taken everything they could get their hands on. Factories were dismantled, and only the old worn-out machinery was left for the Germans. The startup for them was sad and slow. How could they make improvements when there wasn't a nail or screw in the stores? It was very disheartening, not just for the younger generation, but for everyone. The war was over, and people looked for a new beginning. Eyeing West Germany and her visible improvements lured many to leave. Food was still scarce, and they had ration cards for many more years. Coffee was a novelty. Packages from West Germany were opened and censored. Items were often stolen. The economy had to feed the occupying troops, and there were many of them in garrisons and camps.

Even though the border between the two Germanys was established, it wasn't fortified until a few years later. In these first years after the war, separated families tried to get back together. People became resourceful. Illegal border crossings couldn't be prevented. East Germany was still establishing its new country status. Berlin was divided into sectors, with each ally occupying a section, but the city remained open. People went back and forth between the sectors. It was easy; all one had to do was hop onto the subway and ride to the West sector, or just walk. Many worked in one and lived in the other. People saw the opportunities in West Berlin and in West Germany in general, especially the young. People constantly moved.

East Germany became stressed. The workforce was leaving, and in 1961 the wall was built between the two sectors in Berlin, dividing it essentially into the American and Russian sectors. This move was so unexpected that it shocked everyone. The East German government had called upon anyone who had equipment. With a sizeable workforce that was mobilized quickly, the wall was practically built in a day. This was the final attempt of the East to seal the border and keep people from leaving. West Berlin became isolated from the rest of West Germany. Only a few trains a day were allowed from West Germany to pass through East Germany territory to connect with West Berlin. The doors of the train were locked the minute they crossed the border into East Germany, and no one could get off or on. The main highway to Berlin was also monitored. A network of checkpoints controlled the motorists from West Germany who used it. A few checkpoints within the city were established, the most famous one being "Checkpoint Charlie," so named by the West. Buildings on the East side along this wall were vacated, and the windows facing the wall were sealed. The airport in West Berlin became the most important lifeline. The Brandenburg Gate ended up in East Germany.

My First Visit Back to East Germany - 1947

I shortly realized that the eight weeks I had spent with my mother and siblings weren't long enough. I missed them terribly. Of course, I knew how lucky I was to be where I was, but in my heart I wanted to be with them. Over a year had gone by. It was still possible to cross the border illegally. I had kept my ears open about illegal crossings, and where the best areas were located. A surprising number of people still went back and forth, and I toyed with the idea of going back for a visit.

Bamberg was not very far from the border, only a two- or three-hour train ride. I hoped my past experience was helpful and that this time I wouldn't encounter Russian soldiers if I were caught. A flash of that frightful night went through my mind. By now, East Germany had her own police force and border patrols.

I looked at a more southern route, always thinking to have as much daylight as possible for the walk across the border. Though mother knew about my pending trip, I couldn't set a date. I had to play it by ear. There wasn't much to prepare; as long as I had my train fare and a sandwich or two, I was ready to go on any day with good weather.

I left on the earliest train, and disembarked at the last station before the border. Not many people were around, but I needed directions and information about the border patrols and the type of border. How would I know if I were across? Was it a road, a creek, or just woods? I followed an elderly woman, and after catching up with her, I told her about my intentions. She didn't have much to say, but pointed ahead down the road, indicating further along the location of a West German border patrol station. This seemed the best news. Actually, this was the place to avoid; they were there to keep people from crossing the border. I knew I would be pressing my luck. My plan was to go right up to them and ask for the best place to cross. I somehow felt that they would let me go. I had my little story ready for them. All I needed was to get safely to the other side and not to be seen by East German patrols.

Walking at a brisk pace, I headed straight for the West German patrol station. The road was just an ordinary country road with a narrow footpath on one side. I was very much in the open, and a warm breeze fanned my face. The day had turned out nice and sunny. Then I saw in the distance a little wooden cabin; this could be it. I wasn't really frightened, but I was apprehensive, and my heart was beating faster.

No one seemed to be around. Was this my lucky day? But then I saw two young men inside, probably taking a break. I didn't have to explain very much, as they knew what I was up to. Of course, they warned me that it was illegal to cross the border, but they didn't stop me. They even suggested crossing in a wooded area farther down. I had to walk a short distance to find the spot. It would have been helpful if there were border markings, since it was hard to know where I really was. I was following tracks, and was pretty sure they would lead to the border or some kind of crossing, and indeed they led right across the border. When I came to an unpaved road, I knew that had to be the other side. It was scary walking along this deserted border road. My main thought was to stay out of sight. The chance of meeting a guard was obvious; he could be walking or perhaps on a bicycle. I tried to make as little noise as possible. At times, I stepped off the road and walked near trees that lined the roadside. It was very quiet;

my ears were strained for any sounds. I suspected if a guard came on foot, I would have time to hide. The terrain was hilly, and I couldn't see very far ahead. I hoped that I had crossed at the right place, and this road would lead me to a village; I remembered the area on the map that I had studied. But it was still a gamble. Finally, with a big sigh of relief, I saw the first houses. Instinctively, my pace increased. This was my last stretch, and I prayed that this was the place on the map with a train station.

People in this little village appeared to be used to illegal travelers. When I asked about the train station, they were friendly and helpful, and even hinted to act casual if I met a soldier; soldiers often checked the train station. I had only a small bag, and looked like one of the villagers. By this time, the guards on the East side were also Germans. This new division of Germany made for some unnatural circumstances. It was possible that one soldier could have a cousin in the village right across the border, but now he would have to treat him as a foreigner and arrest him by law if he came to visit illegally. Anyone caught by the border patrols was at risk for being sent back. I made it to the train station, and the train came in the late afternoon. From here it was a long way to Tangerhütte. I spent part of the night in a railroad station, and arrived in Tangerhütte the next day.

It was wonderful to be with my family again. Christa worked in the neighboring village, and Werner lived with mother. No one questioned my being there. The little towns and villages had recently established and organized their governments. Briest was a very small village, and no one cared how I arrived there; many people didn't know me.

The biggest thrill was seeing Cousin Sigismund, who had just returned from Russia where he had been held for almost three years. When he was released from the Russian camp, he found that he couldn't return to his hometown, and did not know where his family had relocated. He remembered his sister Brigitta's address in Bamberg and sent a telegram. When the mailman brought his telegram, I was home to receive it. How can anyone forget a moment like that? To think it was I who first knew of his homecoming.

The family had no knowledge of whether he was still alive. Aunt Adelheid had been desperate, not knowing what happened to her boys. She even consulted a clairvoyant, a man who lived in a neighboring town. He did tell her that he felt vibes of Sigismund, but nothing with Hans Dietrich, the seventeen-year-old who had been drafted and was missing in the war.

Now Sigismund, of course, wanted to be with his parents. He went to Briest where they had been relocated. I was very excited to see him again. It was a heartwarming reunion, and I rejoiced with them. Recounting some of our survival experiences reminded us how precious life is. He had endured the Russian camps and the cold winters. He left as a boy of fourteen and came back a man. We had both grown up in a hurry.

My other cousins, Arno and Lothar, from Aunt Lydia and Uncle Ewald, were also living in the big von Bismarck manor, making it easy for all of us to get together. This time was very special and wonderful, since it was the first time ever that six of us cousins were all together, including Christa and Werner.

Sigismund faced the same dilemma I had; where to start and tackle a plan for the future. To stay in East Germany meant little advancement unless he joined the Communist Party. Going back to school was not possible unless one lived in a bigger city. Who could support that? Aunt Adelheid and Uncle Hans had already been working secretly on a plan to leave East Germany and move in with their daughter Elisabeth in the West. Sigismund's advantage was that his older sisters were already well established in West Germany. Brigitta was in Bamberg, and Elisabeth was married to a protestant minister near Heidelberg. The opportunities between East and West were like day and night. He would have help to start anew if he could find a way to West Germany.

My two weeks in Briest went by much too fast. A few days before my return back to Bamberg, Sigismund told me, "I have decided to go with you. My parents and I have gone back and forth with this all week. It'll be hard to leave them so soon, but we decided I should go with you." I wasn't surprised since the subject had come up a few times, but there was always the issue of not parting with the parents.

I dreaded the return. I was always afraid of what the soldiers would do to me if I should get caught. There was no guarantee that it would go well again. Now I was glad to have a companion. Since Sigismund's experiences in the camp, the border crossing might seem just like a stroll in the park to him. He had faced wolves in Siberia; what could be worse than that? Sigismund was willing to take the chance of being caught.

The distance to the border was always important to me. We made a plan and searched for a town close to the border. Wherever we crossed, once on the other side we would have to take the train. This time, I picked a place more in the middle of the border. We needed to travel as close as possible to the border so we wouldn't have to walk very far.

Saying good-bye was never easy for me. I promised to come back soon. Mother's sadness weighed on my mind. Her life had been shattered, but she had to go on; she had to work. I was thankful Werner was still with her, and that they had become very close.

Sigismund and I were sitting on the floor in the crowded train station in Magdeburg waiting for our connection when Sigismund suddenly discovered that his wallet with his ticket and money was missing. It was in his back pocket, and of course our first instinct was to look all around us; it had been stolen. We didn't know what to do; he was crushed. I didn't have any East German Marks to help him out. I had left the rest of mine with mother. The whole incident seemed unreal. We had planned and planned, and he was so looking forward to seeing his sisters and starting his new future. He decided to go back to his parents. I had been delighted that I had company, and now I had to adjust to this disaster.

I was on my own again. I didn't cross in the same place as I had previously. People were always very helpful; they pointed me in the right direction and explained the area a bit. They told me to find a little river, which would be the border. I was in an open field area, and hadn't counted on wading through a creek. Thankfully it wasn't very deep. I took off my shoes and stockings and looked for a shallow spot.

One never knew when starting out what the border crossing situation would be. While I dried my feet and put my shoes back on, a West German border patrolman was heading straight for me. In my excitement, I was almost ready to hug him, since I now knew I had made it safely across. I told him that I was glad that he was a West German guard. He explained that he actually had to arrest me because I had no identification to prove that I lived in Bamberg. I hadn't dared to take my identification passport with me when I left; it was a very precious item. I couldn't take the chance of having it stolen or taken away from me. I don't know if he believed the emotional story I told him, but he eventually let me go.

The 1948 Monetary Reform

The currency was a nightmare; both Germanys were still using the old currency. Coins became rare, and postage stamps were used as change. Often, the stamps were so grimy that one couldn't identify the value. Finally, in 1948, to everyone's relief, the monetary reform took place. Everyone received forty Marks. It was the long awaited break. The new crisp bills felt good in our hands; this was real money. No more paying with postage stamps in the milk store. Almost immediately, the stores had things we hadn't seen since before the war. People couldn't restrain themselves; they bought things just because they were available. It was as if this was only a one-time deal, and it would go away again. I saw a lady buy a glass platter and spend a good part of her new money. The slow recovery of the country began.

The construction of Brigitta and George's house now became their first priority. George had served his two years as laborer, and was glad to be hired again by his former tobacco company and reinstated as salesman. He happily went on the road connecting with former businesses and seeing old friends. He was his old jolly self again doing what he loved best.

After the monetary reform, obtaining loans for construction and material was easier and more available. They hired an architect and had plans drawn up for their new house. After three and a half years, they moved into their new home.

During this time, I had learned to cook, take care of the children, do the laundry by hand as it was done in those days, and generally had become Brigitta's housekeeper.

Visiting Family in East Germany, 1948

Just before the monetary reform, I planned another illegal trip to East Germany. This time Brigitta thought I should take her son Rainer with me so he could visit with her parents, Aunt Adelheid and Uncle Hans. Rainer was about five years old.

As I had before, we set out by train again. I planned to cross at a slightly different place than on my previous trip. My responsibility for Rainer meant I would not take many chances. I planned to cross the border at night or early morning. I didn't want to stay one night with him in a railroad station. We made it to the border all right, but it was a dark night; I hadn't counted on the weather with no stars or moon. I didn't want to walk into the dark woods and become lost. The West German border patrol was friendly, and pointed to the direction I needed to travel. They let us stay awhile in their guard shack while I struggled with the decision of what to do with this black night. I was worried that Rainer might get scared and become homesick. I was scared, too, and decided to take the next train and go back. But that didn't deter me from trying again soon. We waited only a few days and tried again. Brigitta still wanted me to take Rainer. I hoped she would have second thoughts about this trip, as I explained the situation and being in constant danger.

From our false start a few days earlier, I knew a little about the border at our planned crossing location. I planned to arrive there in the late afternoon so we wouldn't have to wait too long. My plan was to start before dawn, as soon as there was enough light to see where we were going. I didn't want to walk with him in the middle of the night. This time, I walked right up to the West German Border Patrol shelter, since it had worked well a few days before. I was hoping they would remember me, especially with a little boy.

They didn't seem surprised; it was strange that they didn't discourage me. I asked about activities on the other side, and if they had any idea when the guards didn't seem to be around. This must have been a routine illegal crossing with the blessings of the West German border patrol. Villages that lay right at the border were the best places, but often there was no easy way to get to them without being seen, due to open areas like fields.

Some villagers on either side were daring enough to help people across for a fee. They knew all the little roads and paths, and in many places the border was between two close villages. The German guards described what the border would be; there were no signs and only woods.

The West German guards knew about what time the East German patrols made their rounds in the area. After they had gone, we set out to cross the border nearby. It was very quiet, and I told Rainer that it would be better not to talk. Stepping very carefully and avoiding anything on the path that could make noise, we reached the other side. I was very grateful to the West German guards for describing the border.

We came to a dirt road which the guards had indicated was the East German side, and going uphill would be the right direction. All we had to do was follow a well-trod path. To avoid the open road, we walked on the side amongst the trees; these low evergreens provided the screening we needed. Interestingly, there was already a path people had made before us. It zigzagged in and out and around trees; we just followed the path. We were never very far from the road. Rainer was a wonderful little travel companion, and he never complained. He didn't know what was at stake, but he must have sensed the risk we were taking. I will never forget when I saw what might be a person in the road and halted. I didn't want to get caught now. I asked Rainer, "Look, is that a man?" pointing into the direction. But he trustingly assured me, "No Aunt Ingrid, it is only a tree." It really mattered what Rainer saw at this moment; I was so glad that he wasn't frightened.

We were still going uphill on the road when streaks of pale yellow appeared in the sky; the early morning hours approached. A few times, men on bicycles going to work came whizzing down the bumpy dirt road. We crouched down or just stood still behind a tree or bush, and let them pass. This gave me an indication that there were villages nearby. Sure enough, when we reached the top of the hill, a plateau spread out in front of us with the first houses of a little farming village.

By now, it was early morning and a small open area of farmland lay between us and a house. There was no place to hide, not even a tree. I was hoping that no East German soldiers were around at this early-morning hour. We walked fast, and aimed for the nearest farmhouse. We crossed the farmyard and entered from the back of the house, and startled an unsuspecting woman in her kitchen. I apologized for our intrusion, and told her that I wanted to go to the railroad station. She was friendly, and seeing Rainer with me probably helped. I asked about the next train station, and was happy to hear that there was one at the bottom of the hill on the opposite side from where we came. The biggest hurdle seemed to be behind us. She assured me that there was a train running in the early afternoon.

The woman was elderly, and must have felt sorry for us. She invited us to stay in her house until it was time to leave for the train station. She made a milk soup for us, and then offered us a sofa where we both slept. It was still very early in the morning, and I gladly accepted her offer; we were both tired. Rainer was wonderful; he was my little buddy and I was thankful that he never complained. I didn't talk about the consequences if we would be caught, and instead made it a game of hide-and-seek. The woman told me all she knew about the border guards and that they in fact checked the train station. That was my only way to travel, so I had to take my chances. The train station was a little brick building with just one large room. I bought our tickets, and then we sat close and inconspicuously together on the floor. A young border guard did come in and walk around, asking some people for identification. My heart was pounding. I busied myself with Rainer and avoided looking at him, and he never asked me. I was very glad when finally the train came and we were on our way to Tangerhütte. Of course, no one was at the train station to greet us in Tangerhutte, since they didn't know when to expect us. We walked to Briest and surprised them.

Rainer had to get to know his grandparents again. He had

only been two years old when they last saw each other. Of course, he couldn't remember them. Soon, little playmates showed up. And there were all the other relatives whom he could visit.

The days I spent with my mother were very precious; we made every minute count. The loss of father and our homeland weighed heavily on her. Adjusting to the life that was forced on her was a bridge she had trouble crossing. The time since this tragedy only a few years ago hadn't been long enough to heal her broken heart. We talked about the good years at home. So many things I wanted to know. I was sixteen when we were separated, and I knew so little about the family and the relatives. We often stayed up late talking.

During my visit, Aunt Adelheid considered going back with us to visit her daughters in West Germany. It was hard enough for me to agree to take Rainer with me, but to take Aunt Adelheid back with me was a risk I didn't want to take. But she decided she wanted to travel with me. She was in touch with a family in the southern part in Thuringia who lived very close to the border. She contacted them and asked them to find someone to help us get across the border there. All this was quickly arranged. With poor train connections, it took us more than half a day to get there. We hadn't counted on staying overnight, but it turned out that the family could only connect us with a so-called "guide" later in the evening. A plan was worked out to start early the next morning and meet this man at a designated place. I was very glad that the responsibility of transferring us all across the border was taken off my shoulders. This man did this for a fee, and sounded confident.

He led us on a very narrow path through dense woods; it must have been his own secret path. Rainer and I already knew to be quiet. Rainer was a great little trooper again, and probably thought we were playing hide-and-seek. We made it across the border, but continued walking through woods until we reached a village. From there we took the train to Bamberg. Aunt Adelheid had a wonderful time visiting her daughters and enjoying the West German life. Even though many items were still rationed in the West, there were different items available, and most important, people were free.

The time came for Aunt Adelheid to return to East Germany. She was on her own now, and frightened, but she had to go back. I went with her to the spot at the border where I had crossed. It was still fresh in my mind, but that was as far as I would go. She was not as lucky as Rainer and I were; she was caught on the East German side. She was held up and interrogated, but eventually let go. It was an ordeal she talked about for a long time. During that time many people were still crossing the border illegally, just like we did. If they had put all the ones who were caught into jail, they probably wouldn't have had enough jails.

Even though the city of Berlin was encircled by the East German border, the four sectors of the allies inside Berlin were without borders; people could still travel back and forth from sector to sector. The subways went in all directions. I recall Cousin Arno telling me his story about how he and his fiancé crossed into West Berlin by subway, and then sat all night on a bench deciding whether to stay or go back. The next morning they went back. They couldn't make the break from their families.

The American sector was the favorite one, and every day people left East Germany to find a place in West Berlin. From there these people would try to leave Berlin to go to West Germany by train or airplane; many to reunite with family or to just leave the East Block.

Stepping Out on My Own

My stay with Brigitta and George eventually came to an end, and I started out on my own. Luckily, I could keep my room. Apartments and rooms were still impossible to find. More than anything else, I wanted to get ahead in my life. I had enrolled in secretarial evening courses, and even learned English stenography using the German symbols. At night, I pounded away on a rented typewriter. I needed to become proficient in typing if I wanted to obtain an office job. I had to find work to support myself. Having been tied down with Brigitta's family, I didn't really make any money. I had worked for room and board.

Anna Keller was overwhelmed by the thought of opening up

her bakery again. Times were getting better, but she had lost her courage to tackle the start-up. All the rooms for her needed help were taken, and besides, she was not that young anymore. She decided to lease it. Finding someone to step into her shoes wasn't hard; there were so many refugees who looked for a new beginning. She soon found a baker to take it over. His idea was also to have a little café.

Up to now I had held on to my little room, but had to give it up when this change took place. My paramount worry now was to find a room. I searched for weeks, going to city agencies; searching in the paper was useless. Finally, the mother of a friend came to my rescue. She worked for American military dependents, and suggested I should find a babysitting job; she was willing to help me with her connections. The German government had built housing for the American dependents near the garrisons on the outer perimeter of the city, which was where she worked. Her suggestion was a blessing in disguise. I met the Garrison family, Dorothy and Leonard, and their three little children, Susie, Kathleen, and David; the latter was just six months old.

This was a big change. I accepted the job just to have a room. On the top floor of these buildings were rooms, and the Garrisons offered me one. I felt this was the best I could do for the moment. My relationship with the Garrisons worked out fine. I had meals and a place to stay, and on top of it, I improved my English. My school English was very good and a big help, but I needed more conversation English. Mabel Clark, Dorothy's mother, had come from Ohio to visit the family and to see her new grandson. She had fallen while she was there and broken her hip, and had to extend her stay. This was the start of my connection that led to America. She was always around when I was there, and we had many interesting conversations. She was sympathetic to the hand that fate had dealt me. But I don't think she really comprehended the tragedy of losing my father, home, and homeland. People who hadn't suffered much during and after the war and now had to deal with all the refugees often didn't have much sympathy. They looked down on the East German refugees, and many times didn't treat them as equals. I had a boyfriend at one time who wanted me to meet his family at a family celebration. They were local Bambergers, and of course all talked with the Bavarian dialect. There I was with my regular high German dialect, a dead giveaway that I was from the East. I was the "Fluechtlings Madla," the refugee girl. They were pleasant, but at that moment it raised my self-worth; I knew I would never fit in. They had a well-established business and I probably would have had a good life.

Mabel Clark told me about her home in Columbus, Ohio, and offered to help me if I wanted to immigrate to the United States. This seemed like a farfetched unattainable idea; it had never entered my mind. When she eventually left after a few months, we agreed to keep in touch. The Garrisons' military tour in Germany finished in about six months, and my babysitting job came to an end.

Another door opened when I met the Crowells, Bill and Evelyn. They lived in a housing block in the city which had been vacated by the Germans. I stayed with the Crowell's girls when the parents were traveling; the twin girls Norma and Nancy were about 10 years old. I also was offered a room in their house, which I desperately needed after the Garrisons left. We became good friends and they often invited me to have dinner with them. By this time, I had an office position. It was great to be back in the city now and closer to my friends.

Visits to East Germany in the 1950s

Later, as the border became more regulated, my family visits to East Germany became a different process. The border went from north to south, and several railway crossing points had been established. Crossing points also were established for a few throughways for automobiles, mainly the autobahn (a highway built during the Hitler regime). The no-man's land became heavily fortified with double fences, dogs, and watchtowers; illegal crossings became almost impossible.

Mother then had to apply for a permit at the local police station that would allow me to cross legally. Sometimes this took many weeks. I had to plan my vacation far ahead. With my permit in hand, I was allowed to enter the country. I could never bear to think of East Germany as another country, but it now had its own government and currency. The local police department was very powerful. They decided who would get a permit; everyone was investigated. Their spy network was unbelievably extensive. I always went by train. The permit was for a certain border crossing, which I could determine ahead of time. The time of my stay was limited by the government; usually three weeks. But I never had much more vacation, so it didn't present a problem for me.

The trip was always stressful at the border; one was at the mercy of the border control police. The train I used always arrived at the border at midnight, an eerie time when one would rather sleep than be confronted with the menacing border control. The train doors were locked, and guards walked outside along the train. Inside the compartments, the passengers barely breathed, anxiety and fear were written all over their faces. Everyone hoped that it would go smoothly and that they weren't asked to open their suitcases and bags. There were so many items which were not allowed to be brought into the country; cigarettes and coffee were always forbidden.

The first soldiers who went through the train were looking for hidden things in the compartments like books and newspapers; they looked under the seats and opened the ceilings. Their behavior was

The Buchholz children, Ingrid, Werner, and Christa, 1940s.

impersonal and unfriendly. I always had the feeling that they enjoyed being so powerful.

Then came the person who checked the passports and permits. Another one came and asked if anyone wanted to exchange money. They loved to get the West German Mark, which they exchanged one to one, a poor exchange since at other places one could get a much better exchange rate. The East German Mark had almost no value outside East Germany.

Once all this was done, one would anxiously look out of the window to see if the guards were getting off the train. Finally, the station master would sound the whistle and everyone breathed a sigh of relief. The doors were unlocked, and slowly the train started moving. People settled back into the seats and relaxed, and a swell of conversation would start as if a great battle had been won.

After arriving at the destination, the first step was to go to the local bank and exchange a certain amount of money, a daily rate fixed by the government; most times it was 25.00 DM per day. With this receipt, one had to go to the police station and register. In all the years up to the 1980s, I was only allowed to travel about in the county of Tangerhütte, but I always applied also for a stay with my sister Christa in Reichenbach, a town near the Czech border. Once arriving there, I had to register immediately at their police station.

On all my visits to my sister in Reichenbach, my mother came, too. We wanted to spend as much time as possible together. Later, on trips from the United States, I had my children with me. Only on my last trip, when mother was already ill, did I go alone. It was in April of 1979. She passed away in 1980.

My Later Bamberg Years

The Crowells were still in Bamberg, but their tour was coming to an end. It was again time for me to move on and find a place to live. The situation with available housing hadn't changed at all in the city. City agencies weren't very helpful. One couldn't blame them, since it was very hard to find a place. Eventually, with help, I found a room in an older Victorian house. It had been a one-family home, but with the rationing of living space by the government, all the housing was registered with a city agency. The family, already tenants, had to give up a room.

I was excited to have my own four walls. It had been an exhausting effort, with much running around to reach this point. The room was empty, with only a large brown tile stove in one corner; a large window faced the garden. I quickly bought a sleep sofa and a wardrobe to start with. The occupants of the house were a pleasant family, with older parents and a young daughter and her child. We had to share the bathroom which was off the main foyer. Not having my own bathroom was hard to adjust to, but I had known worse situations; and having a place to stay was primary. I had a hot plate, and often bought already prepared food on the way home. I also had to buy coal to heat the room. They gave me a corner in the cellar where I could keep the coal, and also my bicycle. I soon found out as it got colder that the big window was not very tight; it didn't have drapes or any kind of shutters. The stove took forever to heat the large room, which also had a very high ceiling. I dreaded the winter, coming home from work to a cold room, and starting this monster of a stove. As it became really cold, the landlady offered to start the stove, probably out of sheer pity. This was a big help, but despite it all, the room was never warm enough when I came home. It was the warmest when I woke in the morning and readied for work. It took actually all night to warm up the room. My thick feather quilt kept me warm in bed. Usually, I went early to bed just to keep warm.

Soon after starting my office job I met Lisa. We worked in the same building and became good friends. She lived with her parents close to the workplace. The engineering offices were at the outskirts of the city and in one part of the garrisons. I had to travel quite a distance. In the winter and on bad weather days, I took a bus, but in the summer I rode my bicycle. I never really cared for bicycling to work; sometimes I felt like the Flying Dutchman with my wide skirt blowing in the wind. Girls didn't wear pants in those days.

Lisa's parents welcomed me into their midst, and I often spent weekends with them. Sunday was always a special day; many times we went on long walks with her parents. Lisa and I usually planned something for Saturday evening; often we had dates.

Bamberg, actually in Franconia, which is the northern part of Bavaria, was a jewel to love and explore. It had many wonderful sights. Old churches and historical building were hidden in corners and narrow side streets where one would never go unless one was looking for antiques, or simply exploring. Old houses had faded frescos on still-handsome facades. It was never boring, even if one saw the same places again after a while.

The symbol of the city was the statue of the "Bamberger Reiter" (Bamberger Rider) in the cathedral on a high wall: a knight on horseback. To preserve the statue during the war years, the city had ordered it encased in cement. The city celebrated when finally, after a few years, the encasement was removed, and one could again view this famous statue.

The stroll to a neighboring village wasn't very far. The little restaurants along the way resembled pubs more than regular restaurants; they all served beer for the thirsty wanderer. Oftentimes, tables were set up in their backyards, where apple trees offered shade. Sometimes a butcher owned the restaurant, and the food was simple and delicious; the sausages were made from one of their secret recipes.

Once in a while, we would go to a restaurant that specialized in serving carp. These were popular places that had their own fish ponds; you could practically pick out the fish you wanted to eat. It would then be served whole if one wanted a whole one, or a half. The front part was always served with its enormous head on. If Lisa and I stayed out late, I went home with her and slept on the sofa in her room; if we had been on dates we had lots to talk about.

It was 1954 when Marianne joined our twosome. She worked as a translator-secretary in a military office for Dependents' Affairs. After the end of the war, the American Field Service had established student exchanges. Marianne had already spent a year in the States as a high school exchange student. Her aim was to go back to America. The American family had promised to sponsor her. I admired her for the future plans she had already made. She was a real local, a "Bamberger," and her parents owned a butcher shop. Many times, Lisa and I stopped by for a crusty roll with succulent Leberkäs, a meat pudding baked to perfection that tasted best when warm. Marianne's mother, who always seemed to be behind the counter, greeted us with a big smile. There was no way that she would let us leave without the roll. With big grins on our faces, we retreated almost on tiptoes to the back of the store, and eagerly devoured our rolls, juices running down our chins.

Marianne introduced us to the American-German Friendship Club. The club was founded to further good relationships with the Germans. She had lots of contacts, and I found meeting some of her friends interesting. People met in one of the nicer restaurants, which had opened its doors to this group. Young American couples and ser-vicemen joined young Germans, and exchanged their views over a beer or glass of wine.

Marianne knew how to organize. She loved activities, and one day surprised us with passes to the tennis courts on the military base. How could we not take advantage of this wonderful opportunity? Even though none of us had ever played tennis, we wanted to learn, and marched right to the next sport shop to buy a tennis racquet. The German Tennis Club in Bamberg was quite exclusive, and too expensive for us to even think of joining. But this was free, and soon I began bringing my tennis things to work. We would play with such enthusiasm that only the darkness could make us quit. This was a wonderful time. The military base courts became quite popular, and more Germans came to play.

A Trip to Paris

By now it was ten years after the war. Life in West Germany was upbeat, and the rebuilding of cities was in full swing. The economy was doing well and people traveled again; we wanted to spread our wings, too. We planned a trip to Paris. Lisa was engaged to a service man, a young lawyer who had a Volkswagen. He was easily persuaded to drive; besides he wanted to see Paris as much as we did. We left on a Friday right after work. To save time, I brought all my travel things to the office with me so we would travel to Paris as fast as possible. Of

Ingrid with glider, Bamberg, 1940s.

course, it meant traveling part of the night. Since neither Lisa nor I could drive, we stopped at the roadside a few times to give the driver a break, and then pushed on again.

We arrived early in the morning, with Paris waking up. We didn't know what to expect. It probably was the quietest time of the whole night after even the last straggler had found his way home. Where was all the bustle? We thought Paris never slept. We had planned to stay in the Montmartre area to see and experience the Bohemian life. Our first task was to find a hotel. Would it be possible to find something this early in the morning, when check-in time was much later? We had to give it a try. Even though we wanted to keep on going, our bodies gave us little signs of weariness. The driver certainly needed a chance to relax and sleep a few hours.

We roused a sleepy concierge in the lobby of a little hotel. His disheveled looks and the musty smell of the place quickly changed our minds. We looked around for another place, and decided on one not far from the first hotel. To our surprise, the same man was there. We were baffled. Was he in charge of this hotel, too? We quickly made up our minds because we needed a place to stay. This was not the right time of the day to get into a hotel, but luckily we persuaded this man, with a tip, to give us rooms. We didn't have much money and certainly didn't want to spend it on fancy hotel rooms.

I soon discovered that I didn't have my wallet; I was crushed. I had left it in my desk drawer in the office—which now meant I had no money. It put a damper on my excitement. Borrowing money now from my friends was not what I had expected. We rested just for a little while, and off we went to conquer Paris. We had to fit as much as possible into the day.

We did not have much time for art galleries, but made a special trip to the Louvre; of course we had to see the Mona Lisa. What a surprise: here we were in front of the real wonderful painting and she was smiling on us—we had expected the painting to be so much larger. It was a very quick visit, and we promised ourselves the next time we were in Paris we would spend more time in the Louvre. Now it was nearly noon; the Eiffel Tower moved up on our list. The day was bright and sunny and the view was fantastic, an amazing panorama. The Seine wound through the city; it all seemed so perfect. We didn't want to leave this place so soon. Then, one of us had the spontaneous idea to have dinner in the tower restaurant and enjoy this time a little longer.

Thinking of food made us all of a sudden very hungry. We realized that we had not eaten anything except some snacks we had brought. Our quest to see as much as possible didn't leave room for taking time out to eat. We soon were seated in an elegant restaurant, and a stern-looking waiter handed us the menu. Eagerly, we tried to read it, but mostly had to guess, with the little French we knew. What a shock when we saw the prices; our minds worked fast converting the money. We looked at each other in disbelief. The waiter had already brought us bread, which we had shamelessly wolfed down in two minutes. We couldn't walk out now, so we timidly ordered. The soup, our first course, arrived. By then, we had gathered enough courage to tell the waiter to cancel the rest of our meal. It was an embarrassing situation; we kept apologizing in French. I felt like crawling under the table or vanishing into thin air.

To save even more money, Lisa suggested walking down the stairs of the Eiffel Tower instead of taking the elevator. I knew I would have a hard time doing that, and elected to be last. Looking at the others in front of me was the motivation that kept me going. It was a terrifying experience. The stairs were metal grids, and open so one could see the ground below all the time. The bottom didn't seem to come any closer. I didn't want to look down, but I had to for fear of missing the next step and sailing down to my death. My knees were trembling. I was so glad to finally have solid ground under my feet again!

Everyone who had been in Paris talked about the Follies Bergeres at the Moulin Rouge. It was an elaborate stage show with topless dancers, and all the rage at the time. We were anxious to find out how we could get tickets. The ticket office was our first try. Having the car was great, and we would have never been able to get around quickly without it. We received a lucky break. We met up with three American ladies who were trying to sell their husbands' tickets. The husbands didn't want to see the show. Of course, later in the show they sat right next to us.

This was a first for Lisa and I; we had no idea what to expect. We had never been to a nightclub, let alone to see a performance like this. Now that we had the tickets stashed away, there was still time to find the much-recommended perfume store. Perfume comes to mind when one thinks of Paris. We wanted to give it a try. After much searching, we finally located the store. Our eyes lit up as we entered the store. It was an elegant place with lots of light, sparkling mirrors on the walls, perfume bottles of all shapes and forms lined up on glass shelves, and the fragrance was enticing. A friendly hostess seated us at a counter, and soon a salesperson—or probably more likely an expert—started to show us perfumes which would enhance and complement our personalities. I sat there thinking how to define my personality—how could she know? It was hard to choose; they all smelled fantastic. After spraying and dabbing perfumes on our hands and arms, we could only guess which we thought was the right one. Finally, we left happily with our purchase beautifully wrapped.

We still managed to find our way into a nightclub, where upon entering, we were hit over the head with a plastic bat; it seemed to be an initiation. It was a rustic place with candles here and there, and a very subdued atmosphere. Obviously, this wasn't a place where tourists stopped by. My eyes took in the scene quickly, wondering if we should stay. Were these people artists, or just vagabonds? It was hard to tell. Small wine barrels had been made into seats, and larger ones became tables. A three-man band played jazz. Our wine was smooth, and just what we needed after the big event at the Moulin Rouge.

On Sunday morning, we headed for the Champs Elysees. All we wanted was to walk a few blocks so we could say we had been there. Stopping at a bistro—even the name had a wonderful ring to it—we bought a baguette and cheese to eat later. The gorgeous fashion displays in the windows made us wish we had more time, but we had to move on. The Arc d' Triomphe was another famous landmark in Paris that we had to see. Later, we had to make a last dash to Sacre Coeur to visit the well-known cathedral. Soon the time came for our departure. Happy and exhausted, we started on our drive home.

chapter fourteen

MAKING PLANS FOR AMERICA

In 1955, my friend Lisa and her fiancé were planning for a future in America. Marianne had already been working on her return to the States. Both my best friends had big plans. They knew about my invitation from Mabel Clark in Ohio; we were still corresponding. If I wanted to take that leap across the ocean, I needed a sponsor, and she would be my link. We spent hours spinning yarns on how wonderful it would be to meet again in America. Of course, that meant I would immigrate, too. It was terribly exciting, and I kept thinking, would it really be possible that I, after all I had been through, might end up in America? The thought seemed overwhelming, especially when I considered my family in East Germany. The idea of not seeing my mother, Christa, and Werner for what might be years felt like a hurdle I couldn't clear. They would never be able to visit me in the U.S. As much as I wanted to go, the thought of how to tell my family put a damper on the idea.

These plans all sounded great, but I hadn't even asked Mabel Clark if she was still willing to sponsor me. She was getting on in years, and perhaps there might be an age limit or a last-minute change of mind. Half-heartedly, I told her about my intentions; she replied immediately with an enthusiastic letter, ready to help me. What a surprise; I couldn't wait to tell my friends. I wanted to hop on my bicycle right away as if it couldn't wait until the next morning. Up to now I had treated all this quite lightly, but now all of a sudden it looked like a good possibility. When I told my friends the next morning, they practically jumped up and down and really encouraged me to get serious. After that, our lives weren't the same; we went to work as usual, but now we had so much more on our minds. Our threesome often met after work to sit and talk about our plans and ideas.

Lisa spent more time with her fiancé making plans for a future living in Baltimore. Marianne was gung-ho with big plans to stay in New York City. To her, that was the place to start. It seemed very courageous to me, but she knew what she wanted.

I started to find out what was required to immigrate, and realized that I had an advantage through immigrating on a refugee quota. This was supposed to make it even easier. It was truly the hardest decision I had ever made. Mabel Clark started the paperwork at her end by connecting with the right people to help her; papers went back and forth.

I was astonished at how thoroughly I was investigated by the American government. I had an interview with what I later found out was a CIA agent. My landlady and friends were interviewed. Probably, this attention was due to having the rest of my family in East Germany and my trips across the border. East Germany was a Communist country, and both sides were suspicious of the other.

Lastly was the heart-wrenching task of telling my mother. Am I deserting them? I asked myself that question a hundred times. I kept putting it off as many weeks went by. I couldn't leave without seeing mother; I knew I couldn't tell her in a letter.

Time went by fast. 1956 came around, and we had Marianne's going-away party; she would depart first. We celebrated with streamers, cake, and signs that we made to send her off with all our good wishes. She left in May. Soon she reported to Lisa and me all about her voyage, and meeting a distant relative from New Jersey. She sounded like her old self: positive and hopeful to settle in Manhattan. Lisa had planned to join her there while she was waiting for her fiancé to arrive. Lisa's parents were saddened and their world seemed to collapse, since much of their lives revolved around their daughter; she was the only child, and they hated to let her go. She left in late summer.

But before she left, we had a wonderful experience attending Bayreuth's Richard Wagner's Festspiele to see the opera "Parsifal." The middle intermission was stretched so that people could go for dinner and return for the final acts. I have kept the dinner menu from that evening all these years because on the menu's cover is a beautiful silk-screen print. Lisa went with her fiancé, and I had a date. Seeing this opera in Bayreuth was a once-in-a-lifetime experience.

When I stopped by Lisa's parents' apartment the day after she left, I found her mother in tears holding a little Dachshund puppy in her arms, muttering, "You are supposed to replace my Lisa? It will never do." To me she said, "I don't want the dog. How could she think this would take her place?" But she kept it and became very close to it.

Lisa's fiancé stayed behind in Bamberg to finish his tour of duty. Both of my friends had left.

Good-bye to My Family

Every year I had gone to East Germany and spent my vacation with my family. Mother was always able to obtain an entry visa for me, and I knew how much she looked forward to my visits. How would she react to my plan? I could see an unbelieving expression on her face and her eyes slowly filling up with tears. Imagining her reaction made me teary. I knew I had to work this through myself, but I also knew I could stop this process at any time. I didn't have to go; there was no pressure from anyone, and this fact was a relief. However, the upcoming visit weighed heavily on my mind, like climbing a mountain without the joy of reaching the top. Though I had mentioned the invitation from Mabel Clark before, it was taken as a gesture and not seriously considered; the idea was too far-fetched for my family to consider.

I planned a two-week trip back to East Germany. As usual, the only way for me to go was by train. Naturally, this visit wasn't the usual joyous trip. It was fall, and my mood reflected the drab gray landscape as the train rattled along on its bumpy rails. My mind was battling with what lay ahead of me. How could I tell my mother that I wanted to leave the country and leave them? Looking out of the train window, I saw that nothing had changed since my last visit. It was depressing to see houses still in ill repair and the roads in deplorable condition. I had to change trains in Magdeburg, and then in about an hour I was in Tangerhütte.

Mother met me at the train station. She was waiting at the gate behind a picket fence at the station. We waved, smiled, and then I rushed to her with my suitcase bouncing over the cobblestones. This old station seemed not to have been improved since it was built, perhaps a hundred years ago. We hugged and held hands, and quietly looked at each other. We left my suitcase with the station master to be picked up by Werner later on.

The little hamlet of Briest was about one mile from the train station. By now, I knew the routine from my previous visits; first exchanging money to pay my daily government fee, and then registering at the police department. I had to prove that the money was safely in their hands. For every day I stayed, I had to exchange a certain amount. The West German money was now more than ever very important to them. The East German Mark had little value. After all this was done, we walked arm in arm along the forest path that led from Tangerhütte to the old von Bismarck manor in Briest where mother still lived.

The forest floor was damp and covered with red and orange leaves; as if a beautiful carpet were laid out for us. Signs of fall were definitely all around. How I loved the musty smell that permeated the air; I will always remember it. The old majestic oak trees were once again getting ready for winter, dropping their fruit for the little red squirrels that were busy stashing it away for meager times.

Mother's sister Lydia also lived in the "Schloss," as everyone called the manor. I wanted to tell her first about my plan and hear her thoughts on it. Of course, it came as a total surprise to her. I waited for the right moment to tell my mother. Is there a right moment to tell your loving mother that you want to go your own way and, in addition, the way is far away, as far as America? Her first reaction was disbelief. But she knew I was serious; we talked for many hours. I so much wanted to make it easier for her, and I tried to persuade her that America wasn't out of reach anymore, assuring her that if I didn't like it I would come back. That was actually my thought all along. I knew I would always be able to make enough money to pay for my fare home.

The day came when I had to leave. We tried to be strong; a last hug and a wave from the open train window. Her figure, with her arm waving a handkerchief in her hand, is forever imprinted on my mind. I stared out of the window for a long time as the landscape rushed by faster and faster away from the one I loved most. Tears ran down my cheeks.

Final Arrangements

Returning to Bamberg, I had surprises waiting for me. Letters from the American consulate in Munich confirmed my immigration status, the date of my departure, and the ship I was to leave on. My mind raced; I only had a few weeks. If I had waited any longer I wouldn't have had time to visit mother. I was very thankful for that. But now I had to work fast. I also had an appointment with the American consulate in Munich to appear before the Consul, including a physical examination. Traveling from Bamberg to Munich couldn't be done in one day, so I had to stay overnight on the way.

I had an unusual encounter as I waited in line to see the Consul. A nice-looking young man, also waiting, started a conversation with me. We exchanged our views and reasons for immigrating. He was a student studying architecture, and was thinking about immigration, too. His parents had died in the struggle of war in East Prussia. He wasn't sure whether he really wanted to leave Germany, but thought it wouldn't hurt to get the immigration papers. I was surprised to see him again after I was finished. He had waited for me, and we both headed for the train station to go back to our respective cities. On the way, he tried to persuade me not to go. He had fallen in love with me in this extremely short period, and before we reached the station, he proposed. This unexpected turn of events stopped me on the spot. I looked at him to see if he was serious and, yes, indeed he was. His notion was that there was very little time left; it was now or never. We were both sorry that our paths hadn't crossed before. We exchanged addresses, and as he walked me to the platform and onto the train, he grabbed me and kissed me in front of all the people. Needless to say, I was very embarrassed. He stayed in Germany, and we exchanged letters for a while.

Now I had to quit my job. I had only 2 or 3 weeks. First I had to let my family know the timing of my departure. I quickly wrote a letter, since I had no way of telephoning them. People in East Germany did not have phones, except for those whose jobs required them.

It wasn't too hard to decide what to take with me; I didn't have much. I sorted out what to take and gave the rest away. I had two wooden trunks made and stenciled, and I bought suitcases. What didn't fit in there I couldn't take. I had many instructions, and one of them was not to bring new items into the country. This requirement seemed very strange. Were we labeled as refugees, supposed to arrive in rags with old towels, or perhaps with no towels? That didn't make much sense. I bought new towels and tableware, including a tablecloth and napkins. These items would help me settle in my rented room at Mabel Clark's.

A friend bought my furniture, and my landlady took my bicycle. I took a last look around my room. I wasn't sorry to relinquish it. With winter around the corner, I looked at the big coal tile stove in the corner. How glad I was not to have to heat that up again! It had been more an enemy than a friend. I spent the last few nights with Lisa's parents. They had practically adopted me after Lisa left, and I felt very much at home with them.

Departure Day

The ten years in Bamberg had slipped by with many ups and downs, and now I was about to enter a totally new phase in my life. What was lying ahead of me was a good friend who offered me a place to stay; the rest was up to me. I was confident that I would find a job, and besides that, I still planned to go to New York to be with my friends.

I had moments, however, when I thought, "It can't be true." How can I leave everyone I love and care about behind? The thought that I could come back if things didn't work out was always close to my mind, and comforting.

It was November 17, 1956. Saying good-bye is never easy. Lisa's parents and several friends came to the train station with little going-away gifts. With some last hugs and promises to write, and a last wave from the train window, I was on my way to the seaport of Bremerhafen. My trunks had been shipped ahead to the port, so all I had to worry about were my suitcases.

The train station in Bremerhafen was bustling—people were everywhere with large pieces of baggage. It looked like they were all heading the same way to the "Überseeheim," the Oversea Home. This was a place where all the immigrants were processed before boarding the various ships. There was a last-minute physical examination. I tried to read people's faces; did they look happy, or did they look anxious? I couldn't imagine that so many people wanted to leave the country. Different languages were spoken. I wondered if all of us would be on the same ship. The waiting period was not very pleasant; I had to stay in a dormitory one night with other single girls.

My dorm had a happy bunch of girls, mainly war brides, who were excited to finally be on the way to meet their husbands or husbands-to-be. They sat on the edges of their cots, celebrating, and exchanged stories with lots of giggling and laughing. It was quite late before the lights were finally turned off. I hardly slept that night. My thoughts were with my family, hoping they received my mail and knew tomorrow was sailing day. I wanted them to think of me, too.

chapter fifteen

VOYAGE

November 19th, 1956 was my sailing date. A nasty gray day greeted us the next morning. Busses lined up, shuttling us to the pier. The air was chilly, with a misty breeze that made me pull my coat a little tighter. One could almost taste the salty air; a musty smell wafted from the water and pervaded the area. Clouds hung low over the pier, and little waves moved dark circles of oil shimmering like kaleidoscopes in the murky water.

There it was—the ship that would carry me across the big ocean. I don't know what I expected, but it was not what I observed. I pictured a big white ship, perhaps with an elegant railing, but here sat this rather small, nondescript, gray ship. There was no doubt that it was my ship; it had the name "GENERAL LANGFIT' painted on the bow. This was my ship. I had written that name quite a few times on tags and papers. This wasn't at all what I had expected.

My heart sank; I was crushed, and stared at it for a long time searching for a little more positive inspiration. Perhaps it might not be so bad inside, but first impressions often matter. Not having been on a ship before, or even seen one, I had the illusion of having a wonderful time cruising across the ocean on an elegant ship. I had thought of pictures I perused in magazines. All my best clothes were in my suitcases for dressing up if circumstances required it.

The ship was one of a series built during the war as a troop transporter. If I had known that, I would have been prepared for this. Gradually, more people gathered, including families with children. Multiple languages were spoken. I could tell there were Italians, and later I found some were also Hungarians. Some of these immigrants had participated in the people's uprising against their leaders earlier in the year, and had fled to Austria for fear of being caught and killed. Hungary was the first country to revolt against the shackles of the Communist government. It was a short-lived attempt, and the Russian Army quickly squelched the uprising with a large force of power. Now some of these people, who were lucky to escape, were immigrating to America.

The crowd was getting larger and larger. I was amazed how many people wanted to board the ship. It seemed everyone had mountains of luggage. Besides the two wooden trunks that were already loaded, I had two large suitcases and two bags, more than I could really carry. Finally, the gangplank was lowered, and a wave of movement traveled through the crowd. A long line formed and slowly worked its way onto the ship. Men hoisted duffle bags onto their shoulders, and mothers held on to their children; the wait was over. For some, the hard times were behind them, and for others, they might be beginning.

I glanced a last time at the ground before I stepped on the gangplank. This was still my homeland, and the next time I stepped on ground, it would be in America. It felt like a sudden force that grabbed me. At that moment I scrutinized my big decision: was I doing the right thing? Did I know enough about America? I thought about my family; there was still time to change my mind. But I had waited for this day for a long time. I felt in my heart that this huge step into a new life wasn't just a fickle idea; I believed in a better opportunity. I had experienced the worst of life; nothing could ever be that bad again. That thought was often in back of my mind, and helped me to be strong; my past experiences had been good teachers.

Both my friends were very happy in New York, and we had planned that I would, after a while in Columbus, Ohio, move there, too. I didn't really feel that I was alone. The realization that I could go back to Germany any time, if things didn't work out, was reassuring.

I began to wonder how all the people would fit into this small ship. I found out after I boarded. Right at the entrance, men and women were separated. There were only large bunk rooms; what an upset that caused. It meant families were separated, with older boys accompanying their fathers. The situation was confusing, and people didn't know what to do with their luggage. Which family member should take care of it? It caused stress and delays and much unhappiness.

Personnel were ushering the group of women I was with into one of these huge compartments. It looked like we were in the bottom of the ship. I was shocked; immediately my dream of a great voyage ended. I recalled the interesting accounts of my friends' voyages when they traveled on regular ocean liners. I felt sad. I wondered how many more surprises were in store for us. All around the walls were three tiers of hammocks, probably the original ones the soldiers used. In the middle of the room were bunk beds fastened to the floor. I headed for the wall and claimed an upper hammock, the third tier, and wondered how I would ever climb in and out of it. My apprehension grew when I looked around; no one had much space to move about. We had to sit on our suitcases. If one wasn't a claustrophobic, this was a quick way to become one. In all the confusion I didn't realize that there were any windows. My only hope was that we didn't have to stay in here all the time. We had to look on the bright side and make this as bearable as possible. All we were able to do was place our luggage right by our bunks, and that left no room to move around. It seemed to take forever until everyone was on board and the gangplank finally was pulled up. Saddened and teary, I made my way to the deck. Slowly the ship moved away from the pier; the sound of the horn reverberated in the mist. Where was the band playing "Ade Du mein lieb Heimatland?" Where were all the well-wishers on the pier waving handkerchiefs?

People were quietly leaning on the railing, gazing into the distance. I wondered what they were thinking, what their expectations were, what they had left behind. Slowly, the skyline receded, and a gray haze soon covered my view. Shrieking gulls circled the ship, giving us a last farewell.

The weather didn't turn any better as we started under way. The sea became rough as we entered the English Channel. People were becoming seasick, and knew they would be better off outside even if it meant moving along the railing in the cold and wind. I was prepared, and made good use of the Dramamine I had packed.

We were entrusted to a motley crew of hired civilians to transfer us safely across the ocean. I was quick to sign up when they were looking for volunteers who spoke English and could type; it was my salvation. On the deck of the ship were a few cabins which were offices for the people who ran the ship. Being on top and having windows helped with seasickness, and, of course, it was wonderful to have daylight. I took my pills religiously, and never became seasick.

My job started right away. The equipment was outdated; the typewriters must have been rescued from a rubble pile. All this didn't matter, since it was a blessing to get out of the bunk room. Most of us hung around in the offices all day. The work was actually fun. We put together a newsletter every day containing some of the events that we caught on the wireless radio, the food menu, and information about activities for the next day. The menu was printed in three languages: English, German, and Italian. An Italian came in and drew little sketches on the backs of our typed sheets. Some sketches were warnings like walking carefully down the metal stairs on the ship. He did a very nice drawing of the Statue of Liberty. I remember we had heard the news on the radio that the United Nations Secretary Dag Hammerskold was killed in a plane accident in Africa. I was wondering who had ever heard of him. No one rushed us; we had all morning to finish the tasks. Two boys worked an old-fashioned copy machine that was another remnant of the past; it stood on the floor and had to be turned by hand.

Food was served cafeteria-style in a large dining room using volunteers who were recruited to help in the galley. It didn't take long to get acquainted with my sleeping companions. Despite the dreadful situation on board the ship, people who weren't seasick were upbeat and amicable. Most of the time the talk was about their aspirations and experiences; most of us were refugees, and everyone had a story. One lady was from Estonia; she was following her children who were already in New York. She wanted me to meet her son, and was doing a little matchmaking. She was a likable person and full of fun. Many times when I was getting ready to turn in for the night, I found my pajamas all knotted or something funny in my hammock. I was usually absent all day from our quarters, and upon returning in the evening would report to them about the things that were happening on the ship or in the world.

Of course, for people who were seasick—some were the whole time—it was a terrible journey. As a whole, people put up with the circumstances; many had surely endured worse. On the upper floor were a few larger and smaller rooms. These were used for many different occasions such as church services and information centers. The ship wasn't equipped for entertainment, but they offered movies for children and sometimes for adults. The everyday English language lessons were popular, as were informative talks about the United States. A small library was also available. Chairs couldn't be set up, so everyone sat on the floor. To keep from sliding as the ship rolled, we sat on brown paper, which was rolled out on the floor. It worked fine.

The sea was choppy as we left the English Channel. Having a view of the water from the offices was great; at least one could follow the weather predictions, which we received from the radio officer. The forecast was not good; the ship was heading into a big storm. It was scary to see the big waves as the weather worsened. We walked out on the deck every day, standing in a protected little niche just to breathe fresh air. This daily ritual soon wasn't possible anymore. The wind whipped the waves, and a salty spray flew through the air.

The conditions became worse. In a few days, the crew strung ropes along the deck, not for us, but for them to hang on to. It looked like a maze. What fun the children would have had chasing each other in the rope playground. The doors to the deck were locked to keep people from going up. The weather worsened more. The fury of the Atlantic had no pity on our little ship. I was glad to be able to escape to my job. Staggering to the window and hanging on to what was next to me, I watched the waves leaping mercilessly on deck of the rolling ship; it was scary. The ocean was churning and white with foaming spray hitting the cabins windows. As the bow dipped down, water was all around; it appeared as if the ocean was swallowing the ship. I silently prayed that this little ship with its many frightened souls, striving for a new beginning, would hold together and transfer us safely across the Atlantic.

Fewer and fewer people appeared in the cafeteria. The long tables had rims so dishes wouldn't slide off; one had to hold on to everything. I had my first Thanksgiving dinner on the ship. What a pity—of all the many passengers, only a few showed up for the special meal.

At night, the swooshing sound of suitcases and bags sliding from one side of the room to the other kept us awake. One sensed how the engines labored battling the storm. Everyone hunted for their shoes in the morning. Keeping all those items tied up and close to us was very hard. Another stormy day passed. How many days had this storm been upon us? Our ship kept wrestling with the raging sea, and then one night—of course it had to happen at night—our poor little ship had had enough. It was rolling from side to side and from front to back, and then a trembling went through the ship before it simply quit. I sat up with a sudden jolt. The lights had shut off and there was ominous quiet; I held my breath waiting. It must have been the height of the storm. I had been so used to the constant drone of the engines that now this quiet was frightening. Was it a foreboding of trouble? Did the little ship just want to rest or had it broken down? I waited, listening to the people murmuring. I thought of the lifesaving drill we learned on the first day on deck. It had been so cold that day I couldn't wait to go inside. How would I ever make it to the deck with all these people storming ahead of me? My mind was racing from one thing to another, and then all of a sudden the lights came back on and the engines started up. A loud sigh went through the bunks. I silently cursed the storm. It took another day or two before the storm let up, and eventually the ship won the battle with the ocean.

Signs had been posted announcing a dance. How exciting! Of course it was a far cry from the "Captain's Ball" on an ocean liner. I'm sure there weren't many people on the ship who could make this comparison. I planned to attend. My "bunk mates" helped me to dress up. We all had to live out of our suitcases, and by now my suitcase needed a good overhaul. I looked for a dress that wasn't too wrinkled, but in the big picture, who cared? With some little heeled shoes, I was ready to dance the night away! A large group of young people showed up; it was the first time I saw so many young men in one place. I was surprised, because I didn't have much contact with passengers during the day; I spent most of my time in the ship's office.

The dancing was hilarious. One had to figure out which was the best way to get around on the rolling floor. It seemed the floor wasn't always there where it should be when you took a step. It was easier to just follow the swaying of the ship and shuffle around the floor.

The weather finally improved after the storm to just rough waves. The gray sky lifted a little. We were craving fresh air, and some of us went on deck again and huddled in a protected corner. We were now nearing New York. I had arranged with Marianne and Lisa to pick me up. I wanted to stay with them for a week in the city before traveling on to Columbus, Ohio.

The voyage had been scheduled for nine days, but actually took ten days. Since we arrived in the late evening, we had to stay on the ship one more night before disembarking. Luckily, I was able to send my friends a message from the ship about the delay, including the change of the docking site. A longshoremen's strike held up the unloading, and delayed us further. It was an advantage to work in the ship's office because I was updated with new information every day and had quick access to the radio officer.

I felt a strange excitement come over me. Only hours now before we docked! The ship docked in a harbor in Brooklyn. Many of us were on the deck the evening before, staring at Manhattan in the distance. The scene was a sea of lights; seeing skyscrapers for the first time was an awesome sight. I stood there for a long time, and a chill went down my spine. Tomorrow was the big day. How would it be meeting my friends?

We were all packed and ready. Finally, early the next morning the moment came to disembark. We had been at sea for eleven days. This was November 30th—a dreary damp day. The sullen sky still hadn't changed much at all. Manhattan across the river looked like a forest of colorless trees stretching up to meet the low-hanging November clouds.

Everyone scrambled to form lines. We were herded into a large hall right off the dock. Here the customs people inspected our baggage. Large cranes with huge nets holding many pieces of baggage dumped them on the floor; we had to sort things out by ourselves. It was all the help we would get. I had two big wooden trunks, and wondered if I would ever find them; eventually I did. I had to have them with me for the inspection, but then they were shipped to Ohio afterwards.

A fence separated us from the waiting crowd. I edged over to the fence to see if my friends were there. They were doing the same thing. Suddenly, I spotted them with their heads turned up and their eyes searching; they hadn't seen me. "I'm here, I'm here!" I shouted and waved. What a joy it was to see them; a weight lifted from my chest. I felt I was in good hands now. They inched closer to the fence, and soon we could talk to each other. It seemed unreal to see both my dear friends.

They had taken off from work that day to help and welcome me. Lisa's mother insisted that I should take a few jars of homemade jam which I reluctantly did, knowing that they could break and be a problem. And now I began to worry what might happen if the custom officers, moving around checking and searching the baggage, would find them, since we weren't supposed to bring along food items.

When the patrolling guard was at the other end of the fence, I just shoved the whole bag under the fence and my friends quickly grabbed it. I was very glad to have one less worry. I still had to have my baggage inspected. The lock on one of my trunks didn't work, and I couldn't open it. I had bought a little tea set which was securely wrapped in the store. I pleaded with the customs officer not to open it. I would have never been able to rewrap it safely again. There were so many restrictions. It took almost all day until I finally could hug my friends. They had patiently waited.

chapter sixteen

AMERICA

A cold driving wind met us as we left the large hall at the dock. It felt like pins and needles in my face, and I wrapped my scarf a little tighter around my neck. Daylight was fading. We tried to hurry and escape the hustle and bustle, debating what transportation to use. There were several possibilities; train, subway, or taxi. But who wanted to get on a train with big suitcases and bags? However, we changed our mind after looking at the taxi fare, which sounded quite expensive. We decided to take the train after all. The trip was a struggle, but between the three of us we managed.

This was the moment I had been waiting for. Ten years ago I had made the leap from East Germany to West Germany. Who would have thought that ten years later I would be walking the streets of New York? It was just incredible, and I wanted to pinch myself to make sure all this was real.

The prospect of spending a whole week in the city before going to Columbus, Ohio was exhilarating. I called Mabel Clark right away. It was the first time I had heard her voice again since Germany. Was this the voice I remembered? She sounded excited, too, and wanted to know all about my voyage. But that had to wait. I told her about my plans, and she understood that I wanted to stay a few days with my friends. We also needed to make plans for my trip to Columbus. At that moment I didn't even want to think about it; I hardly had my feet on the ground. She suggested that I come by train, and that sounded fine with me. Mabel was in her early eighties by then, and I knew she had given up driving. She now needed to make arrangements to meet me at the train station. She assured me, "Don't worry, I will be there." I was glad when arrangements were settled.

I couldn't wait to see Marianne's and Lisa's penthouse apartment. They had described it in letters as a wonderful location on the West Side, practically across the street from Central Park and right around the corner from the Museum of Natural History. All this didn't mean that much to me in Germany. How could I have possibly visualized the scene?

Their apartment was in one of the houses that were built by an affluent family about a hundred twenty years ago. The house next to it was identical. As they told me later, the houses were the same Beaux Art style reminiscent of that period. The girls had been curious about the houses, too, and discovered that they were built and owned by two brothers. There were other houses on the same street built by certain recognized architects. Actually, most of the houses were under historical protection and preservation measures.

Trees were planted along the sidewalks. They were still small, but provided a nice touch to the street atmosphere. One still saw signs that this house had seen better days before it was made into apartments. A fancy parquet floor in the foyer, though worn and discolored in many places, had withstood the challenges of time.

An old-fashioned elevator that looked like a big brass birdcage still with its golden gleam was in one corner, squeaking and rattling when in motion and complaining of its old age. The stairway with its handsome banister and wainscoting was a reminder of the masterly workmanship of bygone days. I pictured a maid rushing up the stairs answering a bell call on the next floor. The building had five main floors and the penthouse on the sixth floor was the maid's quarters. The elevator went only up to the fifth floor, and then stairs had to be climbed to the penthouse. It wasn't a penthouse one would find on Park Avenue; this one was probably the least expensive apartment in the building.

Stepping into this warm and cozy apartment was wonderful. I was really surprised how nicely it was fixed it up. I recognized some of the wall pictures from home—the ties with family and home that couldn't be abandoned quickly. In a special place on her bookshelf, Marianne had a little sculpture of the head of the "Bamberger Reiter" (the Bamberger Rider), which is the famous statue in the Dom and a symbol of the city.

Both of them were living on their own for the first time. Each had their bedroom, and the rest they shared. Marianne, with a twinkle in her eye, walked me to the door that opened to the roof top. Of course, this wasn't the time of year or the time of day to go out on the roof. But she quickly opened the door and braced against the wind gusts to show me. She was already planning that next summer she would have a little roof garden with pots of flowers. I tried to picture how that would be. Thinking of sitting in the summer on a rooftop didn't appeal much to me. But what did I know about New Yorkers? I had just arrived. Maybe that's what people do who live on the top floor.

The first night we talked and talked. Lisa wanted to hear about her fiancé, the young lawyer in the military, who was still in Germany. I told them about their parents and our mutual friends; we had lots of news to report to each other. What an awesome feeling! Here we were—the three of us together again. All these months I had been looking forward to this day, and deep in my heart I wished I could stay with them. Lisa's new home would be in Baltimore after her marriage. We talked about my return to New York after she left. It sounded like a fabulous idea to come back to New York.

Since Marianne and Lisa had arrived earlier in the year, both had jobs and needed to go to work the next day. They left me with lots of good advice to explore the city alone. But they suggested that perhaps I should get a little acclimated first. Why not go to the Metropolitan Museum of Natural History nearby; a good and safe place to start? I was glad to do this, since it gave me a chance to go out by myself without fear of getting lost.

My first time in a museum of this size was awesome. It struck me that everything seemed so much bigger. I spent a good part of the day there, and knew I hadn't seen all of it. That evening, I sat down with my friends and studied the street map. I wanted to act like a New Yorker and mix with the throngs of people in the streets. I wanted to experience the pulse of the big city. Ready or not, I put my best walking shoes on, and with map in hand ventured out the next day.

It was especially delightful being in New York at that time of year. Stores and windows were lit up and sparkled with Christmas decorations; there was definitely a holiday spirit in the air. Street vendors were out selling hats and gloves; this street-selling was something new to me. It had rained one day, and out came the umbrellas from the umbrella vendors. They seemed to have suddenly dropped from the sky along with the raindrops. A vendor was selling them at every street corner. It had never occurred to me that I would just buy an umbrella if I were caught in the rain.

Tiny hot dog stands not much bigger than a telephone booth were squeezed into the entrances of buildings. Smells of grilled hot dogs and French fries permeated the surroundings. Some were even selling pretzels. Would they taste like the Bavarian pretzels, I wondered? They looked like them. I had never tasted roasted chestnuts. Being curious, I ventured to buy some and was surprised with how good they tasted.

Most of my sightseeing was on foot. I soon realized my feet hurt from my marathon strides; I had to pace myself a little more. Broadway was next on my plan. I had an image of great theaters and entertainment. I thought of it as the heart of New York.

When I finally came to Broadway, it looked just like another street. I kept thinking there had to be more to it; it is known all over the world. But I couldn't see anything different. I only knew from my map that it ran slightly on an angle, winding through Manhattan. I realized what a greenhorn I was. I hadn't even arrived at the theater district.

In the evening, I reported my adventures to my friends. They suggested that if I wanted to go into a store, I should try Macy's. What an experience! There were tables with clothing which was all thrown together. I remembered Marianne saying, "If you want to buy anything, look at the tables first, those are the less expensive things." Standing in the store, I knew what she meant by tables. I wasn't ready to buy anything, but it was fun just to look. I had moved aimlessly from one department to another, and after a while I was totally lost.

When I finally found an exit, I came out on a different street, and had to walk to the next street corner to find out where I was. I discovered that the store was a whole block long and had several entrances.

The weather didn't change much during that week; it was nasty and chilly, with wind gusts at times whipping through the streets whirling paper, dust, and dirt into the air. All this landed and stuck in house corners and street gutters, making the sidewalks look dirty to me.

Going out together with Marianne and Lisa was fun, but there were only so many hours in the evening, and they went by fast. The girls tried to show me as many highlights as possible, and thought of what was interesting for them when they had arrived in America. We walked to Lincoln Center, which wasn't very far from them. From there, we headed to Rockefeller Center. Of course, I knew already about Rockefeller Center, but it was also a first for my friends to see it in its Christmas splendor. The huge Christmas tree sparkling with hundreds of lights was a sight I couldn't have imagined. Lights illuminated the skating rink, reflecting on the ice where skaters were gliding around gracefully, turning loops and showing off their skills. It seemed like a scene from a fairy tale.

Lisa and Marianne did their best to entertain me. I had poked around on Seventh and Eighth Avenues, which weren't far, and explored more in their neighborhood. The variety of stores was interesting, such as small clothing stores, food places, and little restaurants. I was exhausted at night and my feet ached, and I swore to rest the next day; but by the next morning I was ready to go again. Venturing a little farther one day, I found Fifth Avenue, which still stuck in my mind as a place of interest. I couldn't leave without having seen this famous New York Avenue and landmark. I wanted to peek at least into one of the great stores. My American friends in Germany had often talked about Bloomingdale's in New York. I knew that it had to be a very special, sophisticated store. After asking people in the street, I finally found the store, and was glad to get out of the ugly drizzly weather and warm up. I thought I was brave going on my excursions every day and braving the weather. When I passed Tiffany's, another big name I knew already, I was curious, and wondered if I could just go in without buying anything. I should have asked my friends about that. I didn't have any problems in other stores, so I walked right in. The festive ambiance and the beautiful decorations for the holidays certainly invited the shoppers to look around and stay a while. Mirrors reflected the crystal on shelves along the walls, and jewelry dazzled in their cases. It all was lovely.

I slowly inched along the counters, and smiled back at the salesladies who asked if they could help me. I was too shy to have them show me a tray of rings or pins, knowing I couldn't buy anything. It would have been wonderful to say, "Oh, I bought this at Tiffany's." When I saw the prices, I knew I wouldn't be buying anything. I thanked my lucky star for being here at this time of year so as to experience the holiday spirit of the city. I was sorry that I never made it to the Metropolitan Museum.

And then there were those ugly brown boxes in windows. I noticed they all seemed to look alike. Could they be birdfeeders or birdcages? There were plenty of pigeons and screaming sparrows around. I was glad that I hadn't asked my friends, since I soon found out, in a roundabout way, that they were air conditioners. I would have been embarrassed. I couldn't remember ever seeing an air conditioner, and had no idea that people placed them in windows.

My friends were wonderful; they rushed back after work every day. One evening we had dinner in Chinatown; two new experiences because we used the subway to travel there. To me, my friends were already seasoned New Yorkers, but my excitement stirred theirs, too. When we poked around Times Square, which is also well known all over the world, I learned that the famous New York Times newspaper offices were there, too. This had to be the busiest place in the city, with glaring neon lights advertising entertainment and people everywhere.

Of course, the Empire State Building was on our list, too. We decided to go in the early evening, and probably would have had a spectacular view, but a wall of fog and mist had rolled in. Looking down from the top, it seemed like a veil studded with circles of faint lights covered everything below us. The lights on the bridges looked like someone had strung up Christmas lights. The whole city seemed unreal. I felt like a country-bumpkin who hadn't seen much of the world.

The time to leave came much too soon. Here I was with my best friends, and even though everything else was unfamiliar, my friends were the same, and this was reassuring. I wasn't really traveling to the unknown since I knew Mabel Clark, but a hint of anxiousness occupied my mind. I hadn't seen Mabel Clark for years, and now she was in her eighties. How would it work out to be with her in the setting of her home?

The train-ride to Columbus took about twelve hours. The night train was a great way to go, since it was relaxing; I even slept a few hours. It was a crisp, clear December day when the train pulled into the Columbus train station. I had reached another milestone. This was the end of my journey. I took a deep breath and gingerly stepped off the train. There, almost in front of me, was my little welcome party. Mabel, with her arms spread out, hugged me; Dr. Berry and his wife showed big smiles.

I knew from Mabel that Dr. Berry, a sociology professor at Ohio State University, was much involved in helping European refugees immigrate to the States. He had helped her with my papers, and was now here to be with her at my arrival and to welcome me. It was a stirring moment to see Mabel again. Although she looked a little older, her eyes exuded the same kindness and gentleness I remembered from our time in Germany. These were the people who had made it all possible. I immediately liked Dr. Berry and his wife; he was a fatherly figure, friendly, and warmhearted.

A New Chapter in My Life

As we parted, Dr. Berry suggested that whenever I was ready to look for a job, I should try the Personnel Office at Ohio State University. I was overjoyed about this prospect. He had made it sound like there wasn't any problem with obtaining a job.

Mabel's house was an older home with a small farmer's porch and a nice little fenced-in garden in the back. All the houses on this street looked the same age. It was in an older section of the city, somewhat on the outskirts, and luckily, near the University.

She lived upstairs, and I settled in a room downstairs. It was small, but had all the basics I needed. It was a room that she rented for additional income. Another room next to mine was rented to a young couple. I was amazed at how well Mabel was doing at her age. We had dinner together during the first few weeks, which helped us to get reacquainted. Even though we had been corresponding, there was still so much to catch up on. I wanted to hear about her daughter Dorothy and her family for whom I had babysat in Germany. Then she sprung a big surprise on me: she was planning for both of us to visit them at Christmas. This was unexpected and wonderful. "Would the children still remember me?" I wondered. Perhaps Susie would, since she was the oldest. Mabel had their school pictures all lined up on her bookshelf, and I was surprised with how much they had grown.

Getting a job was very much on my mind, since I didn't have much money and wanted to work as soon as possible. I was Mabel's friend, and to a certain extent her guest, but I wanted to pay rent and feed myself. Dr. Berry's suggestion about working at the University was so unexpected, I didn't want to let this opportunity slip by. I was barely in America, and doors opened for me. I saw myself already in a pleasant milieu with the prospect of meeting interesting people. Two days later I was on my way to the University for an interview. I took Dr. Berry's advice to start there first. The University was huge. While finding my way, I pictured how nice it would be to work there. All the time I was hoping that my English would be sufficient now that I was in America. The best thing was the fact that the University was within walking distance.

The interview went well, and I was offered a job in the acquisition department of the library. I never expected it to be so easy. My eyes must have visibly lit up watching the smile on the interviewer's face. There was one item I had to ask the interviewer: I gathered all my courage, and explained about my Christmas trip with Mabel. I wanted to start the first of the year. The interviewer agreed, and thought it would be possible. I was still in disbelief when I thought about what had just happened. I was on cloud nine, and felt like skipping all the way back to Euclid Avenue. I hugged Mabel, and told her all about my interview.

The Berrys stopped by one evening and invited Mabel and me for a ride with them to see the city's Christmas decorations. They knew that was something very American. Big-bellied plastic Santas in front of houses and even on rooftops certainly was a sight I had never observed. I was amazed by the effort people made to put up all those lights. I liked the lights on the shrubbery, but having lights all over seemed a little gaudy to me. New to me, too, were wreaths outside on doors and windows; I thought they were charming. I explained to them that in Germany we celebrate advent, and had a wreath with four candles set up in the house. The four candles denote the four Advent Sundays before Christmas, and on each Sunday the proper candle for that day is lit. The last one was then lit on the Sunday before Christmas. I was surprised to not see the custom here.

The reunion with the Garrison family was touching. We traveled by train to their house near Lake Michigan. It was quite remote from a large city. The weather was very cold, with lots of snow, especially there in the lake region. Of course, the children had grown. Susie, the oldest, was almost ten years old; the two younger ones, Kathy and David, didn't remember me. Seeing all of them again was wonderful, and it didn't seem so long ago since our parting in Germany.

How wonderful it was to have children around this Christmas. They were excited, waiting impatiently for that special day, expecting Santa coming down the chimney on Christmas Eve. The bitter cold kept us inside most days. My attempt to go for a walk lasted only a few minutes. It was just too cold; I didn't have the warm outerwear one needed in this area. It would have been nice to see a little more of the surroundings. Leonard, Mabel's son-in-law, took us for a quick ride through the neighborhood, but it all seemed to be covered with a white blanket of snow. This was also Mabel's first visit since her daughter and family had moved here. She savored every moment she spent with her grandchildren, since there hadn't been many visits. Leonard was in the Armed Services, and most of the time stationed too far away.

The New Year rolled in with frigid temperatures. I started my new job the day after New Year's. The students were still on holiday vacation, and everything was quiet around the campus. One couldn't miss the library. It was a large and distinct-looking building surrounded by a grassy area with large trees. Of course, at this time of year it looked drab, with dead grass covering the ground. I imagined that on sunny warm spring days this place would be busy with students gathering and strolling about. Walking paths from different angles all led to the library.

The bitter cold weather made me think of my homeland and school days where we had stretches of very cold temperatures. In Germany, we were so much farther north, so the cold weather made more sense to me. I really hated the cold. On many days, I walked so fast my feet hardly touched the ground.

I steered right to the door with the sign "Acquisition Department." My heart was beating a little faster as I entered a large room with several desks in different places. I saw only young people. A quick thought ran through my mind: I'll be with people my own age; that would be great. The department head was a middle-aged man whose little office was enclosed in a corner of the room. I had another short interview with him. As I had expected, he was the person to really give me the job. I was glad that it went well, and my nerves settled down a bit. As we walked towards a desk where a young woman was working, he began to explain the job responsibilities. Then he introduced me to Joanne, with whom I was going to work. He said, "Joanne will show you the work and will help you along," and that was it!

My station consisted of a desk and a typewriter next to Joanne. The work was typing order forms for new books or writing to other university libraries for book loans. All the information about the books was given to us, including the addresses of where to order. These were requests by students who needed the books for their research and studies. I had quite a time typing these multiple order forms; there couldn't be any mistakes. One wasn't able to erase, and the copies were very thin; the order form had to be just perfect.

Joanne proofread them, and many went into the wastepaper basket, meaning a redo of my work. It was a stressful beginning. Once in a while, we wrote letters using a Dictaphone, a more enjoyable task at least for me, but it had its little pitfalls, too. The department head had a southern drawl which made me sometimes ponder a word that I hadn't heard or didn't know the real meaning of. When I finally had to ask him about a word, he explained with a big smile on his face. It was amazing that despite this large library with so many floors of books and books, books still had to be ordered; to me it looked like this place should have all the books that had ever been written. The infinite numbers of universities and colleges in America was absolutely amazing, too.

One time I had a reprieve from my monotonous typing. I had to correct the cataloging of books written in the old German script that, luckily, I still understood. This also gave me a chance to see what kind of German books the library contained. Some of the books stirred my interest, and I was able to borrow them.

Sewing Adventures

Joanne became a good friend. Her twin sister worked in another department. We made very little money, and I soon found out that Joanne and her sister sewed their own clothes with their mother's help. For the first month, I had traveled downtown every Saturday looking around in the stores, especially in Lazarus', the largest department store. I had fun just looking around. It had never occurred to me to think of sewing my own clothes. But now I had visions of creating dresses and skirts, especially after the encouragement from Joanne who explained the uncomplicated process of following a pattern. I soon started looking at materials and became more interested; I could at least try it. Much of the material was inexpensive, and the choices were overwhelming. I had to have a sewing machine first, and debated if I really should do it.

Joanne suggested I buy a portable Singer sewing machine that also came with three free sewing lessons. That purchase also taught me how business is done in the USA. I wanted to pay for the machine in three installments, but to my dismay I didn't have any credit. I told them that I had money in the bank, but it didn't make any difference. This took me by surprise. I learned the practice in America that by owing money and paying it back, one would establish good credit. Whether I liked it or not, I had to take money out of my savings and pay for the machine.

It was my first purchase in America. How proud I was that I had bought something substantial and sensible, and never doubted that my hidden sewing talent would soon emerge. Shopping for fabric and patterns was my pastime for the next few weekends. What astonished me most were the low prices. I could buy enough material for a dress for one dollar. No wonder the girls made their own clothes. My enthusiasm grew by the minute. I couldn't wait to begin, but first I had to delve into the pattern books, which were a study in themselves. Different books were spread out on long counters in the stores. Vogue was the most sophisticated; I had to look for something very simple to begin with. I spent lots of time in the fabric section choosing the material, which was tough, because the selections were enormous. Finally, I had it all worked out, including thread and a zipper to match.

It was slow going in the beginning, but the three free sewing lessons that came with my machine were a huge help. I learned a little more with each garment I tackled. Picking out a pattern was always a little adventure. I thought it would be fun to make a list of what I spent on each garment; it wasn't more than three or four dollars for a dress, and a skirt was even less. To think I could make a dress for that price seemed unreal to me.

I had a seamstress in Germany who had made some of my clothes. Of course, there was no comparison but I wished she could see my endeavors. I had fun with my sewing adventures, and winter marched on. Many evenings I sat with Mabel watching television. Sometimes on Sundays the Berrys would pick us up to go to church.

Summer weather didn't gradually arrive, but came with a burst. The weather seemed to go from cold to hot in a few days, and skipped spring altogether; by Eastertime, summer was in full swing. I sat in Mabel's little flower garden behind her house, and became sunburned sitting on a bench writing letters. Writing home was the only communication I had with my mother and siblings; there was so much to write about. Calling my family in East Germany was impossible. Trying to be as close as possible with them was very important.

Fun with Emil

The brand new Mershon Auditorium was opening its doors for the first time with a premiere performance of "South Pacific." It was the big event everyone was waiting for. Joanne urged me to definitely not miss this. She purchased the tickets, and promised to pick me up.

I was just beginning to learn a little about American musicals, but didn't know much about famous singers. But my anticipation grew as I listened to the girls. Finally, the day arrived. The evening was delightfully warm, and the play was wonderful and enchanting. The songs were still echoing in my mind as I walked home. As I approached the house, I noticed a car in front of the house.

As I was skipping up the stairs, someone who I hadn't noticed stepped out of the shadow of the porch. I froze. My whole body tightened up. He took another step, and greeted me with, "Guten Abend" (Good evening). The voice sounded familiar, and he spoke German, so my first instinct was that he was someone I knew. My knees were shaking, but the panicky moment passed. He finally turned so I could see his face; it was Emil, a young American I had met in Germany. He used to come to the German-American club now and then, and we always marveled at how well he spoke German. He had learned German from a German family, and even picked up the Bavarian dialect. His real name was Alvin, or something like that; we thought this a funny name, and gave him an even funnier name, Emil.

We sat on the bench, and he told me his story. He was finished with his military service and on his way home to the West Coast with his little Volkswagen, a car he had bought in Germany and had shipped to New York to pick up.

It was late, so we made plans for the next day, which was May 28, 1957. He had practically no money. When he picked up his car in New York, he visited my friends there, and they sent him on to me. I was a convenient way station to help replenish his food supply.

Was I very surprised when he came the next morning dressed in an authentic Bavarian outfit! He had lederhosen, knee socks, buckled shoes, decorated leather suspenders, and the special hat with a chamois tuft of fur. Would he really walk around like this? He was serious. I kept laughing, and then I thought we could definitely have fun if I wore my German dirndl dress. I called the office and took the day off.

Emil and Ingrid in Bavarian outfits, Columbus, Ohio, 1957.

First, I wanted to show him the University campus. Everyone stared at us as we leisurely strolled down University Avenue. I had more laughs as he described what had happened that morning when he was nearly arrested for sleeping in a sleeping bag on the roadside. The person who had stopped thought he was dead and called the police.

It was May, and the campus looked lush and fresh with all the budding trees and shrubs. I had already noticed a young man with a camera trailing us. It had never entered my mind that we could attract that much attention. The young man caught up with us, and of course wanted to know who we were. I gave him my name, and then before

Emil could say anything, I quickly introduced him as Emil Schmid, my German friend. This put the whole thing in a different perspective. We now had to come up with a story, because this man wanted to know more about us, especially Emil, since I introduced him as a German. I wasn't serious, and thought this was all just fun.

The young man was a reporter, perhaps a student working for the University newspaper, the "Lantern." Quick-witted Emil caught on very fast; he started to speak English with a German accent. In between, we would mumble some German words. Emil mentioned that he was on his way to Oregon to go to school there, which was true. We had this young reporter so fascinated with our stories, some true and some not so true, that he kept walking along with us wanting to know more. I made a terrible remark at a store window displaying Ivy League shirts that I thought were so dark and dull. What did I know about the Ivy League? I didn't even know who the Ivy Leaguers were. We had fooled this young man, and there was no return to the truth at this point. I had toyed with the thought of making a joke out of it, but he was so sincere and believed us, telling him the truth would have been too embarrassing for him. I was hoping in my heart that I would never have to regret this.

Emil enjoyed this game, and he was not much help to me. I was afraid that he might make a mistake and not keep up the German accent, so I tried to do most of the talking, since my accent was real. Then I thought of a couple who I had met awhile ago who lived in the vicinity where we were walking. We needed to be rescued; we had played this charade long enough. We stopped at their apartment, and told the young reporter that we would be visiting for a while, thinking he would leave. We dashed up the steps, and I prayed that they would be home, all the while holding on to a serious face. The friends were in. We recounted our path, the stops, and conversations. I pressed my friends to keep this a secret. We looked out of the window, and to our dismay he was still there, sitting on the steps waiting for us. By now he almost seemed like a new friend. We needed help to ease us out of this comical situation, so we all went outside and Emil and I shook his hand in a real German-like fashion. We remarked what a pleasure it was to meet up with him, but that we now wanted to spend time with our friends. He reluctantly left. We spent the rest of the day sightseeing, but every once in a while looked over our shoulders; we had to chuckle about our morning adventure.

Emil left the next day. I hoped he stayed out of trouble. I didn't dare tell my funny story to anyone. I wondered what the young reporter would do. I soon found out. A few days later, right on the front page of the Ohio State Lantern, was his write-up, including our picture. The story mentioned my place of work, and soon several people stopped by. One of them was an architect who was married to a German woman; he invited me to meet his wife. The Santorinis and I developed a long-lasting friendship.

The University hosted an annual dinner party, with entertainment for foreign students and their sponsors. Even though I wasn't a student, Dr. Berry had arranged for a sponsor and an invitation. The sponsor was a lady who probably had volunteered. It started with a nice dinner at long tables, and our lively conversations went right and left and across the table. Some very talented foreign students entertained us with songs and skits.

As summer came around, I felt more isolated from my friends. Marianne had a good job in New York, and she wrote about her new friends and her life in the big city. Lisa's fiancé returned to America, and they married in New York before going to Baltimore, where he planned to practice law in his brother-in-law's office.

Yvonne, who had come from Switzerland the same year I did, was now her roommate and worked in a laboratory. These two agreed to take me in if I came.

It wasn't easy to tell Mabel Clark that I was leaving so soon, but I needed to make my own decision. I had to call Dr. Berry, which was also hard, but he understood. Of course, none of them thought New York was the right place, especially since I was so new in the country. But I thought my friends were surviving there, and so could I. The long train ride was not so unfamiliar this time. I had to send my trunks separately, but all went well, and we even found a place at the apartment to store them.

New York in the middle of August 1957 was hot and steaming. It was quite an adjustment from peaceful and nostalgic Euclid Avenue, with its old houses dating back to the turn of the century.

Even though it was hot in Ohio, there were breezes and delightful cooler evenings.

Mabel and I sat on the porch or in her little garden. I missed that most. I had been watering the flowers and watching the tomatoes we had planted. We had talked of all the tomatoes we would harvest, and Mabel was already planning to make tomato sauce from all the extras we wouldn't be able to eat.

I couldn't waste time in New York; I needed a job. This was my first real challenge. How could I ever find something in the many columns of ads in the paper? Just looking at them was overwhelming. It was an experience I hadn't anticipated. I finally went to a job agency, since it seemed the sensible thing to do. With addresses in hand, I set off several days for interviews, learning a little more about the city every day. I stressed my German language skills. One of my interviews was in the Empire State Building with a Swiss company that made precision instruments. I remember I was stunned as I walked into the beautifully decorated office. It was actually a waiting room with upholstered chairs and paintings on the wall. It was clear to me right from the moment I stepped into this elegant room that I would never get a job here. It was too intimidating; needless to say, I didn't get the job. Several times, I had to take a typing test, and once even an IQ test. It all was so new to me; I felt I was embarking on an adventurous outing. My perseverance paid off, and I found a job in a small magazine and book export company on the West Side. We were only three in the office, and I did all the billing and letters. The others worked mostly in customer service. The billing was easy to learn, and that helped me later when I landed a job in a bank on Cape Cod.

Cape Cod

During the hot summer, Marianne and I remembered a young man from Latvia we had met in Germany whose family had immigrated to Cape Cod. I had kept in touch with him since arriving in

America, and when he heard about our hot weather, he invited us to visit him on seaside Cape Cod. I took him up on the offer, and once again boarded a train for an adventure. The train was the famous "Neptune" weekender that began in Washington, stopped in New York, and ended at Hyannis. This was my introduction to Cape Cod, and in the following year, 1958, the young man and I were married.

Cape Cod proved to be a wonderful place that instantly grew on me. Never having been around the ocean, the beautiful seascapes and natural surroundings made a big impression. I fell in love with the little fishing towns on the Outer Cape, enjoyed learning about the interesting Cape history, and looked forward to pursuing my interest with the local art scene. My love of Cape Cod has remained to this day.

Epilogue

1996: KÖSELITZ REVISITED

It's hard to describe my excitement when the East German regime in 1989 collapsed. I couldn't even call my relatives because no one had a phone. I wanted to hear my sister and brother's voices, and their exhilaration and joy that finally a unification of the two Germanys was in sight. Now I could visit my family without all the red tape that I had had to put up with before. I felt like jumping on the next plane and traveling there. The fall of East Germany also relaxed the borders between East Germany and the adjacent country of Poland, so that a trip to my German homeland was now possible.

Once in 1986, on a trip to Germany to visit my family, my brother, sister, and I attempted a trip to Köselitz in Poland. It required a Polish visa that I had obtained from the Polish Consulate. I thought I was all set to go, but then learned that the East German Government only permitted me one entry and one exit for my entire trip. If I traveled to Poland and wanted to return to East Germany, they would not allow that second re-entry into East Germany from Poland. I was glad I had checked with the local police department before we left, although I was terribly disappointed that I couldn't persuade them to be more flexible. My brother and sister made the trip without me.

In the winter of 1995, about five years after the opening of the wall between East and West Germany, my sister called, and I could tell by the tone of her voice that she was up to something. "How do you like the idea of the three of us trying to visit our hometown together?" Instantly excitement welled up in me. I had often dreamt of trying it again, and now it seemed within reach. My sister loved to plan and organize, and I suspected that she had already started the planning.

She said, "I already talked with Werner, and he is working out a vacation schedule for a few days. What do you say to that?" I was exhilarated; this time it had to work. Now I became busy making my plans. Thankfully, with the fall of East Germany, there was no need for visas and special permits.

We planned the trip for March 1996. It would be exactly fifty years to the month after my last walk on the cobblestone street of our little farming village. That day in 1946 was bleak and cold, and a raw wind blew in my face. I only owned the clothes on my back—a man's old overcoat, and out-of-shape shoes with worn-off heels I had worn all year. I had struggled home after my release from the Russian camp, not knowing whether my family would still be in Köselitz. They had been forced to leave with the rest of the townspeople in the summer of 1945, and were herded across the Oder River, then the new border between Poland and East Germany. When I arrived in Köselitz in 1946 after my ordeal, the Poles who were forced by the Russians to move to Köselitz were just settling in. They had taken over what was there, moved into houses that were fairly intact, and started their own new lives. The Russians had ravished the town and much was destroyed. That was the picture I carried in my heart as I contemplated this trip in 1996.

My sister had come to my brother's house in Tangerhütte the day before, so we could leave early and make a good start. This would be a two-day trip, and Christa had already arranged with friends for us to stay for a night; she had stayed with them before. These were the people who took mother, Christa, and Werner in when they came across the border in 1945. These people lived near the border, and had already taken day trips across the border to Poland. It had become fairly easy for people living on either side of the East German - Poland border to go back and forth. They had visited towns where several of their relatives used to live; for them the connection to the past lived on. For us, it was wonderful to meet with them, since we could learn about the conditions and obtain driving directions.

We stayed up much too long relishing their warm and friendly hospitality. All I could think was that after a few hours of sleep, we would be on our way. The next morning Ursula handed us a picnic basket with sandwiches, hardboiled eggs, pickles, and a thermos of coffee which she had lovingly prepared for us. "You probably won't come across a place to eat," she said with a big smile and a knowing look. It seemed they were as anxious as we were in anticipation of our trip. After a hearty breakfast, we left on our adventure.

As we drove, we reminisced and recalled many childhood events: stories of our school days, remembering who lived where and names of people, the cold winters with lots of snow, and the carefree life we enjoyed in those days.

Traffic was light. There was something sad about the areas along these borders. The villages were sparsely occupied. It was mostly farming, with no industry. The border was actually at the end of the road we were traveling. The road led through the marshy flats of the Oder River; here winter hadn't quite left—scattered icy spots were visible. We saw a large flock of swans with their long graceful necks stretched out to the ground, nibbling on the sprouts of winter rye or wheat, hungry from the long flight north from their wintering regions. The air was heavy with the musty smell of trees decomposing in the marsh. It seemed there was not much life about; songbirds had not returned from their sunny winter habitats.

Soon our road ended at the border; all of a sudden it was in front of us. With IDs and passports in hand, we waited in line; there were only a few people ahead of us. We were across in no time at all. We took a deep breath, and looked at each other, thinking the same thing. "We are here." Werner's voice was hushed. I had to hold my tears back; I didn't think I would get so emotional. So many years had passed, but the memory and how it all happened would never go away.

We stopped on the side of the road and looked around. Of course, nothing was familiar here, but this was part of our homeland. We let the realization sink in. I thought about my mother when she, with my brother and sister and many, many Germans, was driven across this river more than 50 years ago, never to return. What she must have felt!

Our hearts beat a little faster; what would we find? As youngsters, we had never traveled in these areas. In those days, one didn't travel very far with horse and buggy. We couldn't remember the German names of the towns, and now they were all in Polish. My brother was only twelve years old when they had to leave. He relied on my sister and me, and we weren't so sure ourselves. It didn't take as long as we expected to get to our village. As we got closer, the road became more familiar, as did the neighboring villages. The last village was Loist, just three kilometers before getting to Köselitz. We entered the town at the railroad station. This was such a familiar place for me; for almost five years I had ridden the train to school six days a week; now it was abandoned and desolate. Half of the station was in ruins, with bricks scattered around. I looked for something familiar, something to stir my memory. Sometimes on Sundays, on our strolls with friends, we went to the station just to see who was coming on the train. What simple pleasures we had in those days.

Rusty rails overgrown with grass and weeds were barely visible; more weeds were growing on the old platform. Deep beneath all the weeds and dirt must still be my footprints; especially those running steps as I huffed and puffed to make the train, waving my arms for it to wait for me. Was all of this fifty years ago? There hadn't been a train running for all these years. My mind lingered at the skeleton of the stationmaster's house. It had burned down during the very first days the Russians came. His wife was a seamstress. I had just brought her linen so she might sew a skirt for me. I wanted to get ahead of the season. It amazed me that I remembered this.

These were my first impressions as we drove slowly into the village; there was no traffic. On our left was the blacksmith shop; it had survived and the door stood open. The whole village looked so small, even the distances. The bakery, too, had survived. The entrance of the building looked changed, but the rest of house was still the same. I thought of how my sister and I used to argue who should go to the bakery. "It is too far!" we exclaimed. Now looking at it, the bakery sat just a stone's throw from our house. It reminded me of a child's perspective. I closed my eyes for a second, and in my mind I walked through the narrow hallway in the bakery and saw warm crusty breads in neat rows lined up on wooden shelves. A wonderful aroma engulfed my mind; the sourdough had its particular aroma. I pictured the baker all dusty with flour in front of the hot oven; it seemed that's where he always was. We visited the bakery every Saturday. We carried the cake dough on sheets or in forms to the bakery with a little piece of paper stuck in a corner with our name on it just so it didn't become mixed up with someone else's. Many times, we would have our first taste of the sheet cake on the way home, just sitting on someone's doorstep and breaking off a piece. Streusel cake was my favorite; I can still taste the crispy crust and see myself picking the place with the biggest streusels to try.

"Let's park and walk." We couldn't decide. "Perhaps better to drive, we can go slow." "This is our hometown, or is it not? Or shall we think it was?" "It will always be my hometown," my sister insisted. She is the one who clung most fiercely to the past. "We were born here and grew up here, but were thrown out," she declared. "Should we now feel like we are intruding and have no right to walk these streets?" There was anger in her voice.

We looked at the houses that were now occupied by Polish families, calling out the names of those who used to live there. We wondered where our school pals and good friends had ended up in the world. Skeletons of burned barns and houses were still visible. One could see right through them. It was hard to believe that this still existed fifty years after the war.

I felt a big lump in my throat as we were nearing our house. What would it look like? Werner pulled over on the side. We quietly sat in the car and just looked, each of us with our own thoughts and memories and dreams buried here. Mostly, we had memories of only good years and a good life, a place of love and fun and friendship.

I thought of my mother and father, and remembered my father's words when it was imminent that the Russian forces were only hours away. "They can take everything from us, but they can't take our land." But they did. He was shipped to Russia and he never knew what happened.

The exterior hadn't changed much, except the brick front steps were gone. We used to sit on the sides of them. But the two large elm trees, probably two hundred years old, had withstood the war. They stood like sentries in front of the house. The crowns had been cropped; perhaps someone didn't like the shade they offered. I couldn't help but stroke the bark, remembering what a good hiding place they made. Their gnarled roots protruded all around the base, and when we were little, we sat in them and played. My mother said that even she played there.

We decided to try to meet the people in our house and perhaps have a look around. My brother was especially anxious to do that. The owners greeted us with surprised and questioning looks. It was too bad we couldn't communicate; neither spoke the other's language. But with hand signals and gestures, we made them understand who we were. These people were already the second generation of Poles who had grown up there, and they didn't know much about the war and the farm's history.

The man of the house took us outside. The property had been split in half to serve two families. The large barn had burned down, and he had just rebuilt a very small one. Nothing had been done to the other buildings; they looked awful. We had to remember that fifty years had passed, and it showed. Werner pointed to the doors where we had cows and calves, and also to the horse stable, but the man was reluctant to show us. He mentioned that he had pigs in there. We indicated that we wished to see the back behind the barn—that's where the garden was. Also, father had a wonderful orchard right in back of the barn. He enjoyed experimenting with all kinds of fruit trees, especially plum trees. I remember those early, pink plums; they were small, but oh so sweet. There seemed to be nothing left of it. Perhaps those trees had become too old. Gone also was the old crooked apple tree where we always had a swing. My sister nudged me. "Remember the apple tree with the swing?" she asked, pointing to the place where it used to be. "We argued most of the time about who could swing the highest; I still think I did." A sad hint was in her voice even though she wanted the comment to sound cheerful.

We always had a great view from the garden. At certain times of the day, we could see the train puffing its way to the station, usually whistling at that point announcing its arrival. In the winter we skated on the flooded meadow below.

To my amazement, I heard that the storks had come back; many of their nests had burned down with the barns. They usually came back to the same nests. They must not have despaired when they could not find their old nests; the storks were absent when the war raged on. They found new nesting sites after their return. Both of our neighbors' barns had nests, but ours didn't. But we discovered a nest on the horse stable and one on the church, too. Their favorite places were thatched roofs but those were all gone. Storks belonged to our childhood; we used to wait for them in the spring, and later watched the young practice flying. Every place we looked, childhood memories emerged.

A cup of tea in our kitchen was offered to us by the Polish family. I searched around for something familiar; there was the door to the pantry and the door to the maid's room. A stove sat in the corner where ours also was located, probably the best place in the kitchen. Nothing in the kitchen was familiar, but it was the same kitchen where I used to sit down coming home from the train, telling my mother all about my day in school. It all looked very small and felt strange now. It would have been nicer if we could have talked with the people. We said our thanks and good-byes, and had a last look around as we walked out.

We drove a few times up and down the street, and with saddened voices recounted what we had experienced. My brother would have inherited all this; he found it difficult to picture himself living here.

The village cemetery was our last stop before we turned back on the road to Germany. The German graveyard was separate, and surrounded by a hedge. All the gravestones had been removed, and a blanket of ivy covered the ground. Large old trees still kept watch. We were pleased to see that it wasn't destroyed, but it was impossible to find the graves of our ancestors. As children, every Saturday during the summer season, fresh flowers were placed on the graves; something that Christa and I often did. These were all memories from a time long ago.

Unfortunately, this book could have been written about many others, not only the Germans, who went through the same trials caused by the invading forces. Many lost their lives, family and their all. Read the Diary of Anne Frank.

Made in the USA
Charleston, SC
25 September 2013